The Library at Warwick School
Please return or renew on or before the last date below

11/15

The 1975 Referendum on Europe

Volume 1
Reflections of the Participants

Mark Baimbridge (Editor)

imprint-academic.com

Published in the UK by
Imprint Academic, PO Box 200, Exeter EX5 5YX, UK

Published in the USA by
Imprint Academic, Philosophy Documentation Center
PO Box 7147, Charlottesville, VA 22906-7147, USA

ISBN 9781845400347
A CIP catalogue record for this book is available from the
British Library and US Library of Congress

Contents

Acknowledgements

There are many people to thank for their input into making this book possible. Firstly, Anthony Freeman of Imprint Academic for his immediate support for this project and patience over the duration of its development. Secondly, this book could not have been completed without the many and varied contributions. Seeking to undertake a project focusing upon an event that occurred some 30 years ago has posed inevitable difficulties as the march of time has severely depleted the number of participants still able to provide their first-hand account of the Referendum. Thirdly, my colleagues at the University of Bradford in the *Bradford Centre for International Development* and the *Centre for European Studies* for their support for my research on European integration and the work of the multidisciplinary *European Economies Research Unit* (EERU) of which this is a prime example of the intersection between political science and economics. Finally, I owe a deep sense of gratitude to my family for their support and forbearance during the preparation of this book. It is to them that this book is dedicated: Mary, Ken and Beibei.

Any remaining errors and omissions are solely attributable to me.

Haworth
April 2006

European Integration Timeline

From its beginnings, half a century ago, in the immediate aftermath of the Second World War, through the expansion of the seventies and eighties and the great debate surrounding the Maastricht Treaty, here we highlight some of the key events which have shaped the development of the EU towards closer integration.

1948	The Organisation for **European Economic Cooperation (OEEC)** is set up in Paris in April 1948, co-ordinating the distribution of the Marshall Plan financial aid which will amount to $12.5 billion from 1948 to 1951. The OEEC consists of one representative from each of the 17 Western European countries which join the organisation. In May 1948 in The Hague, the Congress of Europe (a meeting of delegates from 16 European countries) agree to form the **Council of Europe** with the aim of establishing closer economic and social ties
1951	The **European Coal and Steel Community (ECSC)** is established by the signing of the Treaty of Paris in April 1951. Along with France and West Germany, Italy, Belgium, Luxembourg and The Netherlands have also chosen to join the organisation. Members of the ECSC pledge to remove all import duties and quota restrictions on the trade of coal, iron ore, and steel between the member states
1952	The **European Defence Community (EDC)** Treaty is signed by France, West Germany, Italy, Belgium, Holland and Luxembourg in May 1952. It includes the provision for the formation of a parallel **European Political Community (EPC)**. However both initiatives are destined to founder since the French National Assembly never ratifies the EDC Treaty, finally rejecting it in August 1954

1955	The process of further European integration is given fresh impetus by a conference of ECSC foreign ministers at Messina, Italy, in June 1955. The meeting agrees to develop the community by encouraging free trade between member states through the removal of tariffs and quotas. Agreement is also reached to form an Atomic Energy Community to encourage co-operation in the nuclear energy industry
1958	The two Treaties of Rome are signed, establishing the **European Economic Community (EEC)** and the **European Atomic Energy Community (Euratom).** As well as stipulating the eventual removal of customs duties on trade between member countries (over a period of 12 years) the EEC Treaty sets out allow the free movement of workers, capital and services across borders and to harmonise policies on agriculture and transport
1960	At the Stockholm Convention in January 1960 Austria, Britain, Denmark, Norway, Portugal, Sweden and Switzerland form the **European Free Trade Association (EFTA)**. The objective of EFTA is to promote free trade but without the formal structures of the EEC
1961	UK applies to join the EEC.
1963	British application for EEC membership fails.
1967	UK submits second application to join EEC
1968	Customs union completed and **Common Agricultural Policy** enacted.
1972	In October, following the recommendations of the **Werner Report,** the EEC launches its first attempt at harmonising exchange rates. The mechanism adopted is the so called 'snake in the tunnel' whereby participating governments are required to confine the fluctuations of their currencies within a range of +/- 1% against each other. The value of the group of currencies (the snake) is also to be maintained within a range of +/-2.25% against the US Dollar (the tunnel). Countries requiring assistance to keep their currencies within the required band may receive help only in the form of loans
1973	Denmark, Ireland and the UK join the EEC.
1975	UK referendum supports staying in EEC.
1978	At a summit in Bremen in July, the French and West German governments announce their intention to create the **European Monetary System (EMS)**. At the centre of the EMS is the **European Currency Unit (ECU)**. The value of the ECU is to be derived from a weighted basket of all participating currencies with the greatest weighting against the West German mark
1981	Greece joins the EC.
1986	Portugal and Spain join the EC.

1986	In October, following the recommendations of the Werner Report, the EEC launches its first attempt at harmonising exchange rates. The mechanism adopted is the so called 'snake in the tunnel' whereby participating governments are required to confine the fluctuations of their currencies within a range of +/- 1% against each other. The value of the group of currencies (the snake) is also to be maintained within a range of +/-2.25% against the US Dollar (the tunnel). Countries requiring assistance to keep their currencies within the required band may receive help only in the form of loans
1990	UK joins EMS.
1992	At a summit of the European Council in Maastricht, Holland, the **Treaty on European Union (TEU)**, also known as the Maastricht Treaty, is signed. Originally intended to include a declaration of an intention to move towards federal union, at Britain's insistence this aspect is played down. Subsequent to the signing of the Maastricht Treaty, the European Community is referred to as the European Union (EU). UK leaves EMS.
1993	The Single European Market takes effect. Trade tariffs are scrapped, but Duty Free shopping remains until 1999.
1994	Stage 2 of EMU is initiated on January 1st with the establishment of the **European Monetary Institute (EMI)** to oversee the co-ordination of the monetary policies of the individual national central banks. The EMI will also work towards the introduction of stage 3 by organising the creation of the European Central Bank
1995	Austria, Finland and Sweden join the EU, bringing membership to 15. The Schengen agreement comes into force and scraps border controls. UK and Ireland stay out of the agreement.
1997	Heads of Government draft a new agreement in Amsterdam which updates the Maastricht Treaty and prepares the EU for its eastward expansion. Qualified majority voting is introduced into new areas, reducing individual countries' powers to veto new measures.
1998	At the beginning of May, at a summit of EU officials and heads of state in Brussels, the announcement is made as to which countries will participate in the launch of the euro the following January. In June the **European Central Bank (ECB)** is established in Frankfurt, Germany. The ECB together with the national central banks of the 15 EU member states form the **European System of Central Banks (ESCB)** which will be responsible for setting monetary policy for the euro countries and managing those countries' foreign reserves. The EU opens accession negotiations with Hungary, Poland, Estonia, the Czech Republic, Slovenia and Cyprus.

1999	Romania, Slovakia, Latvia, Lithuania, Bulgaria and Malta are invited to begin accession negotiations.
	Eleven countries adopt the euro as their official currency (although national currency notes and coins remain in circulation), but Sweden, Denmark and the UK stay out.
2000	The Nice summit agrees to limit the size of the Commission and increase the President's powers. Qualified majority voting is introduced in new areas, but members keep their vetoes on social security and tax. A timetable for taking forward accession negotiations is endorsed.
2001	The Laeken European Council establishes the Convention on the Future of Europe.
2002	Euro notes and coins are introduced in twelve EU countries.
	The European Commission announces that ten countries are on course to meet the criteria for accession to the EU in 2004.
2003	The UK has been a member of the EU for 30 years.
2004	EU enlargement to 25 member states with addition of Slovakia, Latvia, Lithuania, Malta, Hungary, Poland, Estonia, the Czech Republic, Slovenia and Cyprus.

Glossary

Acquis Communautaire

The term 'acquis communautaire' is used to denote all the rights and obligations that bind Member States to the European Union. This common body of law is constantly evolving as a result of the European integration process. It comprises:

- the provisions, principles and objectives laid down in the Treaties;
- the legislation adopted in application of the Treaties, and the case law of the Court of Justice;
- declarations and resolutions adopted within the EU;
- acts relating to the common foreign and security policy;
- acts relating to police and judicial cooperation in criminal matters;
- international agreements concluded by the Community and those concluded between Member States within the framework of the Union.

Bretton Woods Conference

From 4–12 July 1944, an international conference was held at Bretton Woods (New Hampshire, USA) and attended by 44 countries that were soon to be victorious in the Second World War. It created the Gold Exchange Standard international monetary system and several institutions: the International Monetary Fund (IMF) and the International Bank for Reconstruction and Development (IBRD) which after the success of the Marshall Plan became the World Bank.

The Bretton Woods international monetary system was based on fixed yet adjustable exchange rates, in which each currency had an official parity that was declared to the IMF and defined in gold or in dollars. The system endorsed American supremacy by making the dollar the international currency. Having promoted world economic growth after the war, the Gold Currency Standard system ended in 1971 and was replaced by a system with broader margins and subsequently by floating exchange rates.

Common Assembly

The Common Assembly was the parliamentary body of the European Coal and Steel Community (ECSC) established by the Treaty of Paris of 18 April 1951. The Assembly consisted of 78 members, delegated by the national parliaments of the six signatory States. Its first session was held 10-12 September 1952.

It exercised democratic control over the High Authority by means of questioning and by involving its accountability. The Common Assembly was in a position to table a motion of censure which would entail the resignation of the High Authority en bloc. However, the Assembly had no power over the Council of Ministers and had no budgetary powers.

After the Treaties of Rome came into force, the responsibilities and powers of the ECSC Common Assembly, the EEC Assembly and the Euratom Assembly were granted to a single assembly. During its first session in March 1958, this new institution changed its name to the European Parliamentary Assembly. In March 1962, it became the European Parliament.

Commonwealth

The Commonwealth comprises the States that were part of the former British Empire (except for Mozambique), freely accepting allegiance to the British Crown. The founding text is the Statute of Westminster of 11 December 1931.

The Commonwealth has a duty to maintain and strengthen cooperation between its Members. Their Prime Ministers meet periodically at conferences prepared by the Commonwealth Secretariat. Member countries strive to coordinate their policies and maintain their privileged relations with the UK, from which they have retained a number of institutions and traditions.

In 2006, the 53 Members of the Commonwealth are:

- in Africa: Botswana, Cameroon, Gambia, Ghana, Kenya, Lesotho, Malawi, Mauritius, Mozambique, Namibia, Nigeria, Seychelles, Sierra Leone, South Africa, Swaziland, Tanzania, Uganda, Zambia;

- in America: Antigua and Barbuda, Bahamas, Barbados, Belize, Canada, Dominica, Grenada, Guyana, Jamaica, Saint Kitts and Nevis, Saint Lucia, Saint Vincent and Grenadines, Trinidad and Tobago;

- in Asia: Bangladesh, Brunei, India, Malaysia, Maldives, Pakistan, Singapore, Sri Lanka;

- in Oceania: Australia, Fiji, Kiribati, Nauru, New Zealand, Papua New Guinea, Samoa, Solomon Islands, Tonga, Tuvalu, Vanuatu;

- in Europe: Cyprus, Malta, the UK.

Council of Europe

The Council of Europe is an international organisation founded to promote greater unity among the peoples of Europe. The Statute of the Council of Europe, signed in London on 5 May 1949 by 10 European States, came into force on 3 August 1949. The aim of this organisation is to achieve a closer union between its Members in order to preserve and promote the ideals and democratic principles that form their common heritage. It seeks to reinforce human rights and the rule of law within its Member States and to encourage joint action in the administrative, legal, scientific, cultural, social and economic fields.

The bodies of the Council of Europe are the Committee of Ministers, the Consultative Assembly and the Secretariat. By 2004, its membership had increased to 45 European States.

Court of Auditors

The European Court of Auditors was provided for by the Treaty of Brussels of 22 July 1975, and it was established on 18 October 1977. Starting life as an external audit body for Community finances, it was raised to the rank of an institution by the Treaty on European Union (1992). Since the Treaty of Amsterdam (1997), it audits the finances of the entire EU, carrying out its duties under the three pillars.

The Court has two main functions: an audit function and a consultative function:

- Audit function: the general duty of the Court is to audit the accounts: it reviews the legality and regularity of revenue and expenditure, whilst at the same time ensuring sound financial management. The Court assists the European Parliament and the Council in the audit and implementation of the budget. It submits to them reports which are then considered as part of the procedure for giving discharge to the Commission.

- Consultative function: the Council must consult the Court of Auditors before adopting any financial or anti-fraud legislative provisions. The Court may also deliver opinions at the (optional) request of another of the Community's institutions.

Court of Justice of the European Communities (CJEC)

The Court of Justice of the European Communities (CJEC) was set up as a single institution for the three European Communities (ESCS, EEC and EAEC) on 25 March 1957. It ensures that in the interpretation and application of the Community Treaties the law is observed.

In accordance with the decision of 24 October 1988, the Council attached to it a Court of First Instance (CFI) with responsibility for determining at first instance certain categories of actions.

Euro

The euro is the single currency of the EU. The term 'euro' was adopted by the Madrid European Council of 15-16 December 1995.

On 1 January 1999, the euro replaced the ECU and became the book currency in the countries forming the euro zone. On 1 January 2002, euro notes and coins were put into circulation. By July 2002 at the latest, the national currencies were definitively withdrawn and replaced by the euro.

Euro Zone

The euro zone is a geographical area composed of the Member States which have adopted the euro as the single currency.

Eleven Member States adopted the euro at the outset on 1 January 1999: Austria, Belgium, Finland, France, Germany, Ireland, Italy, Luxembourg, the Netherlands, Portugal and Spain. The first enlargement of the euro zone took place on 1 January 2001, when Greece adopted the single currency.

European Atomic Energy Community (EAEC or Euratom)

On 25 March 1957, Germany, Belgium, France, Italy, Luxembourg and the Netherlands signed the Treaty establishing the European

Atomic Energy Community (EAEC or Euratom) and the Treaty establishing the European Economic Community (EEC).

Euratom entered into force on 1 January 1958. Its task was to contribute towards raising the standard of living in Member States and developing trade with other countries by establishing conditions favourable to the rapid construction and growth of the nuclear industries. Its remit was, however, limited to the civil nuclear sector.

European Central Bank (ECB)

In June 1998, the European Central Bank (ECB) replaced the European Monetary Institute (EMI). Since 1 January 1999, it has been responsible for overseeing the implementation of the tasks conferred upon the European System of Central Banks (ESCB).

The ECB decision-making bodies (the Governing Council, the Executive Board and — while certain Member States remain outside the single currency — the General Council) manage the ESCB, for which the basic tasks are to define and implement monetary policy, to conduct foreign exchange operations, to hold and manage the official foreign reserves of the Member States, and to promote the smooth operation of payment systems. The primary objective of the ESCB is to maintain price stability.

Only the ECB has the authority to issue banknotes in the euro zone. It also approves the number of coins issued by the Member States.

In addition to its monetary tasks, the ECB has an advisory function and a role in the collection of statistical data.

European Coal and Steel Community (ECSC)

On 18 April 1951, Germany, France, Italy and the Benelux countries signed the Treaty establishing the European Coal and Steel Community (ECSC). It entered into force on 25 July 1952 and was to run for fifty years.

The ECSC's task was to contribute, in harmony with the economies of the Member States and by the establishment of a sectoral common market, to economic expansion, to job creation and to raising the standard of living in the Member States. Seeking, furthermore, to render any future armed conflict between its members materially impossible, the ECSC constituted the first embryo of a united Europe in a supranational form.

European Commission

The European Commission is the institution responsible for representing the interests of the European Community independently of the Member States. It is the driving force of the EU. The Commission has many powers and responsibilities:

- Guardian of the Treaties: the Commission monitors the proper application of the provisions of the treaties and of the decisions taken by Community institutions;

- the Commission has the right to propose legislation which allows it to propose to the Council measures aimed at developing common policies;

- the Commission has executive power: it implements common policies either on the basis of Council decisions or directly, in application of the treaties.

Its powers and responsibilities also extend into the areas of foreign and common security policy and police and judicial cooperation in criminal matters. The European Commission is independent of Member State governments and operates according to the principle of collective responsibility.

European Council

The European Council provides the EU with the necessary impetus for its development and defines the general political guidelines thereof.

It was established at the Paris Summit of December 1974 and met for the first time on 10–11 March 1975 in Dublin. It is the successor to the European summits which took place between 1961 and 1974.

The European Council brings together the Heads of State or Government of the Member States and the President of the Commission. It meets at least twice a year, under the chairmanship of the Head of State or Government of the Member State which holds the Presidency of the Council.

European Defence Community (EDC)

On 24 October 1950, the French Prime Minister, René Pleven, presented plans for a European Army to the French National Assembly.

These plans were put forward as a solution to the problem of German rearmament and envisaged the involvement of military units from Germany in the defence of Western Europe. The Paris Conference, inaugurated in February 1951, enabled the six members of the European Coal and Steel Community (ECSC) to draw up the Treaty establishing the European Defence Community (EDC), which was signed on 27 May 1952.

The Treaty created a European army under the integrated command of the North Atlantic Treaty Organisation (NATO). It also provided for the creation of a Board of Commissioners (an executive body modelled on the ECSC High Authority), an Advisory Committee, a Parliamentary Assembly, a Council composed of representatives from the Member States, and a Court that would serve as the EDC's international and administrative court.

Germany became a full member of the EDC following the Bonn Convention of May 1952, which restored complete sovereignty to the country.On 30 August 1954, in the French National Assembly, where opinion was polarised, a preliminary motion was carried, which amounted to a rejection of the Treaty. As the Treaty could not enter into force until all the signatory States had ratified it, France's rejection led to the European Defence Community being abandoned.

The failure of the EDC automatically led to the abandoning of plans for a European Political Community (EPC), which was to head the EDC. The rejection of the EDC Treaty, which symbolised the end of the process of European integration at that time, led to the creation, in October 1954, of the Western European Union (WEU), which sought to coordinate European policy in terms of defence and Germany's membership of NATO.

European Parliament

The European Parliament represents the peoples of the Member States of the European Communities.

Created in 1951 by the Treaty establishing the European Coal and Steel Community (ECSC) under the name Common Assembly, it became a single Assembly for the three European Communities with the entry into force of the Rome Treaties in 1958.

Originally a purely consultative Assembly, its powers have increased as European integration has progressed. It exercises three fundamental powers: legislative power, budgetary power, and power to monitor the Executive (the Commission).

Since 1979, the European Parliament has been elected by direct universal suffrage.

European Political Community

In September 1952, the Common Assembly of the European Coal and Steel Community (ECSC) set up an ad hoc assembly with the task of drawing up a draft Treaty establishing the European Political Community (EPC).

Submitted to the six Foreign Ministers on 10 March 1953, the draft provided for the establishment of a Community, federal in nature, to control the future European army. The EPC was to be responsible for coordinating the foreign, monetary and financial policies of Member States. It provided for the creation of a European Executive Council, a two-chamber Parliament (comprising a House of the Peoples and a Senate) and a Council of Ministers.

The EPC project was automatically abandoned following the rejection, on 30 August 1954, by the French National Assembly of the Treaty establishing the European Defence Community (EDC) of which it was the institutional corollary.

High Authority

Created by the Treaty of Paris on 18 April 1951, the High Authority was the executive body of the European Coal and Steel Community (ECSC). It took up its duties on 10 August 1952.

Supranational in character, it was responsible for ensuring the establishment, operation and management of the common market for coal and steel in the six Member States. To this end, it could take decisions, formulate recommendations and deliver opinions. The High Authority comprised nine members acting independently and in accordance with the principle of collective responsibility.

Following the entry into force, on 1 July 1967, of the Treaty merging the executive bodies of the three European Communities, a single Commission — the Commission of the European Communities — assumed the powers and responsibilities previously exercised by the High Authority.

Marshall Plan

The Marshall Plan was presented by the US Secretary of State, George C. Marshall, on 5 June 1947. Also known as the 'European Recovery Program' (ERP), the plan sought to combat hunger and poverty in a Europe following the Second World War.

The Marshall doctrine sought to provide massive technical and economic aid to the countries of Europe and to stimulate growth and trade in those countries. At the same time, the United States wanted to turn Europe into a solvent trading partner so that Europe would purchase surpluses of American industrial products.

In an international context of the Cold War, the American initiative was also part of a policy seeking to contain the Communist threat in Western Europe. Indeed, objections by the Soviets and their satellite countries of the Eastern bloc denounced the ERP as a capitalist manoeuvre.

Subsequently, the United States sought that the applicant countries develop together a method for economic cooperation and for the coordination of investment and of loans granted. To this end, the Organisation for European Economic Cooperation (OEEC) was established in Paris on 16 April 1948. The Marshall Plan, which cost some $13 billion, ended in June 1951.

Organisation for Economic Cooperation and Development (OECD)

On 14 December 1960, the Convention on the Organisation for Economic Cooperation and Development (OECD) was signed in Paris. Incorporating Canada and the United States as members, it replaced the Organisation for European Economic Cooperation (OEEC), created in 1948 as part of the Marshall Plan of aid for European reconstruction.

The OECD's role is to promote economic expansion and social progress in its Member States by assisting governments in the formulation of economic policies and by coordinating those policies. The OECD also seeks to participate in the development of world trade on a multilateral and non-discriminatory basis, in accordance with international obligations.

In 2006, the OECD has 30 Member States which share the principles of the market economy, multiparty democracy and the respect for human rights.

Organisation for European Economic Cooperation (OEEC)

The Organisation for European Economic Cooperation (OEEC) was created in Paris with the signing, on 16 April 1948, of the Convention on European Economic Cooperation.

Its initial objective was to organise the distribution of American aid allocated under the Marshall Plan, and in so doing, lay the foundations for the revival of the economies of its Member States. In particular, it was responsible for programmes relating to agricultural matters, problems of currency convertibility, trade liberalisation, the lack of raw materials and energy sources, transport problems and technological development and productivity.

An intergovernmental organisation, the OEEC expanded to include the other side of the Atlantic with the accession of the United States and Canada. In 1961, it changed its name to the Organisation for Economic Cooperation and Development (OECD).

Paris Treaty

On 18 April 1951, Germany, Belgium, France, Italy, Luxembourg and the Netherlands signed the Paris Treaty establishing the European Coal and Steel Community (ECSC).

The Treaty entered into force on 25 July 1952. It established a common market for coal and steel, as proposed by the French Foreign Minister, Robert Schuman, in his Declaration of 9 May 1950.

Single European Act

The Single European Act was signed in Luxembourg on 17 February 1986 by the Benelux countries, France, Germany, Ireland, Portugal, Spain and the United Kingdom, and later by Denmark, Greece and Italy on 28 February 1986 in The Hague. The Act was the first fundamental review of the basic Treaties establishing the European Communities.

It provided for the creation of a large internal market by 31 December 1992 and for the free movement of goods, persons, capital and services throughout the Member States. To that end, the Act introduced qualified majority voting for Council decisions relating to the internal market, strengthened the powers of the European Parliament and provided for increased cooperation in the area of foreign policy. The Single European Act came into force on 1 July 1987.

The Rome Treaties

The Rome Treaties establishing the European Economic Community (EEC) and the European Atomic Energy Community (EAEC or Euratom) were signed on 25 March 1957 in Rome. The Treaties came into force on 1 January 1958.

Western European Union (WEU)

Western European Union (WEU) was created on 23 October 1954 by the Paris Agreements modifying the Treaty of Brussels (Treaty of

Economic, Social and Cultural Collaboration and Collective Self-Defence) of 17 March 1948.

After the failure of the plans for a European Defence Community (EDC) in August 1954, WEU sought to promote defence coordination between its members which, at the outset, were Belgium, France, Germany, Italy, Luxembourg, the Netherlands and the UK.

In 2006, the organisation has 28 members with four different types of status: Member States, Associate Members, Observers and Associate Partners. Only the ten Member States (the seven signatories of the Treaty of Brussels modified in 1954, together with Spain, Greece and Portugal) have full decision-making rights in WEU.

Promoted by the Maastricht Treaty to become an integral part of the development of the EU, the WEU relinquished its military headquarters and its responsibilities as regards crisis management, after the European Councils in Cologne (June 1999) and Helsinki (December 1999) had confirmed, in particular, the resolve of the 15 Member States to establish a European Security and Defence Identity (ESDI) and, in the long term, to subsume WEU.

List of Contributors

Mark Baimbridge is a Senior Lecturer in Economics at the University of Bradford. He is the author/editor of: *The Impact of the Euro* (Macmillan, 2000), *Economic and Monetary Union in Europe* (Edward Elgar, 2003 & 2005), *Fiscal Federalism and European Economic Integration* (Routledge, 2004), *Current Economic Issues in EU Integration* (Palgrave, 2004), *Britain and the European Union* (CIB, 2005) and *Implications of the Euro* (Routledge, 2006), together with a number of forthcoming texts: *Britain, the Euro and Beyond* (Ashgate), *EU Enlargement* (Copenhagen Business School), *Current Issues in EU Enlargement* (Palgrave) and a three volume series analysing *The EU at 50* (Palgrave). His main area of research is the political economy of European integration (EMU, central bank independence, enlargement, UK-EU relations and elections/referendums).

Tony Benn is the son, grandson and father of MPs. He was Labour MP for Bristol South East (1950–61 and 1963–83) and Chesterfield (1984–2001). He retired from the House of Commons after fifty years in Parliament, the longest serving Labour MP in the history of the party to 'devote more time to politics'. He was a Cabinet minister in the Wilson and Callaghan governments (1964–79), as Minister of Technology, Secretary of State for both Industry and Energy, and President of the Council of European Energy ministers (1977). An elected member of the National Executive Committee of the Labour Party (1959–94), he was also Chairman of the Party (1971–2). His published Diaries in eight volumes cover the period from 1940 to 2001. He has also written seven other books, including: *Free Radical* (Continuum, 2004), *Dare to be Daniel* (Hutchinson, 2004), many pamphlets, and several videos and audiotapes. He is the holder of seven honorary Doctorates from British and American universities, a Visiting Professor at the London School of Economics and is a regular broadcaster.

Richard Body was Conservative MP for Billericay (1955–59), Holland with Boston (1966–97) and for Boston and Skegness (1997–2001). Coming from an agricultural background, he is highly critical of the use of pesticides in agriculture leading to his support for organic farming. However, it is his fervent euroscepticism that led to him becoming one of those condemned by the (then) Prime Minister John Major, which eventually lost him the Tory whip for a period. His publications include: *Agriculture* (Avebury, 1982), *Europe of Many Circles* (New European Publications, 1990), *Our food, our land* (Rider, 1991), *The Breakdown of Europe* (New European Publications, 1998), *England for the English* (New European Publications, 2000) and *The European Union versus Democracy* (New European Publications, 2003). He stood down from the Commons at the 2001 General Election.

Brian Burkitt is a Senior Lecturer in Economics at the University of Bradford. He wrote two widely quoted reports: *Britain and the European Economic Community: An Economic Reappraisal*, and *Britain and the European Economic Community: A Political Re-Appraisal* at the time of the 1975 Referendum on EEC membership. His publications include: *Trade Unions and Wages* (Crosby Lockwood Staples, 1975 & 1980), *Trade Unions and the Economy* (Macmillan, 1979), *Radical Political Economy* (Harvester Wheatsheaf, 1984), *The Political Economy of Social Credit and Guild Socialism* (Routledge, 1997), *The Impact of the Euro* (Macmillan, 2000), *Britain and the European Union* (CIB, 2005) and *Implications of the Euro* (Routledge, 2006). He is a frequent contributor to, and commentator on economic issues to television and radio programmes.

Tam Dalyell was Labour MP for West Lothian (1962–83) and Linlithgow (1983–05). In that time, he has served just two years as a frontbencher, and instead assiduously carved out a niche as a thorn in the side of successive governments of every hue. He is famed for his ability to focus on an issue and pursue it obsessively through the Commons making fine use of parliamentary procedures. He also served as an unelected Member of the European Parliament (1975–79). He became Father of the House of Commons after the retirement of Edward Heath in 2001. He stood down from the Commons at the 2005 General Election. His publications include: *Devolution* (Jonathan Cape, 1977), *Misrule* (Hamish Hamilton, 1987) and *Dick Crossman* (Weidenfeld & Nicolson, 1989).

16/15

Library Book Request Form

Author: BAIMBRIDGE, Mark

Title: 1975 Referendum on Europe

Publisher & date of publication: 2006

ISBN:

Price: £17.96

Requested by: DR Chapman

London

EPQ

Harvey Innocent

h.innocent@oneview
school.org

07811 749404

Eric Deakins was Labour MP for Walthamstow West (1970–74) and Walthamstow (1974–87). He was Parliamentary Under- Secretary of State at the Department of Trade (1974–76) and DHSS (1976–79). He is a member of the Labour Euro Safeguards Campaign. His publications include: *Europe: What Next?* (Fabian Society, 1969), *European Economic Community Problems for British Agriculture*(Fabian Society, 1971),*You and Your Member of Parliament* (Nelson Thornes, 1987), *What Future for Labour?* (Shipman, 1988).

Bernard Donoughue worked on the editorial staff of *The Economist*, *Sunday Times*, *Sunday Telegraph* and *The Times*, and taught at the London School of Economics (1963–74), before he moved to 10 Downing Street as Senior Policy Adviser to Harold Wilson and then to James Callaghan (1974–79). After working in the City, he received a Peerage in 1985 and served as Parliamentary Under-Secretary of State at the Ministry of Agriculture, Fisheries and Food (1997–99). His previous books include: *British Politics and the American Revolution* (Macmillan, 1964), *Herbert Morrison* (Weidenfeld & Nicholson, 1973), *Prime Minister* (Jonathan Cape, 1987), *Heat of the kitchen* (Politico's, 2003) and *Downing Street Diary* (Jonathan Cape, 2004).

John Edmonds began his career in the trade union movement in 1966 and rose to become General Secretary of the General, Municipal and Boilermakers (GMB) trade union (1986–2003) and President of the Trades Union Council (TUC) (1997–98). He was also a Member of Council of ACAS (1992–00). He is a Non-Executive Director of the Carbon Trust and of Salix Finance, Vice President of the National Society for Clean Air, Co-Chair of the Trade Union Advisory Committee on Sustainable Development, Member of Royal Commission on Environmental Pollution, Member of Executive of European Trade Union Confederation, Forestry Commissioner and President of Unity Trust Bank. He was Visiting Fellow of Nuffield College, Oxford (1986–94) and is Visiting Research Fellow of King's College, London (2003–).

Philip Goodhart was Conservative MP for Beckenham (1957–92) following a career in journalism at the *Daily Telegraph* (1950–54) and *Sunday Times* (1955–57). His publications include: *Fifty Ships that Saved the World* (Heinemann, 1965), *Referendum* (Stacey, 1971), *1922: The Story of the 1922 Committee* (Macmillan, 1973) and *Full-Hearted Consent: Story of the Referendum Campaign and the Campaign for the Referendum* (Davis-Poynter, 1976).

Uwe Kitzinger was the first British economist of the Council of Europe in Strasburg (1951–56) and served in Brussels as Cabinet Adviser (1973–75) to Sir Christopher Soames, the first British Vice-President of the European Commission. He has been a Fellow of Nuffield College, Oxford (1956–76), was Visiting Professor of Government at Harvard (1969–70) and at the University of Paris (1970–73). He was Dean of the European Institute of Business Administration (INSEAD) in Fontainebleau (1976–80) and Founding President of Templeton College Oxford (1984–91). He was the Founding Editor of the *Journal of Common Market Studies* (1962), whilst his books include: *German Electoral Politics* (OUP, 1960), *The Challenge of the Common Market* (Blackwell, 1961), *Britain and the Common Market* (BBC, 1967), *European Common Market and Community* (Routledge, 1967), *Second try* (Elsevier, 1969), *The 1975 Referendum* (Macmillan, 1976).

Juliet Lodge is Director of Jean Monnet European Centre of Excellence, Jean Monnet Professor of European Union Politics and Professor of European Studies at the University of Leeds. She was the 1991 UK Woman of Europe and European Woman of Europe 1992. She has published widely on the EU with over 200 journal articles and more than 10 books. She has written and edited work for the UK Office of the Commission and European Parliament, given evidence on EU policy to national parliaments and the European Parliament. Her books include: *European Union: European Community in Search of a Future* (Macmillan, 1986), *The European Community and the Challenge of the Future* (Pinter, 1989), *The 1989 Election of the European Parliament* (Macmillan, 1990),*Euro-Elections 1994* (Continuum, 1995), *The 1999 Elections to the European Parliament* (Palgrave, 2001),*The European Union* (Blackwell, 2003), *The 2004 Elections to the European Parliament* (Palgrave, 2005).

John Mills is an economist who has spent all his working life running companies involved in making and selling consumer products. He thus combines a theoretical background in economics with years of practical experience in international business. He is currently responsible for the budget of a major London borough. He is Secretary of the Labour Euro Safeguards Campaign. His publications include: *Monetarism or prosperity?* (Macmillan, 1981), *Tackling Britain's False Economy* (Palgrave, 1997), *Europe's Economic Dilemma* (Palgrave, 1998), *America's Soluble Problems* (Palgrave, 1999), *Manag-*

ing the World Economy (Palgrave, 2000), *A Critical History of Economics* (Palgrave, 2003).

Andy Mullen is a Lecturer in Political Science at Northumbria University. His research focuses upon the response of the British Left to European integration (1945–2002), examining the European policies of the Labour Party, the trade union movement, the Co-operative Party, the Green parties, the Independent Labour Party, the Social Democratic Party and left-wing pressure groups/think tanks. He is the co-author of two recent articles in *The Political Quarterly*: 'European integration and the battle for hearts and minds: New Labour and the euro' and 'Spinning the European Union: pro-EU propaganda campaigns in Britain, 1962–1975', together with co-authoring the accompanying text to this collection: *The 1975 Referendum on Europe: Current Analysis and Lessons for the Future* (Imprint Academic, 2006).

David Owen trained as a doctor before becoming Labour MP for Plymouth Sutton (1966–74). He held Plymouth Devonport for Labour (1974–81), the SDP (1981–90) and as an Independent (1990–92) until he stood down from the House of Commons. He was appointed Minister for the Navy (1968) before resigning from the Shadow Cabinet in 1972 over the Labour Party's refusal to support British entry to the EEC. Subsequently, he was appointed Minister of Health (1974) and Secretary for Foreign and Commonwealth Affairs (1977–79). In 1981 he was one of the founders of the Social Democratic Party, served as Deputy Leader (1982–83) and Party Leader (1983–87). He was created a life peer in 1992. He went on to become joint author of the Vance-Owen Peace Plan to settle the conflict in Bosnia in the 1990s. He was until recently leader of the 'No Campaign' against British membership of the euro. His books include: *Politics of Defence* (Cape, 1972), *In Sickness and in Health* (Quartet Books, 1976), *Human Rights* (London: Cape, 1978), *Face the Future* (Cape, 1981), *A United Kingdom* (Penguin, 1986), *A Future that will Work* (Penguin, 1987), *Negotiate and Survive* (CLV Publications, 1988), *Our NHS* (Pan, 1988).

Alan Sked is a Senior Lecturer in International History at the London School of Economics where he was Convener of European Studies (1980–90). He stood as a Liberal candidate in the 1970 general election, but later rejected the party's pro-EU stance. He was associated with the Conservative-linked Bruges Group until the early 1990s and founded the Anti-Federalist League (1991) as an anti-EU pressure group. Subsequently, he was the founder leader of the

United Kingdom Independence Party (1993–97). He is a Fellow of the Royal Historical Society and is a member of the advisory board of two historical journals. His major books include: *Crisis and Controversy: Essays in Honour of A.J.P. Taylor* (Macmillan, 1976), *The Survival of the Habsburg Empire: Radetzky, the Imperial Army and the Class War, 1848* (Longman, 1979), *Britain's Decline: Problems and Perspectives* (Basil Blackwell, 1987), *Post-War Britain: A Political History (1945–1992)* (Penguin, 1993).

David Stoddart was Labour MP for Swindon (1970–83). He was against joining the Common Market and vigorously campaigned against the idea in every election. He was appointed as PPS to the Minister for Housing and Construction (1974–75), Assistant Government Whip (1975–1977) and Lord Commissioner of the Treasury (1976–77). However, 'Europe' interrupted his progression when the Labour Government imposed a three-line whip on the third reading of the European Assembly Direct Elections Bill leading him to resign his Treasury post. After his elevation to the House of Lords in 1983, he led the opposition to the Single European Act, resigning as an Opposition Whip and Opposition Chief Energy Spokesman in 1988. He continued to sit on the Government benches in the Lords until 2001, when he was expelled from the Labour Party. He remains active in the House of Lords as an independent Labour Peer and is Chairman of the all-party Campaign for an Independent Britain.

Edward (Teddy) Taylor was a Conservative MP for Glasgow Cathcart (1964–1979), Southend East (1980–97) and Rochford & Southend East (1997–05). He became Parliamentary Under-Secretary of State for Scotland (1970–71 and 1974) in Edward Heath's government, but resigned in protest at British membership of the EEC. He was close to Margaret Thatcher and served as her Shadow Secretary of State for Scotland, but lost his seat in the 1979 General Election. He established himself as one of the most steadfast opponents of the EU in the House of Commons and was one of the most persistent rebels against the Major government over Europe, eventually losing the Conservative whip. He stood down at the 2005 General Election.

Robin Williams was called to Bar, Middle Temple in 1964. He is a longstanding critic Britain's membership of the EU which commenced prior to accession and has been advanced through his leading role in numerous all-party pressure groups. He has been Chair of the Anti-Common Market League (1969–84), Director of the Common Market Safeguards Campaign (1973–76) and Honourary Secretary of the Safeguard Britain Campaign (1976–89) and Campaign for an Independent Britain (1989–).

Ernest Wistrich was Director of the European Movement (1969–86) and continues as one of its Vice-Presidents (2000–). He was in charge of the campaign for the UK's entry into the EEC (1970–71) conducted at the request of HMG. In 1975 he was national organiser of the Britain in Europe referendum campaign. He stood for Parliament for the Labour Party in 1964, 1966, and 1979 and for the European Parliament for the SDP in 1984. His publications include: *Europe: Out of the Impasse* (Fabian Society, 1969), *Steps Towards European Political Union* (European Movement, 1990), *After 1992: The United States of Europe* (Routledge, 1991) and *The United States of Europe* (Routledge, 1993).

Robert Worcester is the Founder (1969), Chairman (1969–05) and Life President (2005–) of Market and Opinion Research International (MORI). Visiting Professor of Government at the LSE and Honorary Professor in the Departments of Politics and International Relations at the University of Kent and Warwick University. He is Past President of the World Association of Public Opinion Research and is an Editor of the *International Journal of Public Opinion Research* and a member of the editorial board of the *European Business Journal*. A former Member of the Fulbright Commission, he was the Senior Vice President of the International Social Science Council/UNESCO. His publications include: *Consumer Market Research Handbook* (McGraw-Hill, 1972), *Political Opinion Polling* (Macmillan, 1983), *Private Opinions, Public Polls* (Thames and Hudson, 1987), *British Public Opinion* (Blackwell, 1991), *Explaining Labour's Landslide* (Politico's, 1999), *Explaining Labour's Second Landslide* (Politico's, 2001) and *Explaining Labour's Landslip* (Politico's, 2005).

Mark Baimbridge

An Overview of the 1975 Referendum

The number of books available to analyse contemporary European economic integration have multiplied over recent years to the point where the 'wood' and 'trees' frequently become inseparable. However, despite this extensive choice of texts, a number of weaknesses remain. Firstly, many of the leading texts have sought to maximise their marketability by attempting to cover the entire spectrum of EU related topics, but ultimately only do so at a superficial level. Whilst certain areas may lend themselves to a brief examination presented in a single chapter, many others are too complex to summarise in such a manner and require a more sophisticated approach if all the principal issues are to be analysed. Clearly, the 1975 Referendum on continued EEC membership based on the renegotiated terms of the 1974 Labour administration of Harold Wilson is one such topic. Even the most cursory discussion of the 1975 Referendum should seek to encompass the considerable underpinnings of this area in terms of its economic and political debate, review its historical background and consider how the Referendum features within the present discussion of Britain's membership of the EU.

Given such a Herculean task it would be a challenge to incorporate even the most important aspects into a single book. Given the significance of the occurrence in terms of the British constitution, cabinet collective responsibility, party cohesion, let alone the possibility that Britain might leave the EEC a mere 203 days after gaining entry, it is therefore surprising how little ink has been spilt on this topic. In the immediate aftermath of the Referendum, three books were published:

- Butler, D. and Kitzinger, U. (1976) *The 1975 Referendum*, Macmillan.

- King, A. (1977) *Britain Says Yes: The 1975 Referendum on the Common Market*, American Enterprise Institute for Public Policy Research.

- Goodhart, P. (1976) *Full-Hearted Consent: The Story of the Referendum Campaign and the Campaign for the Referendum*, Davis-Poynter.

The first was part of the established Nuffield series on General Elections pioneered by David Butler and mirrors the now familiar structure, detail and analysis that have become their trademark. The second by Anthony King follows a similar pattern and indeed pays tribute to the work of David Butler and Uwe Kitzinger, although was written with the benefit of distance from the event itself, both geographic and time. Finally, an insider account is provided by Philip Goodhart who was a sitting Conservative MP and had previously written *Referendum* in 1971. However, the next significant publication is not until *The 1975 British Referendum on Europe* article by Broad and Geiger (1996) in the journal Contemporary Record, which takes the form of a discussion between some of the leading protagonists. However, although numerous politicians and Whitehall insiders have frequently covered this topic in biographies, these are inevitably from a single perspective thereby offering a unique, yet ultimately limited analysis. Therefore, given the relative paucity of credible literature on this topic it was decided to divide the analysis of the Referendum across two separate, yet complementary, texts.

Hence, the companion text: *The 1975 Referendum on Europe: Current Analysis and Lessons for the Future*, also published by Imprint Academic, adopts a more formal approach through reviewing a carefully selected series of themes. These encompass the key areas of: the role of referendums in British politics; the Labour Party and Europe; the Conservative Party and Europe; trade unions and Europe; public opinion and Europe; economic issues of membership; and political/ sovereignty issues of membership. Indeed, I am grateful for the scholarship of my co-authors, Philip Whyman and Andy Mullen, for seeing the merit of the initial concept and executing it in such a professional manner. In contrast, the (modest) ambition for this edited collection is to provide a less synthetic account of the 1975 Referendum as witnessed by its participants, together with a degree of overall analysis. Hence the text is divided into two sections outlining a number of background and analytical chapters before focusing upon the recollections of participants.

A second problem for those seeking a greater understanding of European integration is that many books are 'positioned' and adopt a far from neutral stance when explaining the relevant arguments. It is, of course, natural that academics, politicians, trade unionists and general commentators who have self-selected European integration as their speciality, are likely to posses strong opinions towards this subject. However, it is to be hoped that through the varied contributions from across the political spectrum this book succeeds in portraying the concept of the 1975 Referendum in a balanced light.

Thirdly, the fast-moving events of European integration can result in books becoming out-dated soon after, or even before, their publication! However, for this project it is possible to see the opposite as true, whereby such a period of time has elapsed since the occurrence of the central theme, this danger therefore becomes redundant for analysis. Although, in general, readers should always be aware of the time lag it takes for the latest ideas to be included in texts following their initial publication as working papers, conference contributions and journal articles, the hindsight which this project is afforded can be regarded as a luxury rarely available to authors/editors.

This edited collection, with contributions predominantly from those involved in the 1975 Referendum, seeks to both review aspects of the Referendum and look ahead to the prospect of two further referendums concerning the UK's relationship with the EU. Firstly, there is the longstanding commitment of the current Labour government to consult the people once the Treasury tests of October 1997 are satisfied regarding UK entry into Economic and Monetary Union (EMU). Although a recent speech by Tony Blair (2006) seems to suggest that 'the economics had to be got right and the politics follow', reversing the original position. Secondly, a key EU process has been the process started following the Laeken declaration in December 2001, when the European Convention was established to produce a draft of the Constitution, headed by former French President Valery Giscard d'Estaing. However, the failure of the French and Dutch electorate to support the proposed Treaty establishing a Constitution for Europe in May and June 2005 halted its progress. Whilst neither of these issues are currently at the forefront of political debate, they are nevertheless still on the long-term agenda of the EU and would involve nationwide referendums not previously witnessed since the 1975 Referendum. Hence, a method of resolving significant political and economic issues that has lain dormant at a national level for more than 30 years would potentially be activated twice in a matter of years.

In summary, the present edited collection seeks to minimise the problems that all editors and authors face by bringing together in a single volume a carefully chosen series of contributions written by leading participants in the Referendum. The editorial content of the book endeavours to be neutral in the sense that none of the arguments contained in the volume are presented as being superior to any other. Moreover, considerable effort has been taken to ensure that although the subject matter is rigorous, the 'technical' content is reduced to a minimum, without compromising the quality of its content, to ensure the highest possible degree of 'readability', which is all too frequently absent from contemporary academic texts. Thus it is hoped that the potential audience for this edited collection has been extended to encompass all those academic disciplines concerned with European integration and a general readership however defined.

The Early History of the EU

This section seeks to provide a brief overview of the development of the EU from its immediate post-World War II origins, through its subsequent foundation and initial phase of growth to its first enlargement in 1973. Whilst those familiar with these matters will undoubtedly be acquainted with this story, it nevertheless seeks to demonstrate that the stop-start nature of European integration can be dated back to the early years of the 20th century in a form that we would recognise today. Thus the momentum of the 1920s was destroyed by the economic and political turmoil leading to the Second World War, such that it was not until its aftermath that further impetus was given to this idea. However, the continued economic hostility between France and (West) Germany over control of raw materials, such as coal and steel, almost halted cooperation in its embryonic tracks. Indeed, once founded, the EU has frequently lurched from crisis to crisis, with issues such as agriculture, budgetary contributions and receipts, voting rights, exchange rate mechanisms, democratic deficit and external relations all remaining too familiar. However, key milestones have also been achieved, not least of which was the founding Treaty of Rome, together with the momentum following the 1969 Hague Summit which led to the initial enlargement in 1973. The latter, in the case of Britain led to the focus of this book examining the 1975 Referendum concerning the renegotiated terms of membership. Hence, this section is divided into historical phases that reflect various key time periods of the EU's development. Subsequently, the major events within each period are summarised to give a general introduction to the themes and trends at work surrounding the embryonic EU. To omit the story, albeit briefly discussed, of the evolution of this unique supra-national body that has come to dominate not just the events of 1975 but much of British economic policy and politics for the post-war period would be a case of Hamlet without the Prince.

Pioneering Phase (1945–49)

At the end of the Second World War trade links had been cut off and any heavy industry or vital manufacturing that had not been destroyed was operating below capacity. The continent was rele-gated to playing a supporting role on the international stage owing to the increased might of the United States and the Soviet Union and their growing rivalry.

Beyond the urgent need for the bare essentials, such as coal and steel, the aim was to revive economic activity and to promote trade and the modernisation of production, either via monetary agree-ments or by means of regional measures for dismantling customs barriers. The establishment of Communist regimes in Central and Eastern Europe, as well as the presence of Soviet troops in those countries, fomented a feeling of apprehension in Western Europe. On 17 March 1948, the Brussels Treaty setting up the Western Euro-pean Union (WEU) was signed, marking the start of European mili-tary cooperation. The creation of the North Atlantic Treaty Organisation (NATO) on 4 April 1949 was a further step towards improved military cooperation between Europe and the United States.

In this context, a divided Western Europe could only prosper through establishing effective, common institutions, if necessary with American financial, technical and military support. The debate on the status of Germany, where, from 1961, the division of Berlin was the symbol in Europe of the Cold War, together with the inexo-rable decline in their overseas territories, made Europe's depend-ence on external forces all the more striking. It was at this point that pro-European movements and supporters of federalism began to promote the idea of European unification and established an Inter-national Committee for the Coordination of Movements for European Unity in 1947, which preceded the Hague Congress, from which emerged the European Movement also in 1948.

There were three basic questions for the peoples of Europe:

- how could material damage be repaired and economic activity revived on the old continent?
- how could the return of a conflict which had set Europe and the whole world ablaze be prevented?
- how could the survival and renaissance of European civilisation be ensured in the face of the increasing threats, which seemed to be embodied in the ideological schism and confrontation between the victorious American and Soviet blocs?

The ideal of European unity, which had already been popularised by certain elite circles during the inter-war period, spread rapidly just after the Second World War. While reconstruction was an immediate priority in the post-war period, many advocated the creation of an autonomous European entity, in order to avoid the world being divided into two blocs.

With regard to the form of and procedures for European unification, ideas often diverged according to political and ideological affiliation. While some favoured a federation led by a federal authority, or even a European government, others preferred an association of sovereign States. In 1946, various supporters of European federal unity founded the Union of European Federalists, bringing together some 50 federalist movements.

Within national parliaments, particularly those of the Netherlands, Belgium, France and Italy, the number of supporters of federalism was progressively increasing. In 1947, Richard Coudenhove-Kalergi, founder of the Paneuropean Union in the early 1920s, united these Members of Parliament in the European Parliamentary Union (EPU) to bring pressure to bear on national governments.

At the 1948 Hague Congress, the Federalists called for the rapid creation of a structure for political cooperation. The US, already giving financial backing to the free countries of Europe, also promoted the idea of political cooperation amongst the democracies of Western Europe. In August 1948 the Joint International Committee for the Coordination of the Movements for European Unity, submitted to the governments of the 16 member countries of the fledgling Organisation for European Economic Cooperation (OEEC) a project for a European Assembly that would be the linchpin of a future EU.

France and Benelux proposed the creation of an independent assembly and the transfer of a share of national sovereignty to a higher decision-making body. While the UK and the Scandinavian countries preferred the idea of close intergovernmental cooperation. A compromise was finally reached between British and Continental interests with the governments of the European states appointing an advisory assembly and a committee of ministers, which would make decisions unanimously and would have the final say. In London on 5 May 1949, ten states (Belgium, Denmark, France, Ireland, Italy, Luxembourg, Norway, the Netherlands, the UK and Sweden) signed the Statute of the Council of Europe. It was the very first international parliamentary assembly. The first representatives were appointed by their national parliaments or by their governments.

The Origins of the EU (1950–56)

The pioneering period as outlined above fell victim to events and the inertia of governments, although it was followed by a period when more concrete achievements could take shape, through consensus and intergovernmental measures. Hence, the European Community, through the Schuman Plan, took its first steps and began to acquire organisational shape.

Germany and France, although hereditary enemies, were at the heart of the plans to establish a new equilibrium in Europe, aware of the fact that Britain would not take the leading role. The issue of the mining regions of the Saarland and the Ruhr was, however, damaging relations between the two countries. The two regions in 1949 were placed under the control of the International Authority for the Ruhr that controlled the production, export and distribution of the coal, coke and steel.

To find a solution in May 1950 the French Foreign Minister Robert Schuman proposed to put the two countries' joint production of coal and steel within the framework of a strong, supranational structure as an effective means of avoiding a steel surplus in Western Europe, this sectoral economic integration plan created shared interests that automatically linked the two countries. Consequently, the Schuman Plan led to the signing, on 18 April 1950, of the Paris Treaty establishing the European Coal and Steel Community (ECSC).

The success of the Schuman Plan inspired a number of similar projects, particularly in the fields of chemicals, electricity, fisheries, aeronautical construction, transport, public health and agriculture. All of them, however, failed for a variety of reasons from technical problems to the divergent political and economic interests prevailing in the various countries. Moreover, these projects, although often modelled on the coal and steel, seemed less urgent, and numerous reservations were voiced by the professionals concerned. A supranational approach no longer seemed appropriate for these proposals, which were inspired more by economic than political considerations. However, two of these projects, agriculture and political union, can be seen as forerunners of the Common Agricultural Policy (CAP) and the EU.

Following the rejection of the European Defence Community (EDC) by the French parliament, some European movements together with some Benelux leaders, set about reviving a Community plan that provided solutions to the specific problems of economic integration where the success of the reconstruction of national economies made the development of external trade an even greater priority. Subsequently, two different initiatives were to combine during 1955 to revive the Community ideal: one of them concerned making atomic energy and the other aimed to stimulate international trade by the opening up of frontiers.

In general, in addition to immediate economic considerations, the international climate also helped to speed up the need for a relaunch. The declaration of the nationalisation of the Suez Canal in July 1956 and Soviet intervention in Hungary in November 1956 were forceful reminders that the lone ECSC did not carry much weight when faced with threats arising from international events.

Successes and Crises (1957–68)

In response to the energy crisis caused by the 1956 Suez Crisis, the Common Assembly proposed extending the powers of the ECSC to other sources of energy such as gas, electricity and atomic energy. The Organisation for European Economic Cooperation (OEEC) concluded that there was a need for the countries of Europe to join together in creating a nuclear industry capable of taking up the challenge and filling the energy deficit facing Europe because of the exhaustion of its coal deposits and of its dependence on oil producers. However, rather than a mere Atomic Energy Community, Germany and the three Benelux countries advocated the development of a wider common market. This idea almost floundered on the strong protectionist tradition of the French businesses and even Monnet felt that such a community would be too large and too difficult to manage. However, ultimately, in order to reconcile these divergent interests, Monnet proposed the establishment of both Communities.

The preamble of the Treaty of Rome states that its main aim was to preserve peace and liberty and to lay the foundations of an ever closer union among the peoples of Europe. With a view to forging closer ties between member states, the objective was for balanced economic growth through the combination of:

- a customs union, together with a Common External Tariff (CET);
- a common policy for agriculture, transport and trade;
- enlargement of the EEC to include other European states.

However, by the mid–1960s, the EEC was shaken by a number of crises. The main cause was General de Gaulle's policy on Europe whereby he sought to shift France's position within the EEC by keeping the latter's supranational powers to a minimum and pursuing intergovernmental cooperation among Member States as an alternative. The failure in 1962 of the Fouchet Plan for a 'Union of States' and France's refusal of the British application to join the common market in 1963, built up further tensions with the Five.

Furthermore, even the Franco-German rapprochement embodied in the Élysée Treaty of 1963 was insufficient to defuse the crisis within the Community which reached its peak in what is known as the 'empty chair' crisis of 1965, when French delegates no longer participated in Community activities, effectively bringing the Community's institutions to a standstill.

Consequently, the crisis was resolved with the 'Luxembourg compromise' of 1966, which allowed any Member State to oppose a Community decision adopted by the majority if it considered its national interests to be seriously threatened. Subsequently, the Community was launched anew with the merger of executives and the financing of the CAP.

Crises and Revival (1969–79)

At the end of the 1960s there was evidently a need to end the political and institutional stalemate that had existed since 1967 when de Gaulle had vetoed Britain's second application for membership. Thus, unification had to be given new impetus. Subsequently, the new President of the French Republic, Georges Pompidou, suggested a meeting of the Six to discuss the urgent problems faced by the Community, summarising the EEC's new priorities in the phrase: 'Completion, deepening, enlargement'.

The Hague Summit of December 1969 examined a threefold policy based on completion, deepening and enlargement. In particular, the latter resulted in the opening of negotiations between the Community and the four applicant countries (Denmark, Great Britain, Ireland and Norway).

Furthermore, as part of the package of decisions taken at the Hague Summit, the Six agreed on a system which, from 1975, would profoundly change the EEC's budgetary resources. The aim was to endow it with genuine fiscal powers and confer definitive financial independence from the Member States and their parliaments. Own resources were also designed to enable the EEC to implement the common policies. The new financial resources consisted of agricultural levies, customs duties on imported goods and value added tax (VAT) limited to 1% of the total VAT collected by the Member States. However, most of the new resources of the EEC went towards the financing of the CAP whereby its cost was so much higher than initially forecast that the Commission soon found itself having to consider how it might limit expenditure from its financial instrument, the European Agricultural Guidance and Guarantee Fund (EAGGF).

The 1957 Treaty of Rome also referred to the idea of a common monetary policy (Articles 103–108) and to the free movement of payments and capital (Articles 67–73). Indeed, since the end of the Second World War, the notion of a European monetary system had been a recurring theme of several European federalist movements. However, the idea still met with strong reservations. The founding Treaty's provisions covering monetary issues were therefore rather cautious, and neither the Commission nor the Council had any binding powers in the area of monetary coordination. Moreover, monetary cooperation was not an urgent matter, given that the Six had balance of payments surpluses and the international monetary situation was stable. Indeed, it appeared unrealistic to create an independent monetary system which did not include the US dollar or the pound sterling.

However, in 1962 the European Commission proposed a pathway for an EEC monetary policy through the introduction, after the transitional period, of fixed exchange rates for the currencies of the Six. The Commission also recommended the creation of a Committee of central bank governors, eventually set up in 1964, as well as a procedure for prior consultation on internal monetary policy.

The first tangible attempt in this direction was made in 1969 in the wake of the 1968 currency crisis which affected both the French franc and the German mark. Furthermore, the growing indebtedness of the United States was increasingly eroding the dollar's international credibility and, consequently, that of the system of fixed exchange rates laid down in 1944 under the Bretton Woods Agreements. Subsequently, the Hague Summit agreed to draw up a step-by-step plan with a view to creating a European economic and monetary union. However, it became clear that the international monetary climate was no longer conducive to plans for European monetary union with the international monetary system going through a succession of crises, ranging from a series of speculative attacks on the dollar to the suspension of the dollar's convertibility into gold, which was the mainstay of the Bretton Woods system. This climate of monetary instability forced the European authorities to set up the EEC's monetary system. Hence, in March 1972, the Six created the European currency snake, designed to guarantee a certain amount of stability by narrowing the fluctuation limits for the exchange rates between European currencies.

Although the snake exchange-rate agreement managed to alleviate the 1972 European currency crisis, the relative weakness of the British pound and the Italian lira was such that they could not remain for long within the system (a result echoed some 20 years later within the European Exchange Rate Mechanism following the combination of speculative attacks and the collapse of economic fundamentals). A new devaluation of the dollar resulted in currencies being floated in 1973, and the first oil crisis caused a rapid imbalance in the external payments of the nine Member States. Grappling for the first time for many years with a serious economic recession, the EEC reacted in an uncoordinated fashion, each struggling to protect its own national economy, thereby demonstrating all the more clearly the wide disparities between them.

Since the 1950s, members of the ECSC's Common Assembly had regularly been calling for its successor, the European Parliament, to be elected by universal suffrage. Since it was primarily a consultative body, none of the Member States took any action on the ECSC Treaty provision which, nevertheless, empowered the Member States to hold direct elections to the Common Assembly. Nor was Article 138 of the Treaty of Rome, which provided for the election of Members of the European Parliament by direct universal suffrage, taken into consideration by the Council. However, during the 1960s, the European Parliament itself sought to increase its democratic legitimacy, but the continued objection of France stymied this as a consequence of its belief that the Council of Ministers was the only authorised legislative body in the EEC.

In 1972 it was recommended gradually to increase of the European Parliament's legislative powers with a view to its eventually securing genuine powers of co-decision. The report also proposed that the President of the Commission, appointed by the Council, should subsequently be invested by Parliament before the other Commissioners were appointed. However, it was only in 1974 that the French President Giscard d'Estaing accepted the idea of direct elections to Parliament which he nevertheless associated with the establishment of a European Council instructed to create a genuine European government.

Negotiations with Britain resumed officially on 30 June 1970 in the wake of the Hague Summit, which had associated the strengthening of the Community with its enlargement. Parallel diplomatic discussions were conducted with Denmark, Ireland and Norway, whose economies remained closely connected to the British market, particularly under the European Free Trade Association (EFTA). Nevertheless, the negotiations took place in conditions very different from those of 1961 and 1967. Since then, the Community had consolidated its position, developed common policies and the establishment of the common market had entered its final phase. The entire body of Community legislation, which would have to be accepted by the applicant countries, was therefore much more extensive than it had been in 1961.

The Treaty establishing the EEC laid down two conditions for potential new Member States:

- the applicant country must be a European country;
- the unanimous agreement of the existing Member States of the EEC is required.

The eligibility of an applicant country was also conditional on some implicit criteria:

- the democratic and pluralist character of its political institutions;
- its capacity to take over the entire body of legislation adopted by the Community (the acquis communautaire);

- its acceptance of the fundamental objectives of the basic treaties establishing the Community.

It was therefore upon these seemingly innocuous grounds that negotiations commenced in 1970 between the Conservative government of Edward Heath and the European Commission with a view to Britain being in the first wave of enlargement. The immediate consequences of which are the focus of this book and its companion text *The 1975 Referendum on Europe: Current Analysis and Lessons for the Future*.

Structure of the Book

The book is divided into two principal sections. The first seeks to establish the background to the discussion of 1975 Referendum. Contributions in this section commence with a chapter by the editor outlining the three distinct phases of Britain's relationship with the EEC until the Referendum in terms of the 'road to membership' which was accelerated by various internal and external economic and political forces. Secondly, it describes the difficulties between Britain and continental Europe, in particular focusing upon significant historical, political, legal and economic disparities that continue to exist. Finally, the chapter concludes with a brief description of the countdown to the Referendum following a renegotiation of the terms of entry in 1974–75 by the government of Harold Wilson.

The following chapter in this section is by Andy Mullen and analyses the changing policies of post-war British governments and establishment towards European integration until the 1975 Referendum. Thus the European policy of the British State shifted several times. From 1945–48 it was enthusiastic about European integration, seeing it as a vehicle for its imperial third force policy. However, from 1949–60, it tried to steer the process towards an intergovernmental direction in an attempt to contain the supranational ambitions of the original EU members. Its failure precipitated a process of gradual engagement, including two failed applications to join the EU in August 1961 and May 1967, culminating in Britain's accession in January 1973. Furthermore, Mullen describes how the Conservative and Labour parties were also divided on the question of the EU, with their leaderships generally in favour and their memberships more circumspect, if not opposed. Hence, both leaderships, who essentially shadowed the official European policy of the British State during this period, strove to manage opinion within their respective parties about European integration. Subsequently, these elites joined forces with pro-EU forces within the British State in an attempt to manipulate the state of public opinion, resulting in two national pro-EU propaganda campaigns.

The next chapter is by Robert Worcester and focuses upon the notion that public opinion is important, real, and was well managed by the Government in the 1975 Referendum. In particular, Worcester argues this to be true, especially in relation to the way in which public opinion in Britain was turned around in such a very short time. Between January and June 1975 the British Government and its fellow travellers struck a chord on the deeper values of the British electorate to reverse a 57%/43% 'get out' poll finding to the 67%/33% 'stay in' vote on the day. To explain this reversal in fortunes Worcester briefly discusses the notion of 'public opinion' and argues that a clear understanding is required of this phenomenon and that measuring opinion through polls is very different from actual voting, whether in elections or a referendum. Consequently, he indicates that even from the earliest stages of the campaign, the outcome was secure for those in favour of the continued membership. However, it is his discussion of the private polling carried out for the Referendum Steering Group that aficionados will appreciate since it provides a unique insight into the operation of government.

The final chapter in this section is by Juliet Lodge, who argues that Britain has the reputation of being one of the least constructive EU members. From the time of its accession in 1973 the issue of whether or not it should be in or out plagued every major development in European integration. She indicates that there are external and internal reasons for this. The former relate to the UK's self-deceiving understanding of the nature of the organisation, whilst the internal concern the UK's self-image, its self-projection on the world stage, its divisive and internally troubled tensions between different ministerial departments, and its sometimes insensitive and inattentive actions within the EU. Hence, the balance between the exercise of the exit and voice options changed, with their credibility waning. However, the EU's security blanket was essential to its international standing, but only weakly acknowledged as a continuing reason for UK 'loyalty' to being in the EU. Too often, it failed to present a coherent and positive vision of its role in and obligations to the EU. As a result, there was the appearance of capriciousness, and the effectiveness of its exercise of voice was compromised. Nevertheless, there is little doubt that the UK remains, as it was in 1973, committed to EU membership.

In contrast to these opening chapters by academics, the second section contains chapters by key participants in the Referendum from a variety of backgrounds: politicians, academics, trade unionists and pressure group leaders. Whilst every attempt was made to ensure a representative group of opinions, this proved a problematic task with the passage of time denying us many key participants to these events of 30 years ago and ill health afflicting many of those who remain. However, the contributions in this section are in no means a 'second best' selection. Indeed, the contributors include many eminent names from across the spheres of politics (Tony Benn, Philip Goodhart, David Owen, Tam Dalyell, Richard Body, Teddy Taylor, Eric Deakins and David Stoddart), trade unions (John Edmonds) and academia/think tanks (Ernest Wistrich, Bernard Donoughue, Alan Sked, John Mills, Robin Williams, Brian Burkitt and Uwe Kitzinger).

This second section of the book seeks to develop both chronological and thematic strands to illustrate the process by which the Referendum gathered momentum from the time of initial entry negotiations within both the Conservative (Goodhart) and Labour (Owen) parties. Whilst following the advent of the Wilson government in 1974 this then swung into full-scale renegotiation of membership terms (Donoughue). The story then turns to a strand of chapters which explore the implications of these negotiations and the calling of the Referendum, where some contributors have subsequently seen a reversal in their positions held in 1975 to being less (Sked) and more (Edmonds) favourably inclined to British membership of the EU whilst others have remained steadfast in their beliefs (Dalyell). A second theme echoed in several chapters concerns the imbalance between the two umbrella campaign groups, Britain in Europe (BiE) and the National Referendum Campaign (NRC) in terms of personalities, finances and expertise (Body and Mills). Thirdly, a wider perspective, in terms of a post-Referendum analysis is given in terms of reviewing the subsequent economic and political consequences of UK membership and the implications / lessons that arise from the 1975 Referendum for the proposed future ones regarding EMU entry and Constitutional Treaty (Benn, Burkitt, Taylor, Deakins and Stoddart). Finally, this section of the book is framed by two chapters from two doyens of European integration and in particular Britain's relationship with its continental neighbours (Wistrich and Kitzinger).

Finally, this book concludes with a series of Appendices which contain the key official documents relating to the 1975 Referendum. The first of these is the official government leaflet *Britain's New Deal in Europe* which commences with the uncompromising statement 'Her Majesty's Government have decided to recommend to the British people to vote for staying in the Community'. The next two appendices contain the information leaflets of the two officially sanctioned campaign groups, Britain in Europe's *Why You Should Vote Yes* and the National Referendum Campaign's *Why You Should Vote No*. These three documents were distributed to all UK households in the run up to the vote. However, it is evident that the Yes campaign possessed an inbuilt 2–1 majority in terms of the pro-membership message emanating from these documents, which was subsequently mirrored by the outcome of the vote itself. The final appendix, *Results of the Referendum on Continued EEC Membership*, details by region the turnout, Yes and No vote, together with the magnitude of the Yes-No difference.

Part I

Past, Present and Future
of EU Membership

Mark Baimbridge

The Pre-History of the Referendum

The Referendum of June 1975 was the first, and to-date only, post-legislative referendum to involve the whole of the UK. Theoretically, the issue was relatively simple, namely whether to accept the renegotiated terms of UK membership and remain within the EEC. However, as with so many political events its apparent simplicity conceals hidden depths that were to plunge the then Labour administration of Harold Wilson and every successive British government into the quagmire that Britain's relationship with 'Europe' would become. This chapter outlines three distinct phases of Britain's relationship with the EEC until the Referendum. Firstly, it summarises the 'road to membership' which was accelerated by various economic and political forces, both internal and external, that combined inexorably to suggest that EEC membership would provide a shield from the growing gales of globalisation and match the geopolitical reality of the UK in the post war era. Secondly, it describes both the immediate and long-term difficulties between Britain and continental Europe. Although the focus on renegotiation of the terms of entry was based on the short-term consequences of accession, which were plainly evident to many prior to membership, there are a significant number of deep-rooted historical, political, legal and economic disparities that existed albeit in the subconscious of those who opposed membership. However, it is these factors, that have since been defined and developed, which now clearly formulate the significant barrier that divides opinion so strongly in the UK regarding its relationship with its European partners. Finally, the chapter concludes with a brief description of the countdown to the Referendum which was triggered several years before within the Shadow Cabinet of Harold Wilson in the interests of maintaining Party unity. Hence, following Labour's return to power in 1974 an inevitable series of events were placed into motion that led through a renegotiation process to the Referendum itself in June 1975.

The Road to Membership

During the first accession negotiations in 1961, the Conservative-led British Government had laid down a number of conditions, since it wanted to preserve Britain's privileged economic and monetary relations with the Commonwealth countries. Similarly many Labour politicians were equally concerned at the prospect of throwing away the achievements of the Commonwealth for a Europe that was, in their view, largely capitalist. There was also a fear that they would see the price of Commonwealth imports soar because of the disappearance of the imperial preference system. Hence, senior British politicians were also careful to reassure their partners in the Dominions, who were worried that they would find themselves henceforth relegated to the second rank of British concerns.

However, by the late 1960s, links between Britain and the Commonwealth had considerably diluted. Whilst the Commonwealth countries still provided 48% of British imports and took 49% of its exports in 1954, by 1972 Britain was importing a mere 19% of its goods from the Commonwealth, which was taking no more than 20% of British exports. Simultaneously, the EEC was replacing the Commonwealth's share of UK outward investment. Additionally, political and strategic links between Britain and the countries of its former British Empire, despite a traditional sentimental attachment, had declined during the 1960s.

Accordingly, British negotiators adopted a more flexible line with fewer conditions to be met by their future European partners. The decision to accede was taken on both economic and political grounds. In terms of the latter, the British were well aware that, having virtually abandoned the imperial dimension of their foreign policy, it could no longer stand isolated from the Community which was, in contrast, becoming more assertive on the international scene. It was also increasingly difficult to reconcile the UK's privileged relationship with the United States with its closer involvement in European affairs. Simultaneously, the constant economic growth of the Six made the EEC more attractive. For its part, France, which had previously twice resisted UK membership, was now more favourable to British accession since it was seeking to balance German power in Europe by relying on British support.

The most contentious economic issues were Britain's financial contribution to Community resources and its participation in the CAP. However, these problems, which were closely linked, were never properly clarified. In contrast, a definitive solution was found for the other stumbling blocks, namely West Indian sugar and New Zealand butter.

During the summer of 1971, Edward Heath's Government pursued an intensive campaign in Britain in favour of accession. On 7 July 1971, the Government published *The United Kingdom and the European Communities*, a White Paper which reviewed the advantages of British accession to the EEC on a point-by-point basis.

Although the House of Commons approved entry into the EEC on 28 October 1971 and the UK signed the Accession Treaty on 22 January 1972, British public opinion was, however, divided on the merits of joining the EEC. This uncertainty was evident in the behaviour of Members of Parliament at the time of the vote. The political make-up of the group of MPs who approved the Treaty was just as mixed as that of the group which opposed it. In addition to the majority of the Conservative Party, there were 69 Labour MPs among the 356 supporters of British involvement in European integration. Among the 244 opponents of British membership of the EEC were the majority of Labour MPs, together with 39 Conservatives. Moreover, the number of supporters of British involvement declined further when national legislation was adapted to EEC legislation, although the House of Commons once again declared itself in favour of membership on 13 July 1972, whilst the House of Lords did the same on 20 September 1972. Subsequently, the UK's entry into the EEC came into effect on 1 January 1973, together with that of Denmark and Ireland.

British Difficulties with Membership

Following the UK's accession into the EEC in 1973 under the Conservative government of Edward Heath a growing realisation had begun to develop in the minds of both politicians and the public of the enormity of this decision. Indeed, the luxury of hindsight has illuminated the innate feeling that many had at the time of Britain's accession to the EEC. Thus, accession proved to be the relatively straightforward aspect of EEC membership with a number of problems evident from the outset. These included Britain's financial contribution, the operation of the CAP, the international role of sterling and Commonwealth relations.

The problem of Britain's financial contribution continued to prove to be problematic. Following the arrangements adopted by the Six in terms of the EEC's own resources, there was a danger that the cost to Britain would be extremely large and disproportionate. Furthermore, France called on Britain to pay its entire contribution of almost one-fifth of the entire budget upon accession. The particular difficulty arose given that according to EEC rules, Britain had to pay substantial sums in agricultural levies since it imported most of its food products from non-EEC countries at lower prices; hence the high levies. Simultaneously, as its agricultural sector was becoming less important to the national economy, the financial return from the European Agriculture Guidance and Guarantee Fund (EAGGF) would be small. Moreover, depending on the region involved, British agriculture was either extremely efficient and productive at very competitive prices, or very weak and in need of support by direct subsidy in the form of deficiency payments. However, such a system was now specifically prohibited by the CAP, which preferred a system of levies and refunds. Although the UK did its utmost to secure a reduction in its contribution, the Six were only prepared to offer a longer transitional period, such that Britain finally accepted the system of community agricultural preferences as well as a British contribution that would eventually account for 19% of the total community budget.

A further significant point of discord was the international role of sterling which the Commission had made a point of drawing the attention of the negotiators to, with France calling on Britain to abolish the pound sterling as an international reserve currency in the medium-term. Secondly, the Six had no desire to make an indefinite commitment to support the pound, which had been weakened over a long period by chronic British balance of payments deficits. These were a result of an ongoing imbalance between British revenue and expenditure, as well as Britain's large foreign debt. By increasing their holdings in dollars and their balances with the IMF, the countries of the EEC were in effect financing a major part of the financial aid which Britain was receiving from foreign central banks and the IMF. However, in 1971, a compromise was ultimately reached on the role of the pound and on the level and evolution of the British contribution, although the text adopted included certain ambiguities, which would allow the British to return to the subject of their budgetary contribution in the late 1980s.

As previously outlined, exports of sugar from the West Indies and butter from New Zealand were significant stumbling blocks during the negotiations between Britain and the EEC. As regards the former, Britain was satisfied with a commitment, to be formalised in agreements between the Community and the countries of the Commonwealth, which would agree to sign up to the second Yaoundé Convention that entered into force in 1971. Also that year, a compromise was also reached on imports of New Zealand butter for which the UK was an essential market. Eventually, the EEC granted Britain a special regime and a suitable transitional period to help the country conform to Community rules.

However, the above issues were essentially short-term points of irritation between Britain and its new partners. In contrast, a series of deep-rooted fundamental issues can be identified to illustrate why Britain has so often appeared to be at odds with its European neighbours (George, 1992, 1998). These can be summarised as the frequently expressed questions of: Why does Britain not appear to share the vision of the other member states? Why does the UK so often resists common policies? Why is it that it always seems to be Britain that wants special treatment? Why in spite of its size and international influence is the British government perceived as trying to block or dilute the impact of initiatives from Brussels?

The first theme revolves around the notion of an unbroken history. In particular, this relates to the lack of invasion, absence of revolution and being an 'old' state in a 'new' world. Firstly, it is impossible to understand Britain's place in Europe without appreciating the importance of the institutional continuity of British political structures. Most of continental Europe has been swept by invading armies several times over the last couple of hundred years, whilst England has not been invaded since 1066. Secondly, there has been an absence of revolution, whereby Britain has not undergone a dramatic revolutionary upheaval, such as that which transformed France (1789) or Russia (1917). The closest was the Civil War (1642–8) and the Glorious Revolution (1689) that established the principle of parliamentary sovereignty and a constitutional monarchy, but crucially they reformed the institutions of governance rather than replacing them with new ones.

Secondly, as an 'old' state in a 'new' world, when we look at the rest of Europe most states are either relatively new, or have gone through upheavals in the recent past as a result of wars, revolutions, or the fall of the Iron Curtain. For example, Germany was only unified as a single state in 1870, but it was then divided again in 1945, before being reunified as recently as 1990. Indeed, similar events befell Italy, Spain, Portugal and Greece, whilst more recent entrants have only established their independence since the implosion of the Soviet Union at the start of the 1990s (Hungary, Poland, and the Czech Republic), or have been reconstituted as independent nations following the end of the Russian occupation (Latvia, Lithuania and Estonia).

A second aspect unique to Britain relates to the twin concepts of empire and war. Here both the legacy of empire and the pretence of global influence are regarded as explanatory causes of Britain's non-alignment with the rest of Europe. Although its empire disappeared in a very short time after the Second World War, what the empire left behind, however, was a pattern of international trade and cooperation that looked away from Europe and towards the Commonwealth. One of the major considerations when Britain joined the EEC was the abandonment of its Commonwealth partners, who now found their goods and services outside the Common External Tariff (CET), particularly in agricultural products (Burkitt and Baimbridge, 1990).

Whilst Britain can no longer realistically regard itself as a top power, however, in international diplomacy it still tends to 'punch above its weight', through holding onto its permanent seat on the United Nations Security Council and maintaining a level of military spending that allows it to join the US as a junior partner whereby Britain's reflex reaction is still to look to its 'special relationship' with the USA, rather than to deeper cooperation in Europe. Moreover, when American and European positions collide Britain is still usually to be found, isolated among its European partners, siding with America.

A third element is the development of a distinctive legal system, whereby Britain operates a very different legal system from that found on the continent, where the Napoleonic Code forms the basis of law. In particular, the British system of law differs in many important respects from that in most of continental Europe, for example, the jury system is not generally found in Europe, where magistrates and judges tend to bring in a verdict as well as conducting a trial. Furthermore, the adversarial system of justice is also alien to the European inquisitorial tradition, where an examining magistrate questions witnesses on all sides in an attempt to uncover the truth of a particular case. Finally, Continental law also makes much more use of general enabling legislation, that which hands over to the European Commission the right to issue related directives which have the status of new laws and which do not require parliamentary approval. Instead, the British system relies on common law, leaving it to judges to interpret how statutes should apply in particular cases, and binding them to a tradition set by the precedent of earlier rulings. Consequently, Britain has to make major adjustments that the other member states do not have to make.

A further aspect to the contrasting legal systems concerns the different rights of citizenship. Such that perhaps the most important difference between the British and continental traditions concerns the different conceptions of citizenship based on the two different legal systems. There is a presumption in continental European law that citizens' rights are granted and safeguarded by the state because it is enshrined in a constitutional document. Legal rights in this tradition are therefore prescriptive. In Britain, by contrast, it has been assumed that individuals have the right to do whatever they choose provided the law does not explicitly prohibit it. Legal rights in this tradition are only hampered by proscriptive legislation.

A fourth identified difference is that Britain possesses a distinctive type of capitalism typified by the City of London, liberalised markets and its welfare state regime. Hence, whilst the primary emphasis in the move to closer European integration was economic, such that all member states pursue the capitalist market system, British-style capitalism is distinctive compared with that in continental Europe. Through the City of London, the size and significance of its financial services market is a unique feature of the British economy. Not only does London host hundreds of banks, insurance companies and other financial institutions, but its stock exchange and its futures and bonds markets are also the major trading markets in Europe for shares and securities.

Moreover, profound underlying differences exist between the British and continental capitalist systems in terms of the degree of liberalised markets. For example, Albert (1993) contrasts many of the features found in 'Rhine' model countries with those characteristic of the more liberal systems (neo-American model) of capitalism and identifies three key differences in these alternative capitalism systems. Firstly, share capital plays a much more significant role in funding private investment and thereby promoting a short-term perspective in contrast to relying on bank loans to fund new investment. Secondly, the development of a credit culture where the deregulation of financial services facilitated an increase of credit far greater than anything witnessed in other EU countries. This also contrasts with more of a 'savings culture' in Rhine model countries (excluding private pension funds). Finally, the emergence of a competitive ethos compared to an emphasis on cooperation based on corporatist structures between government, capital and organised labour.

Additionally, welfare state regimes further illustrate the divide between the British and continental European capitalist systems. A key study by Esping-Andersen (1990) identified three distinctive 'welfare regimes' in Europe. Firstly, liberal regimes (e.g. Britain) where there is an emphasis on social security as a 'safety net' rather than universal provision. Here the key concern is that welfare provision should not undermine labour market flexibility through an over-generous provision of benefits. Secondly, corporatist welfare regimes (e.g. Germany) where the emphasis is on socially inclusive forms of insurance, but in accordance to people's position in the labour market. Finally, social-democratic welfare regimes (e.g. Scandinavia) where the emphasis is on equality resulting in benefits being both high and universal.

A final general difference between Britain and other member states is its distinctively individualistic culture. Anglo-Saxon individualism has been identified in the pioneering work of Hofstede (1980) relating to how different countries ranked on an individualism / collectivism scale. Within the Western group of countries the most individualistic countries were the USA, Australia, Britain and Canada. In contrast, most member states came considerably further down the scale. Such individualism found in contemporary English-speaking cultures, it is argued, can be traced back to the end of feudalism with its restrictions on the sale and purchase of land, which remained in force in parts of continental Europe up to and beyond the time of the French Revolution. Hence, people were used to selling their labour for a wage and to exchanging goods and services in return for money, such that market-based individualism seems to have predated Protestantism and the Reformation by several centuries. In this regard it is interesting to note in this regard that it was British thinkers (e.g. John Locke, David Hume, Adam Smith, David Ricardo and John Stuart Mill) who first developed the ideas and principles of liberalism in relation to individual liberty, the free market and the minimal state.

Countdown to the Referendum

During the 1970 General Election campaign Edward Heath indicated that further European integration would not happen 'except with the full-hearted consent of the Parliaments and peoples of the new member countries'. However, no referendum was held when the UK entered the EEC. Consequently, the Labour Party's manifesto for the 1974 General Election included a pledge to re-negotiate the terms of Britain's EEC membership and then hold a referendum. This was as much to maintain the well-being of the Party as to show genuine concern for the degree to which the public was becoming less enamoured with Britain's new European partners.

Although as Prime Minister Harold Wilson had himself sought British entry into the EEC in 1967, as a member of the opposition since 1970, he severely criticised the compromises accepted by his successor, the Conservative Edward Heath, at the time of ratification of the Treaty of Accession in 1972. Thus, on his return to power, Wilson immediately called into question the British conditions of entry into the EEC, whilst the Foreign Secretary, James Callaghan, in his first speech before the Council of Ministers on 1 April 1974, demanded a fundamental renegotiation of the conditions set by the treaties of accession negotiated by the previous Conservative administration. Hence, following Labour's election victories in February and October 1974, which eventually saw the attainment of a majority government, the manifesto pledge to re-negotiate better terms and then hold a referendum on whether Britain should stay in the EEC was initiated.

Although the new British Government did not challenge the principle of British membership itself, it nonetheless sought to obtain improvements and amendments in favour of the UK remaining within the EEC. In particular, it wanted to obtain an extension to the preferential terms agreed with regard to the transitional period to allow the entry of Caribbean sugar and New Zealand butter into Britain. The government also sought the reduction of the financial cost of membership and the renewal of direct subsidies, or deficiency payments, to small farmers in the poorest regions.

The UK's partners in Europe, in spite of French reservations, showed themselves ready to make certain concessions in order to avoid a victory for the opponents to European integration. Thus at the Paris Summit held on 9–10 December 1974, Wilson obtained the creation of the Regional Development Fund, which would generally be of benefit to Britain and a correction to the budgetary contribution mechanism. The UK also obtained partial reimbursement of its contribution on VAT at the European Council meeting in Dublin on 10–11 March 1975. Consequently, on 27 March 1975, the Wilson Government recommended the electorate to approve the results of the renegotiation and published a new White Paper calling for continued British membership of the Community.

Subsequently, on 9th April 1975 the House of Commons voted 396 to 170 in favour of retaining Britain's membership of the EEC on the basis of the newly negotiated terms. Hence, the Referendum date was set for June 1975. An intense campaign then commenced to influence public opinion led by Britain in Europe (BIE), which supported continued membership of the EEC and the National Referendum Campaign (NRC), which opposed continued membership.

Given the longstanding and open division within Wilson's cabinet between strongly pro- and anti-Marketeers, the unprecedented decision was made to suspend the convention of collective Cabinet responsibility and permit ministers to publicly campaign against each other. In total, seven of the twenty-three members of the cabinet opposed EEC membership.

In addition to most of the cabinet supporting the Yes campaign, it was also backed by the majority of the Conservative Party, in particular its newly-elected leader Margaret Thatcher, the Liberal Party, together with other minor parties. In contrast, the No campaign consisted mainly of the left of the Labour Party, including cabinet ministers such as Tony Benn, Michael Foot, Peter Shore and Barbara Castle, together with many Labour backbench MPs. Moreover, further support came from some members of the right of the Conservative Party, together with the Unionists parties of Northern Ireland, a prominent member being the former Conservative minister Enoch Powell. However, the No campaign also attracted support from the extreme right and left, such as the National Front and the Communist Party.

A key event that occurred early in the campaign was the result of a special one day Labour Party conference on 26 April 1975 when the Labour membership rejected continued EEC membership by almost 2:1. However, the margin of the vote was not a surprise, since only 7 of 46 trade unions present at the conference supported membership and the prevailing high unemployment was widely blamed on the EEC in terms of the perceived impact of European imports on Britain's economy. However, this was to prove an illusory indication of both the attitude of the Party as a whole and the wider electorate.

During the campaign, virtually all the mainstream national British press supported the Yes campaign, with the communist *Morning Star* being the only notable national daily to back the No campaign. However, this was seen by many on the No side as a 'kiss of death' and by those campaigning on the Yes side as a clear indication of the political stance of those advocating a No vote. Television broadcasts were used by both campaigns, under rules pertaining to General Election broadcasts, which attracted audiences of up to 20 million. However, the Yes campaign was much better funded from the outset with Wilson meeting several prominent industrialists to elicit support.

The denouement to this long process was the response of the British public to the question: 'Do you think the UK should stay in the European Community (Common Market)?' The result was overwhelming on a 64.5% turnout with every administrative county in the UK declaring a Yes majority, except the Shetland Islands and Western Isles (see Appendix 1). The Yes vote was 17,378,581 (67.2%) compared to the No vote of 8,470,073 (32.8%).

Following announcement of the result, Harold Wilson called it a 'historic decision'. However, the frequently shifting sands of politics has impacted upon the participants of 1975, with Tony Benn pointing out that many of those who were strongly for EEC in 1975 are now more sceptical of the EU, 'you have to make your case – and sometimes you win, sometimes you lose. But in the sense that Margaret Thatcher has now come round to my view, Rupert Murdoch has now come round to my view, it wasn't unsuccessful, was it?' Indeed, back in 1975 the combined forces of the political Establishment, the national press and a sophisticated marketing campaign persuaded a doubtful public of the case for saying Yes. The question is now whether a sceptical, if not outright cynical, British public could be convinced in the same way? Indeed, the governments of France and the Netherlands failed spectacularly to secure a Yes verdict, despite having similar apparent advantages in the Constitution Treaty referendums of 2005. Hence the enduring legacy of the UK's 1975 EEC Referendum through the now contrary positions of many initial advocates and the more complex interrelationship between the political elites and general opinion.

Andy Mullen

From Imperial Third Force to the 1975 Referendum

Introduction

Drawing upon declassified state records and other official publications, this chapter documents the changing European policies of the British State, the Conservative Party and the Labour Party from the end of the Second World War until the 1975 Referendum. This period witnessed a struggle within the British State, between pro-European Union (EU)[1] forces and those who were more sceptical, to determine the official position on European integration and whether Britain should participate. As a consequence of these divisions, the European policy of the British State shifted several times. From 1945–48 it was enthusiastic about European integration, seeing it as a vehicle for its imperial third force policy. However, from 1949–60, it tried to steer the process towards an intergovernmental direction in an attempt to contain the supranational ambitions of the original members of the EU, hereafter referred to as the Six. Its failure precipitated a process of gradual engagement, including two failed applications to join the EU in August 1961 and May 1967, culminating in Britain's accession in January 1973.

The Conservative and Labour parties were also divided on the question of the EU, with their leaderships generally in favour and their memberships more circumspect, if not opposed. The Conservative and Labour leaderships, who essentially shadowed the official

---

[1] For simplicity, the post-war process of European integration is henceforth referred to as the European Union, rather than its previous titles of Common Market, the European Economic Community or European Community.

European policy of the British State during this period, strove to manage opinion within their respective parties about European integration. Furthermore, these elites joined forces with pro-EU forces within the British State in an attempt to manipulate the state of public opinion, resulting in two national pro-EU propaganda campaigns.

Initial Post-War Strategy (1944–8)

The primary objective of state planners following the Second World War was to preserve Britain's role and status as a 'great power'. Following a number of studies conducted in 1944, the Foreign Office concluded that, to maintain its 'great power' position, Britain should restore its empire after the war. However, Britain's economic weakness in the early post-war period negated such a strategy. The war cost £7.3 billion, which amounted to one quarter of Britain's pre-war wealth. Britain had also accumulated £3.3 billion worth of debt (Her Majesty's Government [HMG], 1945). Hence, the *restoration of Empire* strategy was abandoned by the British State in favour of an imperial third force policy.

Following Labour's general election victory in July 1945, the Foreign Office and Foreign Secretary Ernest Bevin pursued an *imperial third force* policy. This envisaged the creation of some form of European entity led by Britain. Three schemes were devised: Anglo-French economic co-ordination, the 'Euro-Africa' plan based on the common exploitation of Europe's colonies (see Kent, 1989), and a European customs union. However, the policy was abandoned in 1948 in favour of a 'special relationship' with the United States (US).

Although Britain was initially resistant to US designs for the post-war world order, exploring the possibilities of a restoration of Empire strategy, plus an imperial third force policy, its dependence on the US precipitated the cultivation of a 'special relationship' as an alternative means of preserving British power. The primary objective of British foreign policy since 1948 has been to maintain the 'special relationship', an objective that has guided the actions of successive British governments to the present.

In February 1949, Bevin sanctioned the creation of the Permanent Under-Secretary's Committee, equivalent to the US State Department Policy Planning Staff, to consider long-term questions of foreign policy and to make recommendations. One such report, produced in March 1949, identified the centrality of Anglo-US relations to British policy. 'In the face of implacable Soviet hostility and in view of our economic dependence on the United States, the immediate problem is to define the nature of our relationship with the United States' (Foreign Office, 1949a). Another report produced in March 1949 highlighted the 'importance of our maintaining control of the periphery' around the Soviet Union 'which runs round from Oslo to Tokyo.' It recommended that 'this policy should be concerted with the United States' (Foreign Office, 1949b). In January 1960, the Cabinet Office (1960a) noted that 'our partnership with the United States is an existing source of world power and our status in the world will largely depend on their readiness to treat us as their closest ally.' In September 1964, the Foreign Office (1964) conceded that the 'alliance with the United States is the single most important factor in our foreign policy. The possibility of a hostile Unites States reaction is as considerable a deterrent to our adopting a given policy as the certainty of United States support is an encouragement.'

Critically, the one-sided nature of the 'special relationship', a situation of British dependence rather than Anglo-American partnership, was acknowledged as early as August 1945. Britain was a 'junior partner in an orbit of power predominantly under American aegis' (Foreign Office, 1945). Likewise, the Foreign Office's 1947 assessment warned that 'too great independence of the United States would be a dangerous luxury'. It also acknowledged that the US was 'consciously or unconsciously tending to claim global leadership' (Foreign Office, 1947). The stark reality of the 'special relationship' was exposed during the September 1949 sterling crisis and the November 1956 Suez crisis. Post-1948, British policy towards European integration was framed within the context of the 'special relationship'.

Limited liability (1949–55)

In January 1949, an interdepartmental meeting of Foreign Office, Treasury and other officials outlined the essential characteristics of the *limited liability* policy, which operated between 1949 and 1955:

> Our policy should be to assist Europe to recover as far as we can. But the concept must be one of limited liability. In no circumstances must we assist them beyond the point at which the assistance leaves us too weak to be a worthwhile ally for the US if Europe collapses, i.e. beyond the point at which our own viability was impaired. Nor can we embark upon measures of 'co-operation' which surrender our sovereignty and which lead us down paths along which there is no return (quoted in Clarke, 1982: 209).

The results of this policy include Labour's rejection of the supranational European Coal and Steel Community (ECSC), and, following their general election victory in October 1951, the Conservatives' opposition to the supranational European Defence Community (EDC) and European Political Community proposals in favour of the Eden Plan, plus their attempts to wreck the June 1955 Messina Conference. The latter established the Spaak Committee, whose report laid the foundations for the 1957 Treaty of Rome establishing the European Economic Community and the European Atomic Energy Community. The Eden Plan, published in February 1952, advocated the reform of the intergovernmental Council of Europe to incorporate the ECSC and EDC. It aimed to provide an alternative to the 'small group of states which are moving towards political federation by the progressive establishment of organisations exercising supranational powers' (Cabinet Office, 1952).

The post-Messina period was problematic for the British. In November 1955, the Foreign Office (1955) declared that Britain was:

> not against special groupings of the [intergovernmental] Organisation for European Economic Co-operation [OEEC] member countries for functional purposes. But we shall remain a bit sceptical and suspicious of the Monnets of the European world who, having failed so far in their special political objectives, are now using the slogan of 'economic integration' as their stalking horse.

Before Messina, Treasury economists who had been studying the customs union proposal for several years repeated their work, concluding that its benefits would exceed any loss of Commonwealth markets. The Foreign Office disagreed, warning that a common market would be 'a discriminatory bloc most unwelcome to us' (Foreign Office, 1955). However, the Cabinet Mutual Aid Committee assessment in October 1955 ruled it out on the grounds that it would 'increase the relative importance of our trade with Europe and reduce our economic links with the Commonwealth.' This would have 'a profound effect on the readiness of other Commonwealth countries to co-operate with us in the Sterling Area' and would 'damage the Imperial Preference system.' Furthermore, 'once we became members of a common market, we should be subject to strong political pressures to extend the 'harmonisation' of our policies with those of other members beyond the field of tariffs into other fields both of internal and external policy' (Cabinet Office, 1955).

Although the Six had invited Britain to join the Spaak Committee without preconditions, in November 1955 the Cabinet decided to withdraw. Nevertheless, by April 1956 it was clear that the limited liability policy was redundant. The Foreign Office (1956) declared that 'if a proposal for a common market of the 'Six' came into being' it would be so 'dangerous to our economic interests that we should have to make special arrangements with it, even at the expense of our interests elsewhere.'

Partial Engagement (1956–9)

The 1956 Suez crisis precipitated a shift in policy, to one of *partial engagement*, as Britain attempted to re-capture the leadership of the European integration process. One manifestation of the new policy was the plan for a free trade area in manufactured goods, presented to the Cabinet by Chancellor of the Exchequer Harold Macmillan in September 1956. 'Plan G' was one of the seven options devised by the Treasury in anticipation of Messina. It envisaged the creation of a 17–member Free Trade Area (FTA), in which the Six would constitute the core of a wider membership. In an attempt to reinstate the intergovernmental principle, and thus supplant the Six, the British recommended the integration of the FTA within the OEEC. However, France and the US rejected the FTA proposal. George Ball (1968: 79), Under-Secretary of State for Economic Affairs, set out why the US supported British entry:

> If Britain is now prepared to recognise that the Rome Treaty is not a static document but a process that could eventually lead to an evolving European Community, something in the nature of a European federation, and if Britain can make the great national decision to join Europe on these terms, I am confident that my government will regard this as a major contribution to Western solidarity and the stability of the free world.

Following the rejection of the FTA proposal in November 1956, Britain opted for the smaller European Free Trade Association (EFTA), whilst Macmillan (1959), as Prime Minister, decided to turn his attention to 'how to live with the Common Market economically, and turn its political effects into harmless channels for us.' However, Sir Roderick Barclay (1960), head of the British delegation to the European Commission, warned that the aim of the EU 'was not merely harmonisation but the unification of policies in every field of the economic union, economic policy, social policy, commercial policy, tariff policy and fiscal policy.'

Near Identification and the First Application (1960–3)

During the early 1960s, a new generation of pro-EU officials joined the civil service, displacing those loyal to the Commonwealth. This precipitated the development of a new pro-entry orthodoxy within the Foreign Office and the Treasury, a process assisted by the transfer of Sir Frank Lee, a pro-EU civil servant, to the Treasury in January 1960. As noted by Bell (1995: i), the shift 'amounted to a revolution in political thought; in a short period at the beginning of the sixties entry to the EU was turned from an impossibility into an imperative.' The rationale behind this new orthodoxy was identified by Evans (1975: 81–82): the Foreign Office began to see the EU as 'an empire on our doorstep', whilst the Treasury believed that 'if Britain could acquire an expanded home market, then industrial revival would follow.'

In March 1960, an interdepartmental committee of senior civil servants, chaired by Lee, was established to review Britain's European policy. The Lee memorandum, published in May, argued that negotiating entry would involve 'difficult and unpalatable decisions', including some surrender of sovereignty (Cabinet Office, 1960b). It recommended a policy of *near identification* that is, accepting many of its obligations without formal membership. Macmillan subsequently stated that the 'policies of "near identification" and of joining the Common Market were so similar that one might well lead to the other, and if we were prepared to accept near identification, it might be preferable to contemplate full membership' (Cabinet Office, 1960c).

In June 1960, Macmillan circulated a memorandum to officials, asking them to answer 23 questions. The subsequent report, discussed by a Cabinet committee, stated that:

> We cannot join the Common Market on the cheap. First we must accept that there will have to be a political content in our action – we must show ourselves prepared to join with the Six in their institutional arrangements and in any development towards closer political integration. Without this we cannot achieve our foreign policy aims. Secondly, there must be a real intention to have a 'common market', in general we must accept the common tariff (Cabinet Office, 1960d).

The memorandum also considered the issue of timing, recommending a delay of between 12–18 months, rather than an immediate application to join.

The Cabinet discussed the Lee memorandum, plus the answers to the 23 questions, in July 1960. However, it was apparent that it was divided on the benefits and costs of entry. Two weeks later, Macmillan restructured the Cabinet in favour of pro-EU ministers. Looking back on this period, Young (1998: 123) noted that no ministerial paper was put to the Cabinet, making this 'an officials' operation'. In other words, Macmillan's new European policy, in effect a decision to join the EU, was made by civil servants. Denman (1996: 211) charged that 'it must be the only occasion in British history when a memorandum by an official was largely responsible for a momentous change in British foreign policy.'

In March 1961, Ball re-emphasised US support for British entry. In a meeting with Edward Heath, the Lord Privy Seal, he stated that 'the United States deeply regretted that the United Kingdom had not yet felt able to accept the Rome Treaty commitments. British membership of the Community would represent a contribution of great importance to the cohesion of the Free World' (Foreign Office, 1961).

Between April and July 1961, several Cabinet committee meetings discussed the implications of entry. The Cabinet considered several papers that had been produced by a number of officials. The Lord Chancellor assessed the legal implications, warning that:

> (a) Parliament would be required to surrender some of its functions to the organs of the Community. (b) The Crown would be called on to transfer part of its treaty-making power to those organs. (c) Our courts of law would sacrifice some degree of independence by becoming subordinate in certain respects to the European Court of Justice. In the long run, we shall have to decide whether the economic factors require us to make some sacrifices of sovereignty. My concern is to ensure that we should see exactly what it is that we are being called on to sacrifice, and how serious our loss would be (Foreign Office, 1960).

Other officials acknowledged the loss of sovereignty, stating that:

> In the past, the loss of national sovereignty has been the most potent argument against British participation in supranational institutions. It was to a large extent responsible for our decision, in 1950, not to join the ECSC and, in 1955, to withdraw from the discussions which led eventually to the drafting of the Treaty of Rome. Although the Treaty of Rome does not express this explicitly, it has underlying political objectives, which are to be brought about by a gradual surrender of sovereignty (Cabinet Office, 1961).

Officials also conceded the risks involved in qualified majority voting. By signing the Treaty of Rome, Britain 'would be committing itself to a range of indefinite obligations over a wide field of action within the economic and social sphere.' Officials warned that these 'might subsequently be translated into specific obligations by means of a decision, regulation or directive adopted by the Council with which we would not necessarily agree' (Cabinet Office, 1961). However, these assessments, and that of Kilmuir, were never placed in the public domain.

In June and July of 1961, Macmillan consulted with the Commonwealth about British entry. In July, the Cabinet agreed to open negotiations with the Six. Macmillan announced his decision to Parliament on the 31st July, giving an undertaking that he would consult parliament before entering into any agreement. However, he refused to publish a White Paper. Furthermore, as noted by Bell (1995: 72), paraphrasing Camps (1964), once the House of Commons 'had approved the government's motion it would be extremely difficult for it to oppose entry unless the terms were clearly unsatisfactory. By the use of the argument that they were seeking approval only for the terms, the government got the House onto the narrow technical ground.' On the 9th August Macmillan formally submitted Britain's first application to join the EU and the negotiations opened in October.

The First National Pro-European Propaganda Campaign (1962–3)

While the negotiations were proceeding, Macmillan turned his attention to preparing public opinion for entry. According to the United States Information Agency, public support for European integration, including Britain, stood at 78 per cent in 1954. However, by 1962, it had fallen to 47 per cent (see Table 1).

There was a significant decline in public support for entry whilst negotiations were proceeding. A Gallup poll in October 1961 found that 48 per cent supported entry. However, by June 1962 support had fallen to 36 per cent (see Table 2).

Table 1 — Public Support for European Integration (1952–62)

Q. *Are you in general for or against making efforts towards uniting Western Europe?*

	For very much (%)	Against to some extent (%)	No reply (%)
1952	58	15	27
1954	78	4	18
1955	67	10	23
1956	65	16	19
1957	64	12	24
1962	47	22	23
Source: United States Information Agency in European Commission (1995)			

Table 2 — Public Support for Entry to the European Union (1960–3)

Q. *If the British Government was to decide that Britain's interest would best be served by joining the European Common Market, would you approve or disapprove?*

	Approve (%)	Disapprove (%)	Don't know (%)
Jul 1960	49	13	38
Jun 1960	44	20	36
Jul 1961	40	24	36
Aug 1961	49	19	32
Sep 1961	51	18	31
Oct 1961	48	18	34
Nov 1961	52	19	29
Dec 1961	53	19	28
Jan 1962	47	22	31
Mar 1962	49	23	28
Apr 1962	47	27	26
May 1962	47	21	32
Jun 1962	36	30	34
Jul 1962	42	25	33
Aug 1962	40	34	26
Sep 1962	46	30	24
Oct 1962	58	22	20
Nov 1962	50	23	27
Dec 1962	37	29	34
Jan 1963	41	30	29
Source: Gallup (1968: 49–50)			

In July 1962, the Cabinet agreed that it 'would be necessary for the government to undertake as soon as practicable a campaign to present membership of the Common Market in a fairer light' (Cabinet Office, 1962a). In September the Cabinet decided that 'public opinion was getting dangerously sceptical and needed correction' (Cabinet Office, 1962b). To counter public scepticism, the Conservatives enlisted the services of Lee, who set about devising a propaganda campaign to sell the concept of entry. As noted by Kitsch (1964: 163):

> At the Treasury, Sir Frank Lee held the national purse strings. He controlled public expenditure. He was at the nerve centre of Britain's communications; in an exceptional position to orchestrate and manipulate the entire complex of Britain's government and civil service communications system with the machinery of private enterprise. The situation was unique. It was the first observable example of the entire machinery of Britain's public and private communications system being co-ordinated and geared for a single objective.

That objective was joining the EU. Kitsch (1964) revealed that 'the planning and co-ordination of the exercise had been intensively organised during the final twelve months of the negotiations'. The Conservatives subsequently launched Britain's first national pro-EU propaganda campaign.

For Macmillan, facing the difficulty of projecting one intention to EU member states and another to its domestic and Commonwealth constituencies, the issue of presentation was critical. For the domestic audience, the Conservatives highlighted the economic benefits of entry whilst minimising its political consequences. The campaign included the publication of a government booklet and another produced by the Central Office of Information, plus the widespread distribution of leaflets and 'fact-sheets' to the business sector, the media, politicians, trade unions and the general public.

Macmillan's campaign was augmented by a number of others. They included campaigns by the Conservative, Labour and Liberal parties, the Federal Union, the United Europe Association, the business sector, and by the EU itself. Furthermore, Foreign Office officials were instrumental in establishing the cross-party Common Market Campaign. Although no official record of the first pro-EU propaganda campaign exists, making it difficult to assess its cost, Kitsch (1964) estimated that millions of pounds had been spent. The campaign's aim was to swing the business sector, the media, political parties, trade unions and ultimately the general public behind entry. It appears to have been a success. A Gallup poll in February

1963 found that 42 per cent felt supported entry. A further poll in March 1965 found that support had increased to 57 per cent (see Table 3). Although Charles de Gaulle, the French President, vetoed Britain's first application in January 1963, the downward trend in public support was reversed.

Table 3 – Public Support for Entry to the European Union (1963–5)

Q. If any opportunity occurs for Britain to join the Common Market, would you like to see us try or drop the idea altogether?

	Try to join (%)	Drop the idea (%)	Don't know (%)
Feb 1963	42	37	21
Jun 1963	46	25	29
Sep 1963	46	36	18
Nov 1963	49	32	19
Dec 1963	42	34	24
Jan 1964	36	40	24
Feb 1964	42	33	25
Jul 1964	41	37	22
Nov 1964	44	28	28
Jan 1965	48	30	22
Feb 1965	53	25	22
Mar 1965	57	22	21
Source: Gallup (1968: 233).			

The Second Application (1964–7)

Following Labour's general election victory in October 1964, Prime Minister Harold Wilson reaffirmed the party's five conditions for entry: safeguarding Britain's trade with the Commonwealth, its freedom to pursue an independent foreign policy, its obligations to the EFTA, its ability to plan the economy and its commitment to British agriculture. However, under the influence of pro-EU civil servants, Wilson began to shift in favour of entry. In April 1965, Michael Palliser from the Foreign Office (1965) announced that Labour was conducting a 'genuine reappraisal' of its European policy and warned that 'any continuing insistence on the five conditions will seriously hamper' Labour's 'efforts in this direction.' Shore (2000: 71) charged that Palliser, then Private Secretary to the Prime Minister, 'ensured that no Eurosceptic argument or critique put to Wilson went unchallenged.' Whitehall's campaign to sideline the conditions also included Sir Con O'Neill's paper, 'How to get into the Common Market', circulated in August 1966. O'Neill went on to lead the entry negotiations. The paper concluded that 'though the consequences of early entry' may seem 'economically bleak, the long-term economic consequences of continuing on our present relatively independent course look much bleaker; and as time passes, the difficulty and price of entering the Community will both grow greater' (Foreign Office, 1966).

By the spring of 1967, Wilson was determined to join and, together with George Brown, the Foreign Secretary, embarked on an official tour of the European capitals to sound out opinion. At the end of April, the Cabinet voted 13-8 in favour of reopening negotiations with the Six, with a view to joining the EU. When the decision was put to the House of Commons in May, three-line whips were imposed on both Conservative and Labour MPs. The decision was carried by 488 votes to 62, with 35 Labour MPs voting against. Britain's second application to join the EU was formally submitted on the 10th May 1967, only to be vetoed by de Gaulle in November. Nevertheless, Shore (1993, 2000) revealed that a Cabinet sub-committee of pro-EU ministers was established in 1969 to prepare positions and papers for a third application. However, the Cabinet as a whole was not informed of this.

Accession (1970–2)

The primary objective of the Conservatives, following their general election victory in June 1970, was to secure entry. Heath (1998: 724) expressed his 'belief in the general benefit for Europe, as well as for Britain, of our being a full, and full-hearted, member.' To achieve this, Heath, as Prime Minister, established the European Secretariat in the Cabinet Office and the third leg of Britain's negotiations began. Heath inherited Labour's negotiating team and proceeded on that basis between July 1970 and January 1972. O'Neill (2000) claimed that there was no discontinuity between the third application and those submitted by previous governments. However, there was one aspect of discontinuity: the direction and responsibility for the negotiations was transferred from the Foreign Office to the Cabinet Office, in order to facilitate direct executive control.

The Conservatives' White Paper, stressing the economic and political benefits of entry, was published on the 7th July 1971. It conceded that food prices would rise and that Britain's contribution to the EU budget may become a burden, unless the Common Agricultural Policy was reformed. However, it neglected to mention Economic and Monetary Union, even though the Six had already pledged to create a single currency by 1980. The White Paper also dismissed the notion that entry would undermine national sovereignty. 'What is proposed' it claimed, 'is a sharing and an enlargement of individual national sovereignties in the general interest' (HMG, 1971).

O'Neill (2000: 355) declared that Britain's priority was 'to get into the Community, and thereby restore our position at the centre of European affairs which, since 1958, we had lost.' However, he acknowledged that post-war US foreign policy, long supportive of European integration, had shifted to a more sceptical position under US President Richard Nixon. The shift was based on the fear that, 'in the long term the EEC may develop into a gigantic trading area which will effectively discriminate against US interests.' O'Neill advised Heath to assuage US concerns by emphasising 'the importance we attach to making progress with the political integration of Europe, including closer defence co-operation alongside the economic development' (O'Neill, 2000: 371–372). Looking back on the negotiations, O'Neill conceded that mistakes had been made, specifically the terms relating to fishing and Britain's contributions to the EU Budget. However, he argued that, on balance, the final entry terms constituted a good deal.

Although most sections of Whitehall were in favour of entry, there were a number of sceptical voices. A report by Permanent Secretary Bill Nield estimated that the annual cost of entry would be 'between £100 million and £8–900 million' (Benn, 1989: 227). Furthermore, the Treasury was officially against entry, submitting a paper to that effect. However, these dissenting voices were sidelined. Meanwhile, in May 1971, following a meeting between Heath and Georges Pompidou, the French President signalled that the veto would be lifted and that a third application would be successful.

The Second National Pro-European Propaganda Campaign (1971–2)

Heath acknowledged the need to win over the Conservative Parliamentary Party, the Conservative associations, the Parliamentary Labour Party (PLP) and public opinion, if accession was to be accomplished. The fourth task was particularly difficult. Gallup polls throughout 1965, 1966 and the early part of 1967 found a clear majority (ranging from 43 to 71 per cent) in favour of entry (Gallup, 1968: 246). However, in the late 1960s, public support began to decline and by November 1970 it stood at 16 per cent, with 66 per cent against. In an effort to increase public support for entry, the Conservatives enlisted the assistance of the Information Research Department (IRD). This covert unit, established by Labour in 1948, financed from the Secret Intelligence Services budget with close links to MI6, was judged to be the most effective conduit for Britain's second national pro-EU propaganda campaign. Additional, secret funding for the campaign, provided by the CIA, was channelled through the cross-party Economic League for European Co-operation (ELEC) (Dorril, 2000).

Following extensive survey research commissioned by the European Movement, the Conservatives, together with other pro-EU forces, decided to concentrate upon several themes for the campaign, found to be effective in influencing opinion. These included the notions that entry would deliver higher standards of living, better social welfare, strengthen trade links, safeguard peace and security, and protect Britain's national interest whilst enhancing its global role. The campaign incorporated three stages.

The first stage began in the spring of 1971 when the Conservatives issued 12 'fact-sheets' and distributed 6 million copies of a booklet outlining the benefits of entry. Pro-EU campaigners flooded the press with letters, whilst ministers made 280 speeches on the issue from July-October. Furthermore, a special IRD organisation, the European Unit, was created to work closely with pro-EU forces to rebut the claims of the anti-EU campaign, which enjoyed less funding and fewer resources.

The second stage witnessed the lobbying of Conservative MPs by the parliamentary Conservative Group for Europe and party whips, plus the negotiation of a secret alliance with the 69-strong pro-EU wing of the PLP to ensure a successful House of Commons vote. Conservative Central Office, the Conservative Research Department and the Conservative Political Centre targeted Conservative associations, through constituency chairs, party agents and officers.

The third stage of the campaign was a national one, aimed at influencing the general public through the media. To this end, Geoffrey Tucker, a public relations expert who had worked for the Conservative Party, organised a series of cross-party breakfast meetings of between 20 and 30 people at London's Connaught Hotel. Business leaders, civil servants, media representatives and politicians attended these IRD-funded meetings. Furthermore, Geoffrey Rippon and Crispin Tickell, from the British negotiating team, reportedly attended some of these meetings (British Management Data Foundation, 2000). Radio and television media were particularly targeted, including such programmes as News at Ten, Panorama, Today, 24 Hours, Women's Hour and World at One. The national campaign was augmented by specific ones organised by the Conservative Party for Europe, the Labour Party for Europe, the Liberal Party for Europe and the European Movement, co-ordinated by a government committee.

The European Movement campaign involved the recruitment of over 200 speakers, who addressed over 1000 public meetings, the publication of over 10 million leaflets and the distribution of the *British European* newsletter. It also included major advertising in the British press, billboard advertising, the distribution of prepared articles and letters to local and national newspapers, plus the release of a pop record called 'We've got to get in to get on'. As with the first campaign, no official record of the second campaign exists, making it difficult to estimate its expenditure. However, Wistrich (2001) reported that the European Movement alone spent over £1 million, in stark contrast to the anti-EU campaign, which only spent £50,000 (Evans, 1975). In terms of countering public opposition, the second national pro-EU propaganda campaign also seems to have been a success; support for entry increased, and was sustained, during the 1970–72 period (see Tables 4 and 5).

Following the successful conclusion of the negotiations, and with public opinion moving in the required direction, the Conservatives decided to act. The House of Commons debated a motion in favour of entry in October 1971. As a result of the 69 Labour MPs defying the party whip and voting with the Conservatives, the motion was carried in the final division on the 28th October: 356 MPs voted for entry with 244 against. In January 1972, the Conservatives signed the Treaty of Accession and published the European Communities Bill. There were 104 votes during the bill's passage, and although government majorities fell to single figures on 16 occasions, not one vote was lost. Using the guillotine measure to expedite its passage, the bill was passed on the 17th October 1972. Britain joined the EU on the 1st January 1973.

Table 4 — Public Support for Entry to the European Union (1970–1)

Q. Do you approve or disapprove of the Government applying for membership of the European Common Market?

	Approve (%)	Disapprove (%)	Don't know (%)
Feb 1970	22	57	21
Apr 1970	19	59	22
Jul 1970	24	55	21
Sep 1970	21	56	23
Oct 1970	22	56	22
Nov 1970	16	66	18
Jan 1971	22	58	20
Mar 1971	19	60	22
Apr 1971	22	60	19
May 1971	23	59	18
Jun 1971	27	58	15
Source: Gallup in Zakheim (1973: 192)			

Table 5 — Public Support for Entry to the European Union (1971–2)

Q. On the facts as you know them at present, are you for or against Britain joining the Common Market?

	For (%)	Against (%)	Don't know (%)
Jul 1971	25	57	18
Aug 1971	39	43	17
Sep 1971	35	47	18
Oct 1971	32	51	17
Dec 1971	38	47	16
Feb 1972	42	41	17
Apr 1972	43	43	14
May 1972	41	45	14
Source: Gallup in Zakheim (1973: 192)			

Labour's European Policy (1974–)

The hope that Britain's entry would settle the issue of European integration was not realised. The general public was divided on the issue. In January 1973, Gallup found that 38 per cent believed that Britain was right to have joined, whilst 36 per cent believed that it was wrong. As a result of Tony Benn's campaign for a referendum, Wilson went into both general elections in 1974 with the pledge to renegotiate the terms of membership and to put the decision to the British people. Following Labour's election, and in anticipation of a referendum, Wilson created two new cabinet committees, one for European strategy and another for tactics. During the renegotiations of 1974–1975, Wilson and Foreign Secretary James Callaghan managed to secure some concessions. However, several commentators believed that the renegotiation tactic was part of a strategy to swing public opinion behind continued membership. Indeed, Palliser stated that 'the whole object of the exercise was to keep Britain in, and get something that could be presented to the British as politically adequate' (quoted in Young, 1998: 281). In March 1975, following the conclusion of the renegotiations, the Cabinet voted 16–7 in favour of continued membership. When the decision was presented to the House of Commons, it received a large majority, mainly due to Conservative support. On the Labour side, 137 voted for continued membership, whilst 145 MPs voted against and 33 abstained. However, at the Labour Party Special Conference in April, 3.7 million votes were cast in favour of withdrawal compared to 1.98 million against. To avoid exacerbating these divisions, Wilson agreed that ministers could campaign both for and against continued membership.

Conclusion

There are two striking features about the European policies of the British State, the Conservative Party and the Labour Party during the 1945–75 period. The first is the tendency of the Conservative and Labour leaderships to adopt the official policy of the British State when in power. The second is that, although division on the EU existed within each of these institutions, pro-EU forces managed to outmanoeuvre their opponents, leaving them free to pursue a pro-EU policy. Pro-EU forces also succeeded in shaping public opinion in favour of European integration. The resultant pro-EU consensus, among the political establishment and the general public, effectively set the scene for the 1975 Referendum.

Robert Worcester[1]

Public Opinion and the 1975 Referendum

In this chapter I argue that public opinion is important, real, and was well managed by the Government in the EEC Referendum in 1975. I believe this to be true, especially in relation to the way in which public opinion in Britain was turned around in such a very short time. Between January and June 1975 the British Government and its fellow travellers struck a chord on the deeper values of the British electorate to reverse a 57%/43% 'get out' poll finding to the 67%/33% 'stay in' vote on the day.

Prime Minister Harold Wilson served in the strategic role as 'Chairman of the Board', sitting back while Foreign Secretary James Callaghan took the campaign leadership as 'Managing Director', an alliance of pro-European leadership which proved effective both in conception and execution.

A Gallup Poll in the Daily Telegraph on 24 January 1975 with fieldwork a few days before found the continuation of a fairly consistent pattern running from mid-1973 to then that if asked in a referendum how you would vote, most people who had decided how they would vote, 57%, said that they would vote for Britain to withdraw from membership of the Common Market, as it was called in those

---

[1] I would like to acknowledge the contribution two Oxford graduate students made. Doug Schoen and E.J. Dionne worked with me during the two 1974 General Elections and are the co-authors of the Referendum Polling Presentations book documenting the work MORI did for the Referendum Steering Group. Doug went back to the US with his DPhil, his book on Enoch Powell, and formed a research company, Penn & Schoen, who were President Clinton's pollsters in his re-election campaign. E.J. returned to the US where he joined the New York Times as the political analyst working with the legendary Johnny Apple and later joined the Washington Post. He is now at the Brookings Institute and may be read regularly in the Washington Post as one of its star columnists.

days. This misled the likes of Tony Benn and Douglas Jay among the leadership of the anti-EEC forces. On the Sunday before the Referendum at a party at the American Ambassador's residence Winfield House, Jay's son Peter, later the British Ambassador to the United States, told me that the polls showing two to one support for staying in would be proved wrong on the day; they weren't.

For the anti-Marketeers didn't see or didn't take on board an adroit question put by Gallup to the British sample in their January poll. A second question asked 'If the Government were to renegotiate the terms, and strongly urge that Britain stay in, then how would you vote?'. The answer, leaving aside the 'don't knows', was 71% stay in and 29% get out. This forecast the result six months later. Indeed, Gallup had earlier, in August the previous year, found a similar result, 69% for staying in, and 31% for withdrawal.

From the start of the campaign itself in April to the end on 5th June, a consistent two to one was measured in both the public polls and in the private research MORI was carrying out for, and I was reporting to, the Referendum Steering Group.

During the campaign a meeting was held daily at 9am in the Foreign Office chaired by the Foreign Secretary. The Referendum Steering Group of eight pro-Europe Cabinet Ministers, supported by the Minister in the Foreign Office Roy Hattersley, the Foreign Secretary's political advisor Tom McNally, No. 10 Policy Unit head Bernard Donoughue, FCO Mandarins Oliver Wright and Michael Butler, Cabinet Office Parliamentary Undersecretary John Grant, who had the government information brief, and myself, providing the evidence from the grass roots of the state of British public opinion.

Public Opinion

In recent times, 'public opinion', is most often used to describe the adult population in a one-person-one-vote model which would have been unheard of a century ago. Yet Abraham Lincoln not only used the concepts of extended franchise and democratic involvement, ' … of the people, by the people, and for the people' in the Gettysburg Address, he is also quoted as saying 'Public opinion is everything'.

Price (1992) neatly defines public opinion in his introduction to the birth of public opinion, saying 'The combination of public and opinion into a single term, used to refer to collective judgements outside of the sphere of government that affect political decision making …', yet I believe this is flawed, for it restricts public opinion to the political milieu. We can observe the impact public opinion makes on business and commerce, industry, fashion, literature, the arts, science, war and on every other aspect where the collective view, expressed or assumed, influences anyone in a position of authority over others.

Necker, Price reminds us, Minister of Finance in the pre-Revolutionary France of the 1780s, popularised the phrase *l'opinion publique*, using the term to refer to a growing dependence of the government's status on the opinion of its creditors. He instituted the publication of national accounts and argued that support from the French elite was necessary for success of the government's policies. To that end he advocated full publication of state activities, thus becoming not only Minister for Finance, but the first to propose systematic governmental public relations, the forerunner to today's government information service, the Number 10 press office, the White House spokesman, etc. 'Only fools, pure theorists, or apprentices fail to take public opinion into account', Necker observed in 1792.

Allport (1937) conceptualised the public as a population defined by geographical, community, political jurisdiction or other limits. Again, as my elaboration of the Price (1992) discussion above indicates, too limited, too timid. A broader approach, yet limited by its projectability, seems to me lacking in everything I have been able to find on this subject. It seems to me that my definition (amended) of an opinion poll will do: 'A survey of the attitudes of a representative sample of a defined population' (Worcester, 1991: 125). Broaden it out: a public I define as 'A defined population', thus: 'Public opinion is the view of a [representative sample of a] defined population.'

Price (1992) argues that opinions and attitudes have been said to differ conceptually in at least three ways. First, opinions have usually been considered as observable, verbal responses to an issue or question, whereas an attitude is a covert, psychological predisposition or tendency. Second, although both attitude and opinion imply approval or disapproval, the term attitude points more toward affect (i.e., fundamental liking or disliking), opinion more toward cognition (e.g., a conscious decision to support or oppose some policy, politician or political group). Third, and perhaps most important, an attitude is 'traditionally conceptualised as a global, enduring orientation toward a general class of stimuli, but an opinion is viewed more situationally, as pertaining to a specific issue in a particular behavioural setting.' (Price 1992: 46–47).

Later Price brings in values, quoting Rokeach (1973: 55), 'Like attitudes, values are conceptualised as evaluative beliefs, but they have a special prescriptive quality', thus adopting the continuum idea of my simple definition.

We measure five things with the tools of our trade: people's behaviour; what they do; their knowledge; what they know or think they know; and their views. Specifically, I break down views into three levels.

The first level is people's *opinions*, the 'ripples on the surface of the public consciousness', easily blown about by the political winds and the media.

Below the surface are the currents of *attitudes*, which people have thought about, care about, have discussed with their families and friends, which impact on themselves and their families. Those attitudes are more strongly held and they are not easily blown about. You must have persuasion, you must have argument, and these must come from someone they respect and will listen to if they are to change.

Deeper still are the deep tides of the public's view which we call *values* (things like belief in God, the death penalty, euthanasia and, for 25% of the British public, animal welfare). Other people's values focus on the environment, global warming and the like.

Whatever it is that people feel deeply about, their values on these things change glacially, if at all. In 1975, I argued that on the question of whether Britain should stay in or get out of the Common Market, few held deeply felt views, more an attitude favourable to the Common Market, and most didn't feel strongly one way or another.[2]

Opinion Polls are not the Same as Referendums

During the 2005 General Election the Leader of the Opposition tried to frighten the electorate with warnings that any Referendum on the Euro would be 'rigged' as to timing and question wording. I consistently and continually hear from politicians: 'What matters is how you ask the question (and so forth) in a referendum'.

They are wrong. Polls are top of mind. Referendums are not. Polls are ongoing; here today, gone tomorrow. They are not binding. When an interviewer on behalf of a polling organisation asks your opinions, your attitudes or your values, your behaviour or your knowledge, it is not binding. You do not feel an obligation to think

---

[2]   For an excellent summary of opinion polls on 'The Common Market' before the 1975 EEC Referendum, see Teer & Spence (1972, pp. 108–20).

carefully and thoroughly about what it is that is being asked. It is relatively unimportant; it is not something you have thought about necessarily, you are just courteous enough to answer the questions. The media will not have covered the question matter in advance, for the most part, and the wording is vital.

Referendums on the other hand are considered. At the end of a three- or four-week campaign people know what is at issue, and the people who cast their vote have thought something about it. It is not sprung on them, nor is it a surprise to them that elicits an instant response. It is on a certain day; you know when it is. It is morally binding because the electorate has been asked by their elected government to help them decide on an issue.

A referendum is by definition nationally important and because of that, it is the subject of media focus. Frankly, the wording is unimportant. For example, because of the wording of the Italian constitution, when they had a referendum on abortion, you had to vote 'No' to say 'Yes'. And so that was the slogan of the people who were for changing the constitution, because you had to vote no to say yes, and everybody knew exactly what was at issue and how they were voting. That is not so in an opinion poll.

Thus when the British Government under then Prime Minister Harold Wilson gave in to the demands facing his Party to provide the British people with a vote on whether to stay in or get out of the EEC in June 1975, the British people (with greater or lesser enthusiasm) took part in a referendum campaign which was concluded with a definitive outcome, that Britain was in, and in to stay.

There were other factors at work as well. It was the first-ever national referendum, and to hold a referendum at all was a subject of great debate. Wilson himself had been sceptical about the initiative, not knowing where it might lead. Others felt deeply that a referendum of the people, whether or not legally binding, threatened parliamentary sovereignty. Many argued that as British membership was a complex matter, it was too complicated for the 'ordinary voter' to make a reasoned judgment, an argument I felt which had been lost by universal suffrage.

The view of the British public on wishing to have their say is clear, as we found in our survey of public opinion for the Joseph Rowntree Reform Trust in 1991. More than three in four, 77%, of the British favoured referendums being obligatory on Parliament on the petition of (say) one million electors.

Public Opinion and the 1975 Referendum

In February 1975 I received a telephone call from Roy Hattersley, Minister of State in the Foreign and Commonwealth Office. He said that the Foreign Secretary, James Càllaghan, had asked him to discuss with me a plan for carrying out private opinion polls for the anticipated EEC referendum modelled on the work I had carried out for Mr Wilson in the two 1974 General Elections.

The cost for nine 'quickie' polls tracking public opinion and a base-line for a panel with two recalls during the campaign was £25,000. Roy had gone to the Permanent Undersecretary in the Foreign and Commonwealth Office who held the FCO's purse strings, and was told that 'Parliament didn't provide funding to the Foreign Office to ask the British public how they should carry out their business'. 'But the Foreign Secretary wants it' was Roy's response. 'Then of course the Foreign Secretary shall have it', responded the mandarin, 'but I shall have to minute it to [the weekly meeting of the permanent secretaries]'.

Roy went to Callaghan and explained the problem. Jim's response was to tell Roy to raise the money from private sources, as Wilson had been forced to do to fund the 1974 election polling. That afternoon Roy made two phone calls, and the money was raised. It may have been entirely coincidental, but a peerage and a knighthood followed. What a way to do business.

Public Opinion Towards Britain in Europe

The British have always been, along with the Scandinavians, 'reluctant Europeans'. Three people in four, 75%, of the British public say they feel strongly that they belong to the local community. 78% of the English say they feel strongly about England. The Scots and the Welsh are up in the 80% range (and 84% of the British say they feel strongly that they belong to Great Britain. But only 35% say they feel strongly that they are Europeans. And that was in the 21st Century, not a quarter of a century before.

In 1975, most polling organisations asked what the trade calls by-polar questions, e.g., of a 'yes/no' or 'in/out' format. However, these questions while measuring direction, fail to say anything about strength of commitment. Further, they were widely reported with three figures provided, voting intention to stay in the EEC, voting intention to get out, and the don't knows.

For instance, Butler and Kitzinger (1976) reported that 'A private poll conducted for Labour [by MORI] in August 1974 ... showed 50%

said they would vote to get out and 32% that they would vote to stay in. A Gallup poll at the same time confirmed these proportions (47% to 30%).' In fact, eliminating those in these samples who said they didn't know how they would vote gives the precise same figures, 61%/39% each. Yet most newspapers and certainly the television failed to understand that unlike statements of general attitudes in which the don't knows are sometimes the most important figure to watch (as in the case of a newly elected party leader's satisfaction ratings), when thinking in terms of comparing to a past election or anticipating a future election, the don't knows should be reallocated, and reported separately. In fact, most don't knows don't vote.

During the early 1960s, Gallup and others found a substantial majority for Britain's membership of the Common Market, usually around the two to one margin for joining. Once de Gaulle said 'non', the mood of the British public changed, and most people were for staying out, bottoming out at a massive 76% against Britain applying for membership in April 1970 just before Mr Wilson called his surprise June election. It wasn't until January 1973, after Britain's then Prime Minister Edward Heath had on a vote of the House taken Britain in, that a majority thought Britain should be a member, but by just 51% to 49%. The pendulum swung back shortly thereafter however, and by just after the October 10th general election, in November, six in ten of those with a view said they thought it was wrong that Britain had joined.

However, during the early part of 1975, public opinion towards Britain staying in the EEC swung back to a majority in favour, and by April, reallocating the don't knows so as to make all the public polls comparable, showed a clear two to one level of support for staying in (Table 1). The 'don't knows/undecideds' ranged from 12% to 18%.

The most extensive public poll was done by Gallup; their most interesting finding showed that the public felt that the things that made the British people feel most favourable towards to the Market were 'wages and working conditions', 'military and defence links with Europe' and 'the people of Europe'.

Table 1: Pre-Campaign National Polls

Organisation	Fieldwork	Stay in (yes %)	Get out (no %)	Method
Harris	12 March–6 April	67	33	Random
ORC	1–6 April	68	32	Quota
ORC	10–15 April	67	33	Quota
Gallup	17–21 April	67	33	Quota
NOP	22–27 April	66	34	Quota
Source: MORI Referendum Polling Presentations, May–June 1975				

Private Polls for the Referendum Steering Group

The private polls conducted by MORI included nine daily polls of some 540 people each using a quota sample of ten electors in each of 54 constituencies, and a panel baseline and two recalls on the same persons using a random probability sample in 40 constituencies.

The purpose of the tracking surveys was to identify shifts in voter attitudes, and in particular to monitor the effect on public opinion of various issues that arose during the course of the campaign. The first results from the daily polls and brief written interpretations of the findings were delivered to key members of the Steering Group on the evening of the day the polls were taken, within about five hours of the time the fieldwork was completed. A detailed slide presentation, together with further analysis of the survey's findings, was presented the following morning to the Referendum Steering Group.

The survey part of the research design concentrated on four areas:

1. Who are the waiverers?

2. What would make them vote for Britain to stay in the Common Market?

3. What should the role of the Prime Minister be?

4. What was public reaction to renegotiation?

The panel study was undertaken to monitor more carefully exactly who was shifting, and why, something that requires going back to the same individuals rather than in the case of the tracking polls, taking a fresh sample each time. Panel members were interviewed three times during the month of May. The analysis of the panel included an assessment of the overall effect of the campaign and in particular, the respective strategies of the pro- and anti-market camps on voter attitudes toward the EEC.

In addition, open-ended questions were put to any prospective voter who had changed his or her mind from one interview to the next, in order to probe for the 'why' of their change of voting intention. The full verbatim comments were incorporated into the reporting-back process. Interviewers provided 'fast feedback' reports, describing the mood of the electorate at the time of the interview. These proved increasingly valuable during the campaign.

In addition, each day's report to the Steering Group included comment on any published polls that day, and special memoranda on topics raised by the meetings, e.g., 'Issues and the Target Voters', comparing the poll findings on women, DEs (unskilled workers and those living on state benefits), 18–24 year olds, and Scottish respondents, and once several waves allowed for analysis of other groupings, e.g. Labour supporters, trade unionists, Wales, readers of daily and Sunday newspapers, impact of concern about food price rises, etc., these were prepared and reported as well.

The first survey was conducted on Monday, 5th May, a month before the day of the referendum. It found that 70% of those who intended to vote (5% said they were not voting) and were decided (17% were undecided) said they thought Britain should stay in the Common Market. Of those, seven in ten said their minds were made up, while 14% said they might change their mind. When asked 'What, if anything, would cause you to change your mind?', 'prices/cost of living' predominated. By nearly three to one, people said they thought the country would vote for Britain to stay in the EEC.

A number of open-ended questions were employed to tease out both the good and bad things about staying in, and also getting out, and these were coded into categories and also reported with selective verbatim comments. The first survey tested the public's demand for Mr Wilson's involvement in the campaign, with two thirds saying it was 'very important' that he take part. Further, by more than two to one the public thought that the renegotiation of the terms for Britain was well negotiated.

A week later, on 12th May, the second poll took place, with consistent referendum voting intentions of a 70% yes vote, and a hardening of intention to turn out, 74% saying they were 'absolutely certain' they'd vote, and a drop in the undecideds; 85% said their minds were made up. Issues that the sample thought would be the key issues were prices/inflation/cost of living (35%), food prices specifically, 24%; unemployment 8% and sovereignty just 5%, the issue that the No campaign was leading on.

At the meeting on the 13th I made the following points in my slide presentation:

1) Targets must be:
    a) working-class women (high don't knows, may change mind)
    b) 18–24 year old group (low interest)
    c) Scotland (high intention to vote; high may change mind)

2) Renegotiation success must be stressed

3) Satisfaction with the government at all time low level. PM slightly higher than government, with satisfaction level higher with the 'outs' than the 'ins'.

4) Prices key issue, sovereignty issue not at significant level

5) Labour 'ins' strengthening

6) Suggest advertising in the Mirror and Sun

7) Two-thirds of trade unionists dissatisfied with the government

8) Three-fourths of Scots are dissatisfied with the government and a quarter say they may change their mind on how they'll vote on referendum.

The third poll was taken on 16th May and presented on the 17th, with voting stable at 69% intending to vote Yes. We measured intensity of support, not reported in the public polls to any great extent. Thirty percent said they are very strongly for remaining in, twice the 15% who said they are very strongly for getting out. Intention to vote, however, had dropped back, to 62%. Concern about prices continued to soar, 45% mentioning prices generally and another 30% specifying food prices as the issue causing people to vote one way or the other.

In response to a request from the Steering Group, I presented a Referendum Campaign Strategy Paper which made the following points:

• The Common Market is of low salience to the average British voter.

• What concerns most citizens is prices and cost of living, therefore the theme of the campaign must be (if it can be said) that the Government will have a better chance of keeping prices down if we stay in the Common Market than if we get out.

- Two thirds intend to vote Yes, so now is not the time to frighten the public with the spectre of communism, fear of the consequences of a No vote, or bogeymen.

- Instead, be reassuring and encouraging for them to cast their vote.

- The PM's popularity is higher than the government's, therefore the PM should take the opportunity to reassure the country, all the country, pro and con, Labour and Tory alike, that 'The Prime Minister says yes'.

- Do not scatter your shots: let the opposition talk about sovereignty / independence, Britain's role in the world, defence, etc.

- Sun readers require special attention. They are the most anti-EEC of any newspaper's readers. 42% of anti-Market voters read the Sun.

- There are nearly 1.5 million potential voters that can be reached through the Sundays who do not read any daily paper, including a quarter of all of the waverers and undecideds.

The panel survey results were also presented. They were consistent with the tracking polls, 67% in the baseline with the fieldwork 6–12 May, and the recall 20–21 May showing 70% intended to vote Yes.

The 'change matrix' which can only be done with a panel methodology showed a net switch of 4% no to yes; 2% yes to no and a net 1% of the undecideds going over to the yes camp, reassuring us of the stability of the public's voting intentions.

Of those intending to vote No, 72% gave as one of their reasons prices and another 41% food prices specifically; even among the No voters, sovereignty was only mentioned by 14%.

One surprising finding was that among 'Powellites', who thought Enoch Powell would make the best prime minister, a quarter were 'strongly' for Britain to stay in, despite Powell being one of the principal 'men with staring eyes' in the media description of the day, along with Tony Benn (Schoen, 1977).

Between the baseline and the first recall (85% response rate) certainty of voting hardened as did the percentage of those who 'care very much who wins'. I reported that 'Attitudinally, people are confused about why we should stay in (57% agrees), and a similar number, 57%, agreed that its important to our children's future that we stay in, 43% agreed that unemployment will go up if we get out, but 56% agreed that food prices will go up more if we stay in'.

To understand why people were changing, among the 9% who did, from Yes to No, No to Yes, DK to Yes or No and vice-versa, etc., a panel allows for the interrogation of 'switchers', such as:

No to Yes

'Newspapers and two TV programmes make me fear coming out. We'll be on our own and we can't afford it out of the EEC' Housewife, B, 25–34 Aberdeen N., Nationalist, Care quite a lot, Certain to vote.

'TV and News of the World. Possibility of food shortages' Housewife, DE, 65+, Buckingham, Labour, Care very much, Certain to vote.

'Since I saw Mr Wilson on TV' Housewife, DE, 35–44, Stoke-on-Trent, Labour, Care quite a lot, Certain to vote.

Yes to No

'Unemployment too high due to us joining the Common Market – even in today's Sun that is what it tells us. Prices are too high due to joining the EEC. I've seen posters at work that are against it as well.' Man, B, 25–34, East Kilbride, Nationalist, DK, Very likely to vote.

'The Government seems set on staying out (sic) so I'll vote with them. I think we'll get better free trade with the Commonwealth again and cheaper goods.' Housewife, DE, 45–54, Newark, Labour, Care quite a lot, Certain to vote.

The fourth tracker was presented on the 23rd from fieldwork on the 22nd. Voting intention to stay in remained 'rock solid'. Over three in four said their mind was made up on how they'd vote, and the figure who said the country will vote Yes jumped from 61% to 70% as the weight of support for staying in, from the business community, the city, the trade unions, and the media became apparent. On the down side, I presented data showing that the good-renegotiation-job was not getting across.

Over three people in four said that he PM was in favour of Britain staying in, 9% thought he was for getting out, and 12% said they did not know.

On the 28th of May however support wobbled in the way that it does in elections in Britain, mid-campaign. I had to report a two percent swing away from supporting Britain's continued membership. Mind made up was up sharply, to 88%, up ten points over a week, as the campaign continued. Prices still dominated the issue list, and sovereignty at nine percent had still not reached double figures. Only 25% said they were satisfied with the way the government was running the country, but 45% were satisfied with Mr Wilson as PM.

The third wave of the panel took place 27–28 May, and although nine percent (later 14%) of the panellists had switched (a somewhat lower figure than the 20% or so in general elections) it continued to show sold support for staying in, 69%. By then, certain to vote was up to 73%. The only bad news for the Steering Group was that readers of the Mirror and Sun between 12 May and 27 May who had been undecided had almost entirely shifter to No. The contact rate was 81%.

The next several days of tracking showed much the same, solid voting intention, high mind made up, and seven in ten still thinking that the country would vote to stay in. By ten to one people knew that Mr Wilson favoured staying in. On Sunday, 1 June, five days to go, the tracker showed 69% in favour, three in ten 'strongly' v. 16% of the 31% who intended to vote against feeling 'strongly' against, two to one. I said then that it is a lot easier to get to the 50+% required to win a referendum from 30% as a core vote, than from 16%. The findings showed that the 'children's future' message was getting across, especially among younger people, and that Britain's voice in the world would be weaker No than Yes.

Table 2: Final 'Predictive' National Polls

Organisation	Fieldwork	Stay in (yes %)	Get out (no %)	Method
NOP	27 May	68	32	Quota
ORC	1 June	74	26	Quota
Gallup	2 June	68	32	Quota
Harris	2 June	72	28	Random
Marplan	3 June	68	32	Quota
MORI	3 June	67	33	Quota
Result	**5 June**	**67.2**	**32.8**	
Source: Butler and Kitzinger (1975: 251).				

Monday of the week of the vote showed a slight dip, to 66% voting to stay in, which I interpreted as the last few who had decided (it was up just three percent, to 77%) would, if they voted (which was unlikely), vote No. At that stage in the campaign, 29% of the intending No voters said they might change their minds while the comparable figure for the 'ins' was 17%. Sovereignty had levelled off at 11%. Strength of support was still about two to one favouring the Yes campaign, 31% to 15%.

The final poll, a quota sample of 541 respondents taken on the Tuesday before polling day on Thursday showed 67% likely to vote Yes; 33% No across the country, 58%/42% in Scotland. On the day, it was indeed 67% Yes and 33% No nationally, and 58%/42% in Scotland.

The national polls did well also, save for Opinion Research Centre with the largest sample, 1,610 respondents, which forecast 74% Yes and 26% No and its sister company, Harris, which forecast 72% Yes and 28% No which employed the only random sample design.

Juliet Lodge

Britain and the EU

Exit, Voice and Loyalty Revisited – Public Diplomacy Failure?

Britain has the reputation of being one of the least constructive members of the European Union (EU). From the time of its accession in 1973 to the then European Community (EC), the issue of whether or not it should be in or out of the EC has plagued every major development in European integration. There are external and internal reasons for this. The external relate to the UK's self-deceiving understanding of what kind of an organisation the European Economic Community (EEC) was and the EU has and will become. The internal concern the UK's self-image, its sometimes rueful self-projection on the world stage, its divisive and internally troubled tensions between different ministerial departments, and its sometimes insensitive and inattentive actions within the EU. The balance between the exercise of the exit and voice options changed. The credibility of both waned. By 2005, the UK's exercise of voice within the EU was often unpersuasive. The EU's security blanket was essential to its international standing, but only weakly acknowledged as a continuing reason for UK 'loyalty' to being in the EU. Too often, it failed to present a coherent and positive vision of its role in and obligations to the EU. As a result, there was the appearance of capriciousness, and the effectiveness of its exercise of voice was compromised. Nevertheless, there is little doubt that the UK remains, as it was in 1973, committed to EU membership. This suggests that UK government leaders and ministers are still acclimatizing themselves to their roles as one among equals in a much changed EU. Where they might lead or take initiatives that commend themselves to their EU partners, they should do so with conviction and in a European voice sans trans-Atlantic twang.

UK Ambivalence

Part of the problem historically lies with the initial presentation of what kind of an institution the EEC was, what membership of the EEC meant for the UK, and parliamentary sovereignty. The EEC had been misrepresented as an economic union and a free trading organisation membership of which would enhance the UK's prosperity and international trading position. The fact that the UK joined for political rather than simply economic reasons was disguised and never fully acknowledged until the Convention on the Future of Europe. Even then, ministerial divisions and antipathy to European integration lessened the effective exercise of voice, drowning the need for treaty revision in dreary presentations to the public of legalistic disputes as to the distinction between a draft constitutional treaty and a constitution.

The UK's exercise of voice from 1975 onwards has been muffled. It is as though its 'loyalty' to staying in and being effective and influential within the EU is a dirty secret to be whispered behind hands even though rational decision makers acknowledge that going it alone is not a feasible, desirable or attainable option. The old idea of the UK having a special relationship with the USA, the Commonwealth and the EU is not only obsolete, but allows the UK to communicate its views on EU policies and developments (in whose development, approval, adoption and implementation it plays a full part) as if it were 'outside' rather than an equal partner inside the EU. It has failed to sustain and capitalise sufficiently on alliances that it should form with states having similar goals and common concerns, and robust reasons for wanting — as former great powers — to exercise leadership in spheres, especially security arenas, where national interests remain critical. The 'special relationship' with the USA has not been an adequate compensation for this omission.

The apologetic exercise of voice by the UK has meant that since its accession, every major development in European integration could be hijacked by others. On the one hand, steps towards union could be damned by those opposed to EEC membership in principle. Even the countervailing all party pro-EU voice of Britain in Europe between 2002–4 could not provide sufficient a countervailing voice to lend greater authority and conviction to government protestations of commitment to Europe. On the other hand, those seeking political advantage could tactically oppose any change in EEC authority to suggest that a major onslaught was being made on British sovereignty which hitherto, they argued, had remained in tact. That they were able to do so was because of public ignorance: the primacy of EEC legislation and law over UK law, in those limited areas where the EEC had competence, had not been effectively explained to the public at the time. Politicians from all parties from the time of the signature of the Brussels treaty in 1972 onwards tactically and cynically exploited the primary information deficit at the heart of the British political class — including parliament — and the public about the EEC. This was not just a matter of political claims-making or spin. It was in essence an obfuscation of the reality of European politics that has persisted since the early 1970s.

The 1970s Legacy: Mind the Communications Gap

Then Germany was divided; the Soviet Union had only just begun to accept a principle of renunciation of force in respect of changing European borders after World War II — something that impacted especially on divided Germany and divided Berlin (where a Four Power Agreement came into effect in 1971), shortly before the renunciation of force treaty between Moscow and Bonn (for West Germany); and where the two Germanies had come to accept each other as independent 'administrative entities' rather than states per se. The Federal Republic of Germany, under the leadership of Willy Brandt, former Berlin mayor and seen as the architect of the policy of small steps using civilian power means — human contact — to prepare the way for closer ties with former adversaries in Eastern Europe, had become a confident player on the European stage, eclipsing in some respects the former dominance of France under President de Gaulle who had been succeeded by President Pompidou.

Both France and Germany — as ever supported by the Benelux — wanted the UK inside the EEC for political and strategic reasons. The UK was to become not so much an awkward partner as an independently-minded, tough negotiator ready to implement EU rules more swiftly and more completely than many of the founding members. The UK became both the screen behind which others opposed to EU measures could tactically hide, while taking on the moral high ground of pro-Europeanism; and an advocate of policy change that objectively was essential if economic and political goals were to be met. This was again true in 2005. From the outset, agriculture and the budget were an issue with the British. That they remain so is not surprising. Agriculture has still not been sufficiently reformed. Income and expenditure still have to be reconfigured in order to achieve a more modern re-distribution of available funds to economic growth sectors to engineer and sustain future prosperity and growth. The difficulty of achieving reform is compounded, as it always has been, by successive enlargements of the EEC/EU in the absence of sufficiently robust institutional reform.

Since institutional reform has, in the British psyche, always raised the spectre of a (deeply misunderstood) federal constitutional bargain entrenched in a written form alien to British practice, it has been easy for political actors and others to make cheap political capital out of exploiting the information and communication gap at the heart of any public vote on matters associated with European integration. This applies as much to the election of the European Parliament as it does to the often timid way in which EU institutional offices within the UK present EU information or rebut often amusing, and sometimes seriously flawed, misrepresentations of EU intent, policy, practice or roles within the EU member states. This is all the more ironic in view of the new Commission's communication strategy: plan 'D'; and in view of the UK's vigorous engagement with Europe, especially at sub-national levels of government and by private and public authorities across the country.

In the run-up to the creation of the Single Market programme and especially until the early part of this decade, the UK office of the Commission, for example, had been visible in the regions at the local level, responding far more effectively to local concerns than what the EU Commission White Paper now advocates as an appropriate communication strategy close to the citizen. The UK had been the one member state where information had been tailored to fit the needs of the target audience; where Commission officials were at the coal-face, engaging in discussions with people, and rebutting some of the more ludicrous myths about the EU peddled by a largely hostile media. The absence of overtly pro-EU Prime Ministers until 1993 and a sense of ministerial disengagement from public political communication about the UK's achievements within the EU. Government abdicated responsibility for communicating Europe to those with an unconstructive agenda.

The EEC and now the EU are portrayed as Anglo-phobic alien life-forms 'out there'. Major constitutional developments are habitually downplayed, so reinforcing low awareness and understanding among the public and political class. In 1975 when the first British referendum on membership of the EC was held, the big EEC constitutional issues of the day concerned whether or not the European Parliament's members should be directly elected by universal manhood suffrage or continue to be appointed from among the members of the national parliament. High profile Government MPs with EU insider track records, like Deputy Prime Minister Prescott and former Commissioner Neil Kinnock, and Commissioner Peter Mandelson, as well as some Conservative MPs and former MEPs and Commissioners, also appear to have had little success in redressing the domestic communication deficit about the UK in Europe.

Regardless of the positive outcome in the 1975 referendum, opponents of European integration per se, as well as tactical opponents to integration jostling for public support as part of a party campaign for election, have continued disingenuously to present EC/EU membership as optional. The claims that exiting from the EU would enhance British prosperity, strengthen British sovereignty regardless of globalisation and make Britain altogether more effective internationally and more homogeneous domestically lacks plausibility. Thirty years have elapsed since Britain first joined the EC in 1973. It is striking, but rarely underscored that no UK Government since 1975 has seriously suggested that exiting from Europe is a viable option.

Exit: All Mouth and No Trousers?

The persistence of the demand for exit is matched by another slightly more plausible claim for a renegotiation of some of the key terms of membership. In 1974–5, the demands were for a renegotiation of the terms of entry. They were represented not altogether unconvincingly as improving the UK's financial position in respect of its contributions to the EC budget, long before the famous 'rebate' associated with the Thatcher government. The rebate formula basically prevents the UK from becoming the largest net contributor to the EU's budget and adjusts its contributions to reflect more accurately its relative wealth measured by GDP.

There have been two core elements to the British arguments about whether British interests are best served by being in or outside the EU: the first concerns money; the second, the future constitutional direction of the EU in the world. The 'money' argument relates to the relative balance between contributions from the UK to the EU budget compared to receipts from it via structural policies to compensate the UK for its relatively low income derived from the CAP for its highly efficient farming sector and its (then) relatively high 'contributions' by way of agricultural levies on imports from non-EU suppliers in both the developed world (such as Australia and New Zealand) and poor countries in Africa, the Caribbean and Pacific. This remains out of kilter with EU averages and since the Thatcher government 'rebate', Britain has tenaciously defended its 'clawback'. The budget problem in 2005 related not so much to the principle as to the UK's position expressed in terms of a relative wealth index in the enlarged and enlarging EU.

Significant cuts to the rebate would make the UK the largest net contributor to the EU budget, but hovering just above mid-point on the index of highest gross net income in the EU 25+. In 2004, Germany made the highest net and gross contributions to the EU's budget. Without the 'rebate' the UK contribution would have been over double France's. Whereas France and Italy make higher gross contributions to the budget than the UK, they also recoup more via the CAP. Among the EU25, the gap between payments and receipts is biggest in the UK.

Not surprisingly, the impending review of the EU's Financial Perspectives 2007–3, was bound to challenge the budgetary status quo. Newer and applicant members sought more support from the older members. The contentiousness of the UK rebate meant that sensitive handling of the issue was essential if the British Government was to preserve its position and rebate, and persuade and convince its partners that this was both legitimate and just. Delicate private and public diplomacy was an essential precondition to success. The UK's exercise of voice seemed unconvincing on all fronts. Even after the end of its Presidency in December 2005 it continued to be criticised.

Opponents of British membership of the EU traditionally use the rebate issue to press for secession or at the very least a renegotiation of its terms of engagement in the EU. Surprisingly, the UK Independence Party (UKIP) and other anti-European voices were muted in 2005. Even so, the UK Presidency's handling of the Financial Perspectives discussions resulted in the UK arguments in favour of three related issues being negatively received by its partners. These issues are: budgetary reform per se (less spending on CAP, more on R&D); CAP reform; and a common foreign policy. Yet, in all three, the British government has put forward constructive ideas, though not altogether compellingly.

The UK exercise of voice lacks credibility and consistency. This results in confusing messages, discrepant positions, and an impression of a lack of conviction at best. Consequently, it has been easy for an anti-European (British) press to disparage the sagacity of the European venture. This has been done by linking it to constitutional questions. In the past, these were masked by the rhetoric of federalism. Today, they are laid bare in the rumblings over British adoption of the euro and the question of a referendum to approve the draft Constitutional Treaty signed by the UK government along with the other 24 EU governments. The signals point to domestic political pusillanimity and nervousness. Pre-decisional information seeking and compromise packages worked out with national administrations have been either inadequate or drafted in a way that leaves the door open for domestic interests with destructive intent.

The November 2005 Anglo-Dutch initiative to appoint a watchdog to oversee subsidiarity in the EU barely masked British dissimulation in respect of the EU. Any such watchdog would inevitably seek legal force to give effect to its judgements. This would place a faceless supremo above politics, raise legal processes to new heights, render EU integration bureaucratic and faceless, deprive the European venture of its great and laudable politico-economic and social intentions and so rob one of the successes of the post-war period of teeth at the very point when it should be demonstrating robust resilience to anti-democratic forces and commitment to upholding the liberal principles of democratic accountability, responsible governments, freedom, security and justice to the people.

The perverted claim that this is about finding a means of appeasing the disaffected voters who rejected the draft Constitution in referendums in France and the Netherlands is disingenuous. This is about appeasing governments, not voters. Quangos, which are how the watchdog will start, are notoriously opaque, and subject to clientelism and patronage rather than due democratic process, accountability and scrutiny as required by parliaments. Is it not strange that this coincides with the European Parliament's efforts to wrest back some of the decisions that have become clouded in the opacity of the comitology processes behind closed doors? It coincides moreover with damning reports on inadequate transparency by the EU's watchdog: the EU Ombudsman.

The linking of these financial and constitutional issues at the crudest level suggests that British understanding of membership of a supranational community dedicated to achieving an ever closer union has not progressed much since it acceded in 1973.

Voice as Exit from an Integrative Bargain

At the best, the European strategy of successive UK governments can be called confused and confusing. At times, the Blair government's tactics are close to those of Prime Ministers Wilson and Callaghan in 1974–77. Why is exit voiced, if not from the organisation per se then from its explicit constitutional bargain, when voice has been the perennial strategy of even overtly isolationist, anti-communautaire British (Conservative) governments that historically have shown themselves committed to remaining in the EU? All point to confusing and confused communication that obscure loyalty, as typified by the 2005 UK Presidency whose expected exercise of voice was expected to override decades of ambivalent exit from the constitutional bargain in favour of action to strengthen the EU per se and British influence in shaping its strategic global direction and priorities. Once again, the budget issue masked real achievements on policy and diplomatic fronts across the board. The UK's use of voice contested the constitutional bargain on which the funding of the EEC was founded.

The UK Presidency was criticised for being partial instead of objective. It is incumbent on Presidencies to facilitate EU goal attainment rather than prioritising its own national interests. As EU President, the UK was confronted by an intractable responsible department (the Treasury) and a more pliant Prime Minister, ultimately chairing the European Council. Coherent exercise of voice slipped as the anti-EU Chancellor of the Exchequer Brown opposed pro-EU Prime Minister Blair. Britain's insistence on re-directing available spending away from agriculture to new industries, notably R&D as a condition of the UK agreeing that its budgetary rebate should be cut, seemed rational and desirable in order to boost EU competitiveness in the face of the imperative of globalisation. Many other states, led by France and Poland, implacably opposed this until a final agreement exempted spending on the new states from cuts. The issue was tied into the thorny matter of the future financial perspectives and spending priorities of the EU.

EU member governments and the Commission broadly agreed in principle on a budgetary review to meet the globalisation challenge. However, they disagreed on the means to do so. After the inconclusive Hampton Court Summit, the EU Commission President wrote to the Council President in October with five proposals to relaunch negotiations.[1] The Commission had presented several documents on the Financial Perspectives over the past year. These focused on three main priority areas:

- Integrating the single market into the broader objective of sustainable development, and mobilising economic, social, and environmental policies to that end. The goals under this priority, which corresponds to new headings 1 and 2 in the budget, are competitiveness, cohesion and the preservation and management of natural resources.

- Making EU citizenship a reality by completing the area of freedom, justice, security and access to basic public goods and services – a priority embodied in new heading 3.

- Establishing a coherent role for Europe as a global partner – inspired by its core values – in assuming its regional responsibilities, promoting sustainable development and contributing to civilian and strategic security. This corresponds to heading 4.[2]

Following deadlock at the Hampton Court summit, the UK held bilateral meetings with its partners and the Commission, the Baltic governments and then, in late November and early December the Visegrad four whom the UK would like to count among its allies. By then even though they shared the UK position that CAP reform was a bigger problem than the UK rebate, compromise seemed increasingly elusive.

The UK focus on modernising the budget, both income and expenditure sides, touched the raw nerve of the own resources arguments and the issue of achieving comparable contributions from states with comparable levels of prosperity. Deadlock persisted over a timetable for reviewing the budget, and the scope of any such review. The UK's delay in presenting appropriate Financial Perspectives 2007–13 (Council of the European Union, 2005) tarnished its image, reinforced the notion that the UK was 'deaf' to its partners' needs, 'blind' to the EU's common goals, and unwilling to articulate compromises to resolve the matter. Accordingly, the credibility of its professed commitment to the EU was tarnished. A negative image did nothing to engender confidence in its willingness or ability to be an effective leader within the EU. The early optimism that EU governments had of the first and less so of the second Blair govern-

[1]   Council Presidency CANREFIN 227, 28 October 2005.
[2]   http://europa.eu.int/comm/budget/index_en.htmuropa.eu.int/

ments' ability to lend some direction to the European venture, evaporated.

Why did the UK Presidency engender disappointment? The UK government seemed capricious and unfocused. Priorities were ambiguous. Insufficient urgency seemed to be attached to the EU's (rather than the UK's) agenda, notably in respect of the budget. Britain neither demonstrated leadership, nor exit, voice, or loyalty to the agreed priorities of the European Council. Instead, there was silence. The UK's apparent failure to communicate effectively or in the spirit of seeking solutions augured ill and allowed others both to hide behind UK intransigence and to portray it in a negative light at a time when it was imperative to initiate a political demarche of EU leaders to find a workable resolution. The UK failed to display diplomatic negotiating skills geared to finding the necessary compromise and consensus when the EU most needed it. In November 2005, as Germany grappled with an unstable Grand coalition, and France with rioting, the UK seemed to have emerged from its toddler tantrums of the 1980s and junior playground antics of the early 1990s into a full-blown adolescent sulk: voice as non-verbal communication.

Voice as Non-Verbal Communication

The appearance of a sulky ineffective and semi or non-verbal communication by the UK allowed others to portray the Government as not only being a passive aggressor within the EU, but of it not being part of the team. This may have been simply the product of domestic inter-departmental rivalry and clashes between the Chancellor of the Exchequer and the Prime Minister, but it was something that should have been resolved before the December 2005 European Council if its commitment to Europe was to be credible. Instead, its partners resented UK wavering and drew political and economic advantage from the situation which allowed them, posturing aside, to wrong foot the UK. The position of the UK Presidency was all the more problematic in view of the rhetoric of the UK's past exercise of voice. Anti-supranational pro-intergovernmental Mrs Thatcher brashly and vociferously wanted to persuade the EU to her line of argument: UK self-isolation and a reduction of influence in the EU resulted. Her successors' exercise of voice echoed with the rhetoric of pro-European sentiment and loyalty but at times seemed to lack credibility. They tried to escape the shadow of self-isolation but the image of a disappointingly diffident Britain remained. Once the threat of exit ceased to be whispered, the UK exercise of voice did not lead to effective communication. Instead, the UK seemed unsure of its vocation. Espousing European ideals whilst expounding a trans-Atlantic agenda in the most sensitive of politico-security arenas meant that its partners' pro-European leadership expectations were thwarted. The UK seemed ambivalent, unnerved, unable to follow and equally unable to lead. Why?

Britain's problem is that it is not part of the gang. It communicates badly partly because it does not quite know how to communicate effectively, and partly because it is unsure of what it should be communicating. For far too long, Britain has followed 'public opinion' instead of leading it. There has been a public diplomacy failure at home as well as at EU level. The UK government is unable to persuade its domestic audience, far less its EU partners of what it wants for itself and for the EU. Lacking in precision, its voice slips from platitudes into uneasy silence. There is no withdrawal just the sense of a sulk compounded by an astonishingly ineffectual public diplomacy. The UK's inability to communicate its position publicly and competently dulls its 'voice' which, if heard by its partners, seems unimpressive and convincing. It appears to be 'loyal' by default and lacking imagination. Alliances are both difficult to forge and impossible to sustain.

Exit: So What?

Whereas in 1975, it is conceivable that some member governments would not have wanted to see British withdrawal, thirty years later exit was publicly recognised as highly improbable. Equally improbable was the scenario of the UK (or any other member state) obtaining the agreement of its 24 partners to unilateral opt-outs of policies, or parts of agreements, that were inconvenient, politically inexpedient or financially onerous. Exit, without the unanimous agreement of its partners, or Treaty amendment, was also not on the cards. Legally, this would be in contravention of the 1972 European Communities Act, the legal basis for the application of EU law in the UK. If the Government nevertheless insisted on some kind of exit, it would have to negotiate one with partners. Diplomatic face-savers are commonplace, but not necessarily propitious. The UK needs to make common cause with its EU partners in order to retain influence and a voice on the world stage. EU membership is a pre-condition to exercising influence. The UK Government appreciates this in theory. It is careless, however, in acknowledging this truism in practice both on the world stage and more especially within the EU. It is not sur-

prising therefore that other member governments seem unper-
suaded of its posturing, and weakly disposed to conceding
concessions, even when objectively the UK Government has rational
suggestions that, if adopted, would be in the common good of the
Union. By being an adolescent at the diplomatic table, it inadvertently seems to weaken its own position and the collective voice of
the EU.

UK Exercise of Voice

The UK's exercise of voice is characterised by under-performance
and implausibility: under-performance in the context of European
diplomacy and implausibility vis-à-vis the public. This represents a
departure from its exercise of voice until 1997 when petulance and
volubility chimed with limited but sporadic successes in (a) securing
the adoption of measures by the EU that the Government had
sought; and (b) commanding the attention of the core drivers of EU
political initiative: France and Germany. Self-isolation characterised
the UK's position during the Thatcher and Major governments'
terms of office. The UK's exercise of voice had not developed much
from the time of the UK referendum in 1975: UK contributions to the
EU budget remained as problematic in 1985 as they had been in 1974,
and as they were to be again in 2005. The context and fine detail had
altered, but the way in which the Government pressed its case had
not matured significantly. Its voice was softer but hardly more com-
pelling. Had Britain been mindful of its partners' needs over the
years, it might have developed an appropriate strategy to confront
the financial problems facing the EU of 25 member states as it prepared for further enlargement to more relatively poor states. Both
the UK and its partners wanted this issue resolved but the manner in
which the UK went about securing agreement frustrated resolution.

As a result, some of the very important EU policy objectives that
the UK Presidency did push failed to get either the recognition or
priority that was necessary. The budget issue masked the positive
input made by the UK presidency in the R&D agenda, specifically
advancing the EU's e-government and knowledge society goals.
Instead, progress on these seemed mired in a trade off negotiation
over the British rebate and curbing agricultural subsidies. Not only
were the issues not mutually exclusive but the future oriented R&D
agenda needed to be seen as defensible and non-negotiable in its
own right. The British position of rejecting a cut in its budgetary
rebate unless its partners agreed to structural reform of the EU bud-

get, complete with further cuts in agricultural support, seemed justifiable on the surface. It was a threat but one which others could
invert to reveal as being counter-productive and contrary to the original constitutional bargain and UK commitments to EU enlargement. A freeze on the UK rebate would have effectively meant that
over time it would rise. By failing to adjust the mechanism by which
the UK 'rebate' is calculated, the UK's net contribution to the EU
budget would have slipped to 0.23 per cent of gross national income
against France's 0.4 per cent. Politically, the French Government
could not entertain this.

This meant that the UK had to find a compromise to show a rising
UK contribution to the EU budget, even though any such compromise could be depicted as a climb down by the Opposition and tab-
loid media. Once funding to new and applicant members' structural
and regional development programmes had been excluded from the
calculation, UK net contributions would rise by over £6bn between
2007–13. Had this been communicated earlier, damage to the UK's
EU Presidency image might have been contained and Britain's overall performance and voice may have been positively evaluated with
important implications for its future role. Once again, the UK's exercise of voice seems to have been muffled by domestic political division: UK officials had long recognised the need for a compromise;
politicians had refused to negotiate. This had ramifications beyond
the EU because refusal to re-structure the budget and re-visit agricultural reform risked any international agreement on trade as
espoused by the UK at the Commonwealth meeting in Malta and the
WTO in Hong Kong[3]. The public presentation of the issues and the
appearance of diplomatic deadlock at all levels meant that internationally attention focused on the EU rather than or as well as other
heavy subsidizers of agricultural production, notably the USA. Consequently, it is clear that ineffective exercise of voice by one of the
EU's major states, has negative, indirect consequences for the EU as
a whole.

The exercise of voice is legitimate and is essential to sustainable
democracy in and the political vitality of the EU and its member
states. It is a valid, lawful, justifiable, indispensable tool of negotiation. The UK, like any other state, has a legitimate right to articulate
its own interests, needs and visions and to seek compromise to reconcile them with the overarching common interest. The UK case on

---

[3]   For details see http://www.euractiv.com/Article?tcmuri=tcm:29-150179
      -16&type=News&_lang=EN&email=4120

the budget and Financial Perspective had plenty of merits that were drowned by others exercising voice more effectively and coherently, even though their politico-economic case was possibly weaker. They were able to do this because of a consistent practice of coalition formation, engagement and more coherent public diplomacy on the EU than the UK. The UK is not low on voice but low on appropriate tactics and strategies to succeed in a convincing manner that commends the UK government to other states as a desirable, honourable, loyal, reliable, resilient and fair partner and ally in the EU.

Loyalty

The way in which the UK exercises voice gives the wrong impression of the UK as disloyal to EU working methods, objectives, strategic goals and visions. The UK habitually opposes further integration of a constitutional nature, treaty reforms and procedural steps to make decision-making more accountable and transparent—such as revisiting the undemocratic system of comitology that MEPs want curbed, and the opaque open method of coordination. Yet, the UK is among the more reliable of states in implementing EU legislation effectively and in championing much that others value. For example, one of the insightful and knowledgeable advocates of amending comitology to effect parliamentary accountability is a UK constitutional expert, and Labour MEP Richard Corbett. The UK exercise of voice and ineffective communication are all the more problematic therefore.

The UK's position on foreign policy and defence policy, where it generally advocates Union loyalty, collective security, and Union cohesion is undermined by the tunnel vision caused by Iraq and apparent adherence to US rather than independent EU goals. This again creates the impression of the UK being not entirely at one with its partners even though there are many examples to the contrary in respect of other, lower visibility foreign policy involvements. British EU public diplomacy on EU issues seems inexcusably inadequate. Its position, however legitimate and well-founded, rarely seems to be conveyed in a positive light. Consequently, when the issue does surface in the media (and above all in the UK media) it is often not until sharp conflict among governments is evident. The effect is to distort the facts of the issue and divert attention to the players in diplomatic spats. That weakens the effective exercise of voice.

Similarly, British public opinion is traditionally among the least favourable to the EU. The legendary media misrepresentation or quasi-denial of the EU and its relevance to everyday life in the UK is dishonest and at sharp variance with reality. It conveys a sense at worst of UK alienation from, and at best UK disinterest in, the EU. Positive engagement in all things EU from local level to national government level by public and private sector agencies are discounted rather than ignored. In the UK, only rarely have EU institutions' representations been in a position to refute half-truths robustly. This owes something to British practice and the relative constitutional timidity and impotence of the House of Commons vis-à-vis the executive in general and in respect of EU affairs in particular (Morgan, 1999). Feeble rebuttal of misinformation by either government Ministers or MPs means there is a lack of countervailing evidence communicated consistently and vigorously to the public arena.

As a result of weak transparency and sometimes effective voice on core British EU interests, an element of government complicity in disowning the EU exists. This is not the finest example of mediated governance. The sterling work of UK officials with their EU counterparts on a daily basis within the EU and across their EU partners' administrations is lost to the public eye. This is not simply the product of an inadequate representation of European issues arising from the major parliamentary parties' political self-interest, proprietorial demands, sometimes poorly informed journalists, press performance, or dominant commercial interests regarding the press (Anderson and Weymouth, 1999). Media coverage of the EU has improved somewhat over the years in terms of scope and volume if not in terms of reliable information and criticism. It has much to do with the UK political class remaining ignorant of, or in denial about, the reality of the EU and forsaking its responsibility to the electorate.

Where Next?

It would be misleading to assume that the UK exercise of voice is homogeneous or consistently poor. The UK government, like other governments, sometimes speaks with a single voice. Its message is coherent, persuasive and consistent. Rifts between government departments compromise this, as do unclear goals and poor public diplomacy and communication. Alternative voices, from other levels of government—from the regions, local councils, private sector bodies, other public agencies, MPs and MEPs are appropriate in different settings, at different stages of the negotiation processes, and at mediating the presentation of the UK's position. It would be especially appropriate for them to exercise voice in expounding UK interests when the UK next assumes the EU Presidency in 2017. It is then that the UK President has to desist from partiality and mediate a compromise that satisfies common goals as agreed in the EU's multi-annual strategic plans. Using alternative routes, they can give a more positive impression of the UK's actual involvement in EU policies (such as mobility in education where UK take-up has been among the highest of the EU) or social and regional policies. Of growing interest is perhaps the blogosphere of civilian, de-territorialised voice. This may complement citizen information initiatives within the states. It is not, however, coherent or persuasive. Communication just to be heard lacks purpose: Commission online chats with citizens therefore need capturing in political processes to transform 'chat' into something coherent and intelligible in order to have a chance of being heard by those in a position to influence, shape or initiate policy.

In short, the UK remains committed to EU membership. Experience and practice at all levels of government confirms this. For domestic political reasons, a more ambiguous message is conveyed. Exit was never a realistic, credible option. Eurosceptic voices are loud, but without a sustainable, credible strategy for exit, are unproductive, notwithstanding the UKIP's success in winning seats in the 2004 European Parliament elections. UK ministers and politicians need to exercise voice confidently if they are to be persuasive and influential in the enlarging EU. This requires the political class to accept and articulate credible, realistic and plausible objectives for the UK in the EU. So far, their exercise of voice smacks of a failure of public diplomacy vis-à-vis domestic politics: they have not communicated political priorities and choices within their EU frame of operation. This is at the heart of the public trust deficit. It is one reason why it is relatively easy, at a superficial level, for Eurosceptics to hijack major flash points in European integration—from Euro-elections to referendums on the draft constitutional treaty. Paradoxically, it is also the reason why the UK nevertheless, if sometimes limply, asserts its EU loyalty. It is time that it articulated in a more mature voice its commitment to being critically positive in developing the EU and shaping its future. It cannot afford to abdicate this responsibility to others.

Part II

Reflections of the Participants

Ernest Wistrich

Lessons of the 1975 Referendum

Following the return of a Labour government to power in 2005 a referendum on whether to adopt the single European currency and the Constitution remains on the agenda. This will be the second national referendum on Europe, the first having been held in 1975 to confirm continued British membership of the European Economic Community (the predecessor of the European Union). That referendum took place following the renegotiation by the Labour government of the terms of membership on which Britain entered in 1973. Although the issues to be considered are different this time, the same broad topics will be debated: the economic costs and benefits and political arguments about the loss of national sovereignty.

The purpose of this chapter is to look at the issues before both referendums and at public attitudes now and then and to see whether any lessons can be drawn from our experiences of the 1970s which could assist the pro-Europeans in the conduct of the campaign preceding the referendum on the euro and Constitution.

Public Opinion on Membership

From the Eurobarometer survey of public attitudes, conducted for the European Commission in July 2000, it appears that support in Britain for the EU has fallen to its lowest level since we joined the EEC in 1973. Only some 25% believed that EU membership was a good thing for our country. 24% thought it was bad for us, with 29% thinking that it was neither good or bad, leaving some 22% who did not know. Support for the Euro dropped from 36% in the autumn of 1998 to 28% in 1999 and then fell to only 22% by 2000. However, a large majority of those questioned said that they did not know enough about the issues to make up their minds and wished to be better informed. A recent Eurobarometer asked people to rate their knowledge of the EU out of 10. 10 means 'know a great deal', 1 means 'know nothing at all'. The British gave themselves 3.49 out of 10.

If we look at public opinion during the period preceding our entry into the EEC and before the referendum on staying in, we find that British attitudes on joining the European Community were highly favourable when the Conservative government under Harold Macmillan applied for membership in 1961. Nearly 50% approved with less than 20% against joining, and the rest did not know. After the first veto against our membership by French president Charles de Gaulle in 1963, enthusiasm for membership declined somewhat, but then rose quite dramatically when the Labour government under Harold Wilson applied again in 1967. 70% were in favour with less than 10% against. The House of Commons, after a week-long debate in May 1967 voted in favour of a second application to join by an unprecedented 85% of its membership of all political parties. However, when de Gaulle vetoed British entry for the second time at the end of 1967, public opinion changed dramatically. Nearly 50% became opposed to membership with those in favour dropping down to about 35%. Favourable attitudes declined even further, in spite of de Gaulle's resignation in 1969 and a new opportunity being offered to negotiate entry once again. In preparing for the negotia-tions, the Labour government produced a White Paper in the spring of 1970 to set out the costs and benefits of membership. The costs, largely related to food price increases likely to follow British accep-tance of the Community's Common Agricultural Policy, were clearly spelt out. The benefits on the other hand, whilst described in general terms, were not quantified. Public reaction to the White Paper was dramatic with support for membership plummeting even further. By December 1970, when negotiations for entry by the new Conservative government were in full swing, 70% of the public declared themselves against membership with only some 18% in favour. During 1971 support improved and by the time the negotia-tions were successfully concluded the public once again moved in favour with a small majority of 45% against 41%.

Britain entered the EEC in 1973. At the end of the year the war in the Middle East precipitated a world economic crisis following the quadrupling of oil prices and similar massive increases in other raw materials. Soon these affected all price levels. Many in Britain identi-fied the price increases as a direct result of our entry into the EEC. By

1974 opinion turned against EEC membership once again with some 40% wanting to leave the Community and only 24% in favour of continued membership.

These polls illustrate the volatility of public opinion on European Community membership which, certainly up to then, had had little direct effect on the lives of British citizens, their uncertainty about the issue and a strong desire for more guidance. Indeed it was significant that, when Edward Heath's Conservative government and Harold Wilson's Labour administration concluded their respective negotiations and recommended acceptance of the terms, public opposition declined and support for membership overtook those against. In 1975 the change in public attitudes was quite dramatic. Once the renegotiations for new terms of membership had been concluded and the government recommended their acceptance in April 1975, public opinion followed suit and moved to a 2 to 1 majority in favour.

Role of Campaigns

The debates concerned with membership of the EEC in the 1970s, similarly included arguments about the economic costs and benefits. The costs were largely related to rises in food prices as a result of the Common Agricultural Policy. The benefits were seen as a result of joining an economically fast growing Community, most of whose members had overtaken British living standards over the period since its formation. Although the arguments about the loss of political independence played a role, the potential rise in the cost of living dominated the debates. Arguments about the loss of national sovereignty were much less used and less significant in the 1970s than they are now.

As indicated above, the attitudes of governments to the issues being submitted for decision in a referendum can sway the public substantially. But referendums conducted on European issues by our EU partners did not always result in decisions recommended by their governments. Several referendums in Norway and Denmark went against their governments' advice and the French referendum on the Maastricht Treaty was only approved by a minuscule majority, Furthermore politicians in Britain no longer command the same trust and respect amongst the electorate as they did in the past and the public are less likely to be swayed by their arguments. In consequence the nature of the campaigns conducted ahead of a referendum can play an important role in influencing the results.

The attitude of the press has changed since the 1970s. In those days there was almost universal press support for British entry into the EEC, with only the Daily Express and the Communist Morning Star arguing against. Now the position has changed. The majority of newspapers, especially those owned by Rupert Murdoch and (formerly) Conrad Black have consistently opposed both the Euro and any further European integration, and proposals by the European Commission are always castigated. The hostile papers include the Times, Telegraph, Daily Mail, Sun and their Sunday titles. The opinion of the remaining papers is more balanced and a number are good supporters of the Euro and further European integration.

The Referendum Campaign 1974–5

The Labour Party did not reject British membership of the EEC but objected to the terms negotiated for entry by the Conservative government. To avoid a split between Labour pro and anti-Europeans the party had made a commitment that, once returned to power, it would renegotiate the terms of membership and if successful, submit the results to a national referendum, which would allow party members freedom to campaign on both sides of the argument. When Labour was returned to office in 1974 a referendum was clearly on the cards. This was to be the first national referendum in British constitutional history, without precedent or experience to guide its conduct.

Once again the European Movement started to plan for the forthcoming campaign. An in-depth survey of opinion was conducted in June 1974 to determine the state of public opinion on the issue. The results of survey showed a two to one majority against membership. The survey also set out to discover the reasons of those questioned for their attitudes and their reaction to various arguments advanced during the interview.

Because Britain lacked experience of referendums, it was decided to investigate the conduct of the campaigns on EEC membership organised in 1972 in Ireland, Denmark and Norway. In the first two countries substantial majorities were obtained in favour of membership where reports on the experiences of the referendums provided valuable guidance for the conduct of the British referendum campaign. It was agreed to adopt a strategy largely based on the Norwegian anti-EEC campaign. However, the European Movement had a problem vis-à-vis the British electorate. After its wide-ranging, vigorous and highly partisan campaign in favour of entry in 1971 it was seen by many as a movement of federalist Euro-fanatics with excessively partisan views. A number of favourably inclined organisations in the country would therefore have found it difficult to cooperate with the Movement. To overcome this handicap it was agreed to create a new organisation called 'Britain in Europe' and suspend the activities of the European Movement for a period of six months before the referendum. All Movement staff, members and supporters were to act under the common Britain in Europe umbrella.

After the second General Election in the autumn of 1974, which was won by Labour with an increased majority, negotiations for changing the terms of membership were started. Legislation was introduced to hold the referendum after the negotiations were completed, with two official organisations being recognised as the protagonists of the Yes and No votes, each allocated a government grant of £125,000. They were allowed to raise their own funds from private sources, but, once the official campaign started, the names of all donors above £1000 had to be declared.

Britain in Europe, leading the Yes campaign, received endorsement from business, the trades unions, academics and from well known politicians. The campaign was put into high gear at the beginning of 1975 and its slogan 'Keep Britain in Europe' received the widest publicity.

To build up an active army of supporters the European Movement had, already in the autumn of 1974, distributed a leaflet to nearly every household in the UK. Entitled 'Out of Europe – Out of work' it appealed for volunteers to help in the forthcoming campaign. A distribution of some 6.5 million leaflets yielded about 12,000 volunteers. Seventeen regional organisers were employed with the task of organising the helpers into appropriate groups and give them guidance. Some 600 speakers were trained and they addressed several thousand meetings.

In every town committees were formed which had a non-party chair but included representatives of all the major political parties. Co-operation between them was often a novel experience, but was generally highly successful. Every local society and non-governmental organisation favourably inclined was invited to take an active part. The committees' principal role was to work out the reasons why their locality would benefit from membership of the EEC, and then to publicise them. They recruited further supporters, distributed leaflets supplied from the centre, organised meetings and conducted local press campaigns through letters to the editors and articles. They were also encouraged to take part in local and regional radio and TV programmes. Whilst receiving a small grant of some £30 each to get them started, they were expected to raise their own funds locally, no other financial support being given to them from the centre. As the referendum date approached, 374 local groups had been established and, under the guidance of the regional organisers, they were active in preparing for the vote and getting out the voters.

Every conceivable professional and cultural organisation was approached, encouraging their members to set up a group of supporters from their ranks. Posters of well known supporters from the world of art and sports were printed and displayed. Particularly active were specially formed organisations of 'Christians for Europe', 'Women for Europe' and 'Youth for Europe'. Every one of these groups had the task of promoting the European cause amongst their peers from the point of view of their professional or sectoral interests.

Shops were rented in prominent positions in several dozen urban centres to assist the distribution of millions of leaflets, pamphlets, posters, campaign buttons, car stickers, window bills and other promotional material. Large window displays attracted visitors and stocks of the promotional material were freely handed out to all comers for wider distribution.

The major political parties ran their own campaigns within the general framework agreed by Britain in Europe. To accommodate the distinct national interests within the UK, separate organisations were set up for Scotland, Wales and Northern Ireland. To counter the widespread hostility to the EEC amongst trade unions, several hundred industrial and trading enterprises were encouraged to study the effects of EEC membership on their businesses and then communicate the largely favourable results to their employees.

Mass public meetings were organised throughout the country with prominent politicians and other speakers from professional organisations and universities. Training was provided to assist speakers taking part in daily debates between pros and antis on radio and television. A television film was prepared for screening on the lines of a party political broadcast which was shown on all channels alongside one produced by the No campaign. An extensive newspaper advertising campaign was conducted through both the national and regional press, accompanied by a large number of posters displayed on billboards throughout the country. The campaign cost about two million pounds and this sum excluded funds raised by the local and professional groups.

The National Referendum Campaign for the No vote was backed by a number of Labour cabinet ministers who had the government's dispensation to work against its recommendation to approve the renegotiated terms of membership of the EEC and also included politicians like Enoch Powell, Ian Paisley and Tony Benn. They had the support of the majority of trade union leaders and a number of Conservative MPs, but also the neo-fascist National Front and the Communist Party. Although their motivations against membership were often quite divergent, they presented a unanimous front using the same arguments. It may be that the uniformity of the views expressed lacked credibility amongst the electorate and that is why they lost support during the course of the campaign. Their financial resources were much more modest than those of the Yes campaigners, largely because they had difficulties in finding support from business, most of which backed Britain in Europe. They spent about £250,000 including the £125,000 government grant.

Lessons For Future Referendum

The tasks of those campaigning in favour of the EMU and the EU Constitution are likely to be harder than it was for the Yes campaign in 1975, due to the volatility of public opinion on European issues. The economic issues should not present greater difficulties this time round, but much more emphasis is likely to be given by the opponents to arguments about the loss of national sovereignty and the dangers of an emerging European 'superstate'. The opponents will have much bigger financial resources, already promised by wealthy contributors and probably the support of the majority of the national press, although newspaper reading has declined since the 1970s. The nature of the whole debate promises to be heavily influenced by nationalist and xenophobic sentiments of many of the opponents.

To win the case for these referendums it will be important to extend the debate well beyond arguments in its favour. British membership of the EU and pressure by its other leading members for further integration will come under attack. The 1975 referendum was held some two and a half years after our entry into the EEC and the Yes campaign was conducted in favour of the status quo under the slogan 'Keep Britain in Europe'. The adoption of EMU and Constitution requires votes in favour of change, which are harder to achieve.

On the other hand the Labour government recommending each cause will be fully united, unlike its predecessor in 1975, and will be backed by the party. The Conservatives are more divided between Euro-enthusiasts, sceptics and outright opponents of British membership of the EU.

The actual planning and conduct of the campaign by the current Britain in Europe organisation could do well to replicate some of the strategy adopted by its namesake in the 1975 referendum. The essential feature of the latter's success was to speak with many diverse voices in favour, each constituent group arguing the case from its own distinct interest. Equally important could be the grass roots activities of local groups of supporters, well guided by regional organisers acting under central control. Organisers will have to take into account the new factors affecting campaigning, the increased influence of multiple channel television, the emergence of web sites, the fall in newspaper readership, and the current practice of news 'management' by political leaders.

Philip Goodhart

Full-Hearted Consent

Of all the television programmes mounted during the 1970 General Election campaign, none had a greater impact than *Election Forum* when Robin Day, television's leading inquisitor, confronted the leaders of the three main parties in separate interviews. There was only one subject on which Harold Wilson, the Labour Prime Minister, Edward Heath, the Conservative Leader and Jeremy Thorpe of the Liberal Party were united. They were all firmly opposed to the idea of holding a referendum on British entry into the Common Market.

In fact, the idea of holding a referendum was clearly a fringe issue, while the wider question of British entry into the Common Market also failed to attract much attention during the campaign. The Nuffield study of Conservative candidates' election addresses showed that 62% of them did not mention the Common Market at all, while a further 15% referred to the subject without any discernible commitment. Of the remaining 23% who made some comment on the issue, 11% were opposed to entry and 12% were in favour. Among Labour candidates 6% declared some degree of enthusiasm for British entry while 9% were opposed. 8% seemed entirely neutral and 77% made no mention of the issue.

In Beckenham, where I had been the Conservative Member of Parliament since 1957, I made several speeches in which I said that I thought that there ought to be a referendum before we joined the EEC. As all three of the main party leaders had declared their firm opposition to a referendum it was pointed out that my enthusiasm was meaningless. I therefore rashly promised that I would hold a private referendum in Beckenham when the moment of decision came. I had not expected that I would actually have to hold a Beckenham poll. President De Gaulle had already vetoed our application twice and his successor, President Pompidou, seemed unlikely to take a different line. I had also not expected that Ted Heath would replace Harold Wilson in 10 Downing Street.

Once again, I was wrong. The new French President and the new British Prime Minister became friends, the French veto was withdrawn and on 19 May 1971, President Pompidou of France and Ted Heath, the Prime Minister of England, spent a whole day locked in negotiation. At a banquet that evening President Pompidou said 'through two men who are talking to each other, two peoples are trying to find each other again...'. After a press conference on the following day it seemed almost certain that the terms for entry would soon be agreed.

Even before the agreement on British entry, an important part of the British Trade Union movement had been attracted by the idea of a referendum. It would be a sort of national pithead ballot. At the Labour Party Conference in September 1970 Harry Urwin of the Transport and General Workers' Union had moved a motion opposing British entry to the Common Market. He pointed to a public opinion poll which suggested that only 22% of the British electorate wanted to join 'yet no political party represented in the House of Commons is willing to identify itself with the views and fears of the vast majority of the British people'. On a card vote of six million the Transport and General Workers' resolution was rejected by a majority of less than 100,000. Jack Jones, Vie Feather and Clive Jenkins were among the prominent trade union leaders now calling for a referendum.

Once the agreement on British entry had been signed the time had come for me to deliver on my promise that Beckenham would have its own referendum. Between July and October 1971 no less than 16 constituency referendums were held, 15 of them in Conservative-held seats. The Beckenham campaign was the best organised, despite murmurs of disagreement from the Beckenham Conservative Association, and the only one in which there was a majority in favour of British entry. After the agreement had been signed the main tactical argument in Parliament concentrated on the question of whether there should be a free vote in the House of Commons on the EEC bill. One week before the Second Reading debate, the Conservative Chief Whip announced that there would be a free vote. The Labour Party had already decided that their members would be whipped to vote against. When the vote was taken at 10:00 p.m. on 28 October, 356 members voted in favour while 244 voted against. 69 Labour members voted for the bill while 39 Conservatives and Ulster Unionists voted against. Of the 237 members who spoke in the debate only 23 mentioned the possibility of holding a referendum or a special General Election.

Neil Marten, Enoch Powell and I now put down an amendment to the Bill calling for a consultative referendum. For years Neil Marten had been the most persistent critic on the Conservative benches of the idea of British entry. In May 1970 he had noted that Ted Heath had given a speech to the Franco-British Chamber of Commerce in Paris saying that it would be wrong for Britain to try and enter the Community without 'the full-hearted consent of Parliament and people'. In fact, the author of that ringing phrase was Ted Heath's temporary speech writer, Douglas Hurd who had inserted the words 'and people' after 'Parliament' to give an oratorical rather than an ideological balance to the sentence.

It seemed unlikely that the referendum amendment would cause much excitement; and then, on the eve of a visit to Ted Heath at Chequers, President Pompidou launched a bombshell. He announced that there would be a French referendum on British entry 'It is a new Europe that is coming into being, that is going to assert itself, and on which will depend the future of the European peoples and consequently of all French men and women ... And that is why I say that the enlargement of the community must be ratified by every Frenchwoman and Frenchman ...'. At a stroke President Pompidou had transformed the referendum question into a live political issue.

In a letter to *The Times* a Mr G.R. Nottage wrote: 'All is now clear. When Mr Heath, a man of undoubted integrity, said that he would not take us into the Common Market without the whole-hearted support of Parliament and people, he forgot to mention that he meant the *French* Parliament and the *French* people.'

On the day before President Pompidou's announcement the Labour Party's Shadow Cabinet had narrowly decided that the Parliamentary Labour Party would not support Neil Marten's referendum amendment. On the day after the Pompidou announcement Tony Benn submitted a new resolution to Labour's National Executive which 'invites the PLP to consider the desirability of moving or supporting other amendments which would make a referendum necessary before entry'. By 13 votes to 11 the National Executive passed Tony Benn's resolution. Ten days later, the Shadow Cabinet again discussed the Parliamentary Labour Party's attitude to the referendum amendment. Harold Wilson, who had voted against supporting the amendment, now changed his mind.

A few days later, Roy Jenkins resigned as Deputy Leader of the Labour Party. As Roy Jenkins wrote in his letter to Harold Wilson the incident which led to his resignation 'was the narrow decision of the Shadow Cabinet to reverse its much more clear cut decision of two weeks previously and recommend a whipped Labour vote in support of the Tory Backbench referendum amendment ... This, in my view, is not the way in which an Opposition ... should be run ...This constant shifting of the ground I cannot accept. Save in the very short term it will be far more damaging to the Labour Party than to the present government.'

The split in the Parliamentary Labour Party meant that the slim chance of wining the vote on the referendum amendment had finally disappeared. After more than eight hours of debate on 18 April the amendment was defeated when 237 members voted for it and 286 voted against. Three Liberal MPs voted for the amendment. Three Liberal MPs voted against it. To our astonishment the amendment which I had almost casually put down with Neil Marten and Enoch Powell had split the Labour Party.

Although the referendum amendment did not lead directly to the Referendum of 1975, the small earthquake which it started in the Labour Party did lead to a prolonged period of alienation which rumbled on until Roy Jenkins, David Owen, Shirley Williams and Bill Rodgers left the Labour Party to form the SDP.

David Owen

Manoeuvres Towards the Referendum

The 1975 referendum was shaped by what happened in May-June 1972 inside the Parliamentary Labour Party. I wrote this account shortly afterwards in the summer of 1972:

The Shadow Cabinet met on Wednesday, 24th May 1972, for the second time to discuss the call for a referendum on entry into the European Economic Community (EEC), which they had, only a fortnight before, decisively rejected. On this occasion they were discussing the Labour Party NEC resolution which Tony Wedgwood Benn, the then Chairman of the Party, had managed to push through by 13–11 votes. Harold Wilson apparently spoke early, advocating acceptance of the referendum. Jim Callaghan spoke, saying that he had come to the conclusion that it was now necessary to give all possible support to the Leader of the Party on every issue; that the Leader's position was weak, he was under constant attack and that he would do everything to support him. Tony Crosland spoke against the referendum, but the surprising decision came from Ted Short who accepted the referendum. The proposal was eventually carried by 8–6. Shirley Williams, Harold Lever, Roy Jenkins, George Thomson, Douglas Houghton and Tony Crosland voting against: Bob Mellish, Harold Wilson, Jim Callaghan, Tony Wedgwood Benn, Fred Peart, Peter Shore, Michael Foot and Ted Short voting for. It was alleged mainly by Bob Mellish afterwards that, if only Roy Jenkins, then Deputy Leader of the Party, and the others had indicated at that meeting that they would resign on this issue, then the meeting might have taken a different course.

I met Roy Jenkins who briefly mentioned the outcome of the meeting the night before. It was clear that he believed that resignation was inevitable and essential. Roy had previously talked to George Thomson who had made it clear that he felt he had no option other than resign, that he was personally deeply committed in numerous speeches up and down the country. Roy told me later on 8th June that, at this meeting George had told him that he had been approached by the Government, offering that he should go to Brussels to be one of the two UK European Commissioners. This was very important because Roy knew throughout that George's own personal position could not but influence his position over the referendum and Roy could and, I believe, did subconsciously from then on compensate for George's advice.

I photocopied Harold Wilson's two election interviews — on 'Panorama' and on ITV — where he had categorically stated his rejection of a referendum on the EEC. I read the statements to Roy as he drove his car. We began to explore the options: the one option which, on reflection, we were perhaps too dismissive about was that of abstaining and sitting tight, refusing to resign from the Deputy Leadership and the Parliamentary Committee and challenging our critics to put down a motion of no confidence for a PLP meeting. The reason this never looked attractive was the wording Roy had used in the statement he had made to the PLP before running for Deputy Leader after the October vote.

The real issue was why had Harold Wilson and Bob Mellish switched and the more he looked at it the more Roy was led to the conclusion that Wilson had switched, not so much as on previous occasions to cover his flank from Benn and the Left who, on this issue, could have been easily held, but to engineer an open breach with the promarketeers in the Shadow Cabinet. There was no evidence that on this issue Jim Callaghan was pushing him. It is easy to forget that all through the period shortly before October 28th, and afterwards, it was Roy who had held the pro-EEC members in the Shadow Cabinet together and ensured they did not resign.

Discussing the situation I was certain of one thing that, on this occasion, like most of those in the past, Roy would make his own decision. Looking ahead, Roy was also worried about voting on Clause 2 of the Bill. Was he expected to vote against this as well, and if the Shadow Cabinet could reverse its decision on the referendum with such apparent disregard for everything that had been said before, it was only a matter of time before they could engineer another crisis. The key question remained, was Wilson deliberately provoking a crisis; did he want Roy to resign? Perhaps it was not as clear as this, but did he want to force Roy into a humiliating position.

It was understandable; Roy was being projected every day as a man of principle, Wilson as devious.

I was left with the firm view that Roy felt that Wilson had now decided that whatever the short-term cost to his own credibility he had decided to force his Deputy Leader to severe humiliation and compromise so that his image would be tarnished. He probably had a vague recognition that this could mean resignation, but he was astute enough to know that resignation would not help Roy's position and, in consequence, he had no doubt that Roy would swallow this compromise as he had swallowed voting for the Second Reading of the EEC Bill

When discussing the referendum, Roy had asked me if I could ever support referenda, even apart from the EEC controversy I had wondered whether I had been too definite about this. In particular, I was not so certain that conceding a referendum on the EEC would lead on inexorably to referenda on all major issues. It did seem just possible to believe that this one occasion could be isolated and treated exceptionally. Certainly the Government's recent decision to introduce a periodical plebiscite in Northern Ireland had not helped. It was yet one more twist to the Government's inept handling of the EEC question: on this, of all issues, to concede anything was to imperil the Bill, for the lobby in favour of referenda on EEC entry on the Tory side, included people like Philip Goodhart and other less militantly hostile anti-EEC who would feel far less inhibited over supporting an amendment at the Committee stage of the Bill. It had all along been recognized that the Neil Marten amendment on the referenda, if supported by the Opposition, would be one of the closest votes for the Government of the whole legislation.

Having put my point vigorously about the need to regularly attend Prime Minister's questions and Party meetings, I left Roy under no illusion that whatever decision he made on resignation, whether I agreed with it or not, I too would resign. I felt he needed to have the certain knowledge that some would come with him — in these situations we simply had to retain a basic cohesion and loyalty and though I felt still unsure which was the right course, I had developed enough confidence in his judgment over the last year to accept the outcome.

I became very worried that we were in danger of making the decision to resign without looking at the options. I had had a telephone conversation with Roy when he was clearly very disturbed by the massive majority in favour of a referendum, which was revealed by the Sunday Express poll. Even allowing for the loaded way in which the question was put, it was clear that this poll would only serve to put greater political pressure on pro-EEC Labour MPs and luke-warm Tory anti-EEC MPs. As had always been envisaged, the cry, 'let the people decide', was a heady brew, hard to counter and with public opinion still very divided on the issue, if a referendum was conceded, entry to the EEC might well be blocked. On top of this, there were the 'elitist' jibes. The escape hatch of the referendum was a tempting one for anyone under pressure in their constituency, and from those who had taken up the various new constitutional themes thrown up by the issue, like parrots.

The most serious pressure, however, was that coming from left-wing activists who had taken up the cry that the pro-EEC Labour MPs were keeping in power the most reactionary Tory Government since the 1920s. It was no surprise that in this climate, Bill Rodgers, who had as close an idea of what the pro-EEC section in the party thought as anyone, warned that there was little chance of any large number of abstentions; for example, at the most no more than 25–30, if Roy and other Shadow Cabinet members voted for the referenda. This might have been sufficient to ensure that the referendum amendment was defeated, but even this was not absolutely certain with the Northern Ireland Unionist MPs threatening to use their EEC voting as a lever against the Government's policies in Northern Ireland.

Extracts from memo to Roy Jenkins:

I start from three basic assumptions. Firstly, the PLP will support a consultative referendum before ratification, despite any opposition we might put up at the Party meeting. Secondly, less than half of the 89 European voters or abstainers will consider abstention, even if Roy and the other members of the Shadow Cabinet resign. Finally, the Labour Party Conference in October will support the commitment for any incoming Labour Government to have a referendum on whether or not Britain should stay within the EEC.

If these assumptions are correct, by far the most important is that relating to the likely position of the Party at the next Election. To vote now against a referendum, quite apart from any short-term problems, will make for immense difficulties over the General Election Manifesto. Given that the pressures for a commitment to come out of the EEC are now pretty strong, it can be fairly argued that the only way of holding off such a commitment would be to compromise on the referendum. It is clear, therefore, that to vote against a referendum now could well start a process whereby a group of us would have no option other than to reverse our earlier position or not to stand at the next Election.

The Shadow Cabinet's about-turn on the referendum poses a very serious challenge to us. It will almost certainly divide our own forces and we will be depicted, unless we are very careful, as adopting an inflexible position and, at the same time, allowing Michael Foot to pose as the great unifier of the Party In short, we are in danger of being boxed in and it is vital that we should look at ways of breaking out of this position. Up to the present we have seen our position solely in terms of ensuring that the legislation is passed. It is becoming more and more clear to me that we cannot ignore in our calculations two other factors: the need for Britain to enter the EEC reasonably united and with a commitment that will last the difficult period of transition and the need for the Labour Government to take office without an overriding commitment to come out and this critically depends on our section of the Party still retaining a powerful position.

In accepting, under these unique circumstances, the desirability of a referendum, I must stress that to have any meaning it must be genuinely democratic. The argument must not be allowed to polarise entirely on political lines and it is, therefore, crucial that certain safeguards would have to be built into the referendum. Firstly, all political parties would accept that this referendum would not establish a precedent and its introduction would not be used as an argument for the extension of referenda into the British system of Parliamentary Government. Secondly, the political parties would agree to conduct a referendum, not on the basis of a party-political confrontation, but would allow MPs and other politicians the normal party facilities to put forward their views, even if they conflict with the general position of the political party to which, under normal circumstances, they owe their allegiance. Thirdly, there would be a responsibility on the BBC and ITV to reflect a fair balance in the factual arguments and the Press Council should be asked to ensure that this is done as far as possible in the national and regional newspapers. Fourthly, there would be no advertising or free or subsidised propaganda published relating to the referendum.

It will be said by some that these suggestions are being put forward purely to heal the differences in the Labour Party. This is not so. Genuine differences exist on this issue in all parties. Those of us who believe strongly in the desirability of Britain's entry into the EEC, risk through agreeing to a referendum, a rejection by the people whose best interests we believe are served by Britain's entry. I will do everything in my power to see that the result of the referendum is a decisive Yes and I believe that this decision can be taken with the full-hearted consent of the British people.

Roy, when discussing my memo, raised many questions:

Whatever might be said at the start, as the campaign progressed, a referendum would become identified with a general election in party workers' minds. He was convinced that, whatever were people's intentions at the start of the campaign, before the end he and others would inevitably run a very substantial risk of being expelled from the party To the argument that he would have to have a written undertaking that those of us pro-EEC would be free to campaign, he forcefully reminded us of other similar pledges. Though Roy was well controlled, one could detect very considerable emotion, he was reaching the limit of his tolerance. He said that before polling day some action of the Government, the writing of the referenda question, or the conduct of the poll or a completely extraneous issue, would be used to invoke one theme, this was the issue on which to get the Government out. It was clear beyond argument that Roy was not prepared to break up the Labour Party; he was prepared to concede that a referendum with full Government backing and a split Labour Party could and probably would, despite the opinion polls, be won. But, even so, it would put at risk a centrally important issue and there were also the powerful principled argument against referenda.

I left Roy totally convinced in my own mind that he was now going to resign and, to some extent, this judgment of his intentions began to alter my own judgment. I was determined, on no account, to leave him alone and isolated: he not only needed politically a few people to resign with him, but I had felt a sufficient doubt all through, to be content to accept his judgment. In this situation, one instinctively tries to go along with the arguments in favour of the course one intends to follow.

In retrospect, writing in 2006 I do not regret my resignation. I hated voting against the Bill to take us into the EEC when I believed it was then and still is today, important for the UK to be a committed and constructive member of this grouping of our European neighbours, which now numbers 25 and could be 35 within a decade. To be able, after my resignation in 1972, to abstain on all future votes, knowing that we would therefore ratify was a relief. I was pretty confident we would stay in the EEC because the issue would no longer be in any referendum whether to risk going in, but whether to risk coming out. I believed that both Harold Wilson and Jim Callaghan would, if we won the General Election, be saying in any referendum that we should stay in and their view would carry considerable weight with Labour voters. In the event their views mattered far more than those of us in the official Yes campaign.

In 1977 as Foreign Secretary in a paper for a one-day political Cabinet meeting, I committed the government to support enlargement as the counter to federalism. Also proportional representation for elections to the European Parliament, or Assembly as it was then called. Both became policies of Conservative as well as Labour governments. Labour's decision to fight the 1983 Election on a pledge to come out of the EC without even a referendum was one I could never have fought an election on as a candidate in Plymouth. The SDP can fairly claim to have been a crucial factor in Labour's conversion to wholehearted belief in membership of the EU by the 1997 General Election, as well as so many other SDP policies. As so often, the zealotry of the convert meant that many of those who had fought the 1983 Election on coming out, by the 1990s embraced the eurozone and then in 2004 the new Constitution with all too little attention to the detailed economic and political problems inherent in both ventures. Fortunately the necessity of having to win over British public opinion in a referendum on both issues may force a more rational reappraisal of Labour's policy in both areas.

Bernard Donoughue

The Inside View from No.10

The first government thistle which we had to grasp was the renegotiation of the terms of Britain's membership of the European Economic Community (EEC). This was to dominate the Prime
Minister's and our time over the next nine months, concluding with
the Referendum which had been promised in both recent election
campaigns, and I and the Policy Unit were heavily involved
throughout in detailed briefing to the Prime Minister.

The political background was that in 1972 the Labour Party had
been seriously split, with Roy Jenkins resigning the deputy leadership, over Edward Heath's successful application to join the EEC. A
majority of the Labour Party in Parliament and in the country, and of
the Prime Minister's senior colleagues, were against membership.

So in 1974 Wilson saw the issue not — as did Jenkins for the 'pros'
and Benn for the 'antis' — as one of principle, but as a question of
political party management. His twin objectives were to prevent
Labour from inescapably committing itself to withdrawal from the
EEC, and from breaking up the Party over the issue. He successfully
achieved these by offering at the two 1974 elections the immediate
prospects of renegotiating better terms for Britain's membership,
followed by a referendum of the whole British people.

Fulfilling this promise was not to prove easy, since Jenkins and
many on the right were uncompromisingly committed to EEC membership while Benn, Shore, Foot and the left were opposed with
equal dogmatism.

Wilson was also assisted by the use of two rare political devices.
First he suspended normal collective responsibility and in the
Referendum campaign allowed dissenting colleagues to oppose
whatever was to be the Government's formal decision on Europe
without resigning. This so-called 'Agreement to Differ' gave Wilson

useful political elastic to avoid splitting the Cabinet asunder. The referendum mechanism itself was also novel and convenient to Wilson. It was originally advocated by Tory and then by Labour anti-Common Marketeers seeking a way to block entry to the EEC and was opposed by Jenkins because of that extremist support. In the event it sank Benn, who proposed it to Wilson, and confirmed the victory of Jenkins, who had passionately opposed it. Wilson at first rejected the whole concept of a referendum; but then on second thoughts he shrewdly saw its utility to him. He realised that a vote of the whole British people would dilute and swamp the opposition from Labour activists, who were strong in the Party, but small in the country as a whole.

Wilson typically approached the EEC renegotiations with the recent election manifesto permanently in his pocket to serve as his guideline. He knew that, providing he stuck to the manifesto and then secured a majority in Cabinet, he could not be attacked in the Party.

The renegotiations were thrashed out in broad principles at a succession of summit meetings of Heads of Government, while the critical details were settled at lower diplomatic levels under the shrewd leadership of Jim Callaghan, and these two experienced politicians worked together in close tandem. My Policy Unit was busy throughout drafting briefings for the Prime Minister. I attended all the Summits as his Senior Policy Adviser and also had regular discussions with Foreign Office and Trade officials to advance the Number 10 view.

Just before the Paris Summit in December 1974, Wilson held a critical private meeting with Germany's Chancellor Helmut Schmidt at Chequers. Schmidt promised to secure the necessary Budget reforms, providing Wilson agreed that he would then come out clearly in public in favour of Britain staying in the EEC. Wilson agreed the deal and decided to announce it in his next public speech. Once the speech had been made to the audience of unsuspecting mayors of London boroughs, the path was prepared for a successful summit conference in Paris.

There we made considerable progress, particularly on the Budget and the Regional Fund. Wilson confidently described how he would complete the negotiations by March 1975 and hold the referendum by June. He told me that Roy Jenkins had agreed this timetable and so for the first time had implicitly accepted the referendum device.

The second day in Paris we faced typical French hostility, but Schmidt privately reassured us that this was only a rhetorical gesture to President Giscard's nationalist constituency and that the Germans would settle the Budget problem through a 'correcting mechanism' (for which they would themselves of course pay, leaving the French as usual a net beneficiary).

The next summit in Dublin on 10–11 March 1975 proved not too difficult, though it had its odd tricky moments. On the final afternoon, all was deadlocked until Wilson came out smiling to tell us that the Germans had produced their helpful Budget mechanism and suddenly the tension lifted. Everyone was laughing and chatting except Germany's Chancellor Schmidt, who would have to pay for our Budget achievements. Our EEC partners had delivered what the British wanted. Wilson and Callaghan now made it clear in private, though not yet in public that they would recommend staying in the Community.

Wilson took his EEC package for approval or rejection to a tense two-day Cabinet on 17–18 March 1975. Roy Jenkins and Shirley Williams had made it clear in advance that they would resign if Cabinet decided not to approve staying in the EEC. Others in more junior ministerial office would certainly follow them. On the other side were Benn, Shore, Foot and Castle, weighty politicians who were equally passionately opposed to continuing our membership of the EEC. The atmosphere inside Number 10 was electric and unforgettable. The Cabinet seemed in danger of being torn apart. If that happened, the Government, with such a weak parliamentary position, would surely fall.

Wilson prepared for and handled his Cabinet with consummate skill. He chaired the proceedings with the express object of preventing any open confrontation and allowed everyone the chance to speak. He also provided, rare for a cabinet, a break for coffee. At the start of the concluding votes around the table, he and Callaghan gave a lead by announcing that they accepted the terms and would recommend Britain staying in the EEC. They personally swung several doubters, and the Yes vote won by 16–7, an encouragingly large margin, given that only a year earlier five of those Yes votes: Rees, Peart, Morris, Prentice and Shepherd had been opposed to our continuing membership. Jim Callaghan's personal influence almost certainly swung the first three. Without these five switches, the vote would have been lost 11–2.

Wilson's style of consensual agnosticism, legitimised by an election mandate, made it easier for him to hold the cabinet together,

though a majority of Labour MPs, the National Executive Committee and Party conference voted against the EEC.

The long referendum campaign was masterminded by a specially
established Referendum Unit which met each day in the Foreign
Office. Jim Callaghan, or, more often, his junior minister Roy
Hattersley, took the chair, with other relevant ministers and FCO
officials present, and the Prime Minister asked me to attend as his
personal representative. Throughout the campaign our polls
showed roughly two thirds of the electorate in favour of staying in
the EEC, so we did not feel under great pressure.

Wilson himself showed little enthusiasm for the campaign, and
for much of it made no speeches. When this was queried by Jim
Callaghan at the morning strategy meeting on 15 May 1975, I raised
it with Wilson, who then at least arranged some engagements and
spoke on each of the final days of the campaign, dictating his long
and rambling speeches himself to demonstrate that he was not in the
hands of the so-called 'Euro-fanatics' surrounding him.

In the referendum poll on 6 June 1975, 67.2% voted Yes and 32.8%
voted No, closely in line with our MORI findings. It was an overwhelming victory. Our Yes majority was greater than the entire No
vote.

But Harold Wilson did not seem to enjoy the victory which he had
secured. He spent the day of the result at Chequers, from where he
wired to us in Number 10 a flat and impersonal draft of his proposed
victory statement, with no welcome for the result, as if he had never
been involved. I telegraphed back to him some amendments, including suggesting that as the Prime Minister who recommended a Yes
vote, he should personally welcome the result. He accepted some
amendments but still omitted any personal welcome for Britain taking a more positive position in the future of Europe. He came up
from Chequers in the evening and read out his little statement on the
steps of Number 10.

Wilson's own personal position was agnostic, mentally, but only
at the cerebral level, accepting the arguments that it was on balance
better to stay in. Over the past decade he had coolly taken many
positions on the EEC. In 1967 he had first proposed Britain's entry to
a sceptical De Gaulle, then had opposed the terms of Heath's entry in
1972, and at one time opposed a referendum while later supporting
it. He never displayed strong feelings either way on the EEC itself.
He supported the concept of a Community of Europe, never wishing
again to see it wracked by nationalist conflicts. But he did not have a

broad vision of the political future for the EEC, seeing it as just a trading organisation, and was deeply sceptical that Britain would derive much net economic benefit from a more integrated Europe.

Wilson's main concern in my time with him on this issue was political: to trim, and to manage, the Labour Party mood so that he could hold the Party together. During the negotiations he did his homework, constantly asking me for more Policy Unit briefings because he said that he did not trust the official advice, especially from the Foreign Office, which he saw as too 'Euro-bureaucratic'. But I felt that had we been arguing against these particular points and for the opposite, he could have accepted it and done it just as well, professionally and pragmatically, like the good civil servant he once was. Only on the issues of New Zealand food and the protection of poor Third World countries did he show any personal commitment.

He was never warm to things European, nor indeed to anywhere abroad other than through his sentimental attachment to the old Commonwealth, especially Australia and New Zealand. Indeed, he was probably mildly anti-European in the sense that he did not seem to like the continental style of life or their politics. Politically, he believed that British democracy and the British Parliament were the most wonderful political systems and institutions ever invented. His observation of continental politics from the 1930s onwards did not convince him that very many Europeans were fundamentally democratic or had much to bring for Britain politically to learn.

Harold Wilson was, on my observation, basically a provincial, nonconformist puritan, with all the virtues, vices and inhibitions of that background, including touches of the 'little Englander' and a healthy suspicion of metropolitan glitz and cosmopolitan glamour. He would probably have preferred that the EEC did not exist. Now that it did, he adjusted to that reality. He was also a sensible mainstream professional who was usually prepared to take the advice of Whitehall, and his official advice was to stay in the EEC. As a pragmatist, he knew that a Yes vote was the most practical choice, because to stay in would be less disruptive politically, economically, industrially than to pull out.

As a national leader, he believed that a victory for the No campaign would empower 'the wrong kind of people' in Britain: the Benn left and the Powell right, who were often extreme nationalists, protectionist, xenophobic and backward-looking. As a party leader, he saw the positive 'Yes' vote as the best way to hold Labour together, because Benn's antis would not finally leave the government over Europe, whereas the Jenkins Europhiles would and their resignation could effectively destroy it. Perhaps, as a statesman which part, but only part, of his complex personality was he sensed that Britain ought to be placed at the centre of Europe's future. Certainly, as a shrewd politician, he saw the Yes position as the likely winner. So, for this mixed bag of reasons and motives rather than for any enthusiasm for the EEC, Wilson fought and won the battle to stay in. His whole conduct of the issue was, to me, deeply 'Wilsonian', consultative and consensus-seeking. His approach was flexible and not 'theological'. Throughout, he fudged and ducked and weaved. But he succeeded. He kept Britain in the Community as he always wished; he achieved the terms which his manifesto demanded, and he held together by Wilsonian elastic bands his cabinet and party.

By his overwhelming victory in the referendum, he gave Britain's position in Europe a democratic mandate. Edward Heath had in 1972 taken the British political establishment into Europe. Harold Wilson and James Callaghan now brought in a majority of the British people. This positive outcome was a great relief to me personally. I had never been what Harold called a 'Euro-fanatic'. I opposed political union and was sceptical of monetary union. But I did believe Britain should be in the EEC, and when we came into government in March 1974 I was the only, very lonely, member of his personal team who was in favour of our membership of the EEC.[1]

---

[1]   This chapter first appeared in *Heat of the Kitchen* by Bernard Donoughue (Politico's 2003). Reprinted here by permission of Methuen Publishing Ltd.

John Edmonds

Learning to Love the 'Rich Man's Club'

The last day of May 1975 and I am sitting in the departure lounge at Heathrow waiting for the flight to Aberdeen. The weather is chilly and it matches my mood. The next week will be spent at the Congress of my trade union in an even colder Scotland listening to the union leadership trying to persuade sceptical delegates that Britain should stay in the Common Market.

A group of us pass the time in a desultory debate about the Referendum. I wave my postal vote. 'I am certainly going to vote No'. The theatrical gesture impresses no one. 'So our youngest national officer has decided to reject the future', says one know-all. The remark is sharp enough to stay in the memory. I protest, but the argument is over even before we board the plane. Five days before the Referendum and experienced trade unionists already know that the result is a foregone conclusion. Harold Wilson will win, the Yes campaign will win, and the UK will stay in the EEC.

The 1975 Referendum split the Labour Movement, but not down the middle. Most of Labour's leaders were in favour of voting Yes and most grassroots activists were determined to vote No. Indeed, many Labour Party supporters regarded the Referendum as little more than a sham, designed to get Harold Wilson off an uncomfortable hook. Their argument was that the Labour Party Conference had consistently voted against membership of the EEC. The Party Leader had a responsibility to implement Party policy and take the UK out. If he was not prepared to do so, he should face the consequences. For many activists, the use of the Referendum, a device previously unknown in the UK political system, was a typical piece of Wilsonian chicanery.

In the trade union movement the debate was less about constitutional purity than about how best to pursue trade union interests. In 1975 Britain's trade unions were at the height of their power. The miners had just won a stunning victory over the Heath Government. The TUC had the confidence to believe that we did not need the EEC or any other external organisation to advance the living standards of working people in Britain. Properly mobilised, trade union members could win higher wages and better conditions of work by their own efforts. The unions were also worried about the EEC's sense of priorities. With all its talk of sound money, low inflation and increases in productivity, the EEC sounded more and more like a 'rich man's club'. The TUC, on the other hand, had a well rounded view of what was important to British working people, and as General Secretary Len Murray observed, 'the most important decisions about our future can only be taken here in Britain.'

Regretfully, I have to admit that mixed in with that new found confidence was more than a modicum of contempt for our Continental colleagues. The French trade unions were weak, the German trade union movement had been recreated by the TUC after the War, and the trade unions in Italy, Belgium and Holland, were split every whichway on political and religious lines. So when people in the Yes campaign pointed out that French and German workers had more legal rights than workers in Britain, the ready response was that British workers had something better: a strong trade union movement. Our experience with 'In Place of Strife' and the Industrial Relations Act had also taught us that Governments do not give away free gifts. Every offer of legal rights for workers comes with a price attached: usually some limitation on trade union power or some restriction on the right to strike. After the battles with Barbara Castle and Edward Heath, the British trade union movement was in no mood to see the advantages of an industrial relations system based on legal rights and responsibilities.

In 1975 I was convinced by these arguments. The trouble was that my Union, the GMB then called the GMW, was one of a small minority of trade unions who were part of the Yes campaign. This put me, like so many others, in a very uncomfortable position. A natural loyalist, I had decided to vote against the recommendation of my Party Leader and against the policy of my Union. Of course, Harold Wilson had given us all permission to be rebels, but in the rather unsubtle world of the trade union movement things were not quite that simple. A trade union official who went around contradicting the policy of his Union would quickly find himself in a stressful discussion with his Union Executive. So I expressed my views with rather too much bluster in private and with rather too much caution in public.

At the time I thought that my decision to vote No was the result of a balanced consideration of all the issues. Looking back, I now appreciate the extent to which my personal experience in representing a particular group of vulnerable workers influenced my thinking. The trade unionists who worked in Britain's sugar refining industry, my members, were likely to lose their jobs if Britain remained a member of the EEC.

For centuries the sugar trade had been controversial and highly political. Originally cut by slaves in the sugar cane plantations of the West Indies, sugar production was extended to Swaziland, Mauritius and Queensland. Sugar became one of the great trading commodities of Empire. The sugar cane was crushed in mills near to the plantations and the raw sugar was then transported to the great imperial ports of London, Liverpool and Glasgow, where it was refined into the familiar white granules. by the 1970s, a whole system of Commonwealth preference had been constructed and was underpinned by the Commonwealth Sugar Agreement.

Continental Europe was very different. The Common Market had no cane sugar industry of any size. Since Napoleon, sugar had been supplied by European farmers growing extensive fields of sugar beet. Subsidies to sugar beet farmers became a pillar of the Common Agricultural Policy and European beet farmers were not inclined to open up their comfortable closed market to the import of some two million tonnes of cane sugar from the British Commonwealth.

If Britain remained in the EEC, the prospects for Britain's 5,000 sugar refinery workers were bleak. British negotiators had managed to achieve a form of words by which France, Germany and the rest agreed to 'keep in mind' the interests of the Commonwealth sugar producers. And so they did ... up to a point. The Lomé Convention allowed the continued import of something over half the previous supply of raw cane sugar. So the industry did not crash overnight, but pretty soon two of the smaller refineries closed and then, most traumatic of all, the massive Liverpool Refinery shut down. That factory had been an icon of Merseyside life and culture, immortalised in the song Maggie May. She would never again push a sugar barrow down Love Lane.

In 1975 the Common Market seemed to that young trade union official to be very much designed for rich businesses with little concern for the welfare of ordinary people. And at one level, that is the way it turned out. In the few years following the Referendum, some 3,000 British sugar workers lost their jobs. The Commonwealth sugar Industry lost part of its secure market and another 5,000 people were thrown into unemployment. But there were some winners. The bigger refinery company, Tate & Lyle, bought out its smaller competitor and reinvented itself as a successful and highly profitable multi-national food company. Continental farmers continued to profit from the over production of sugar beet, either dumping the surplus on the world market with further damage to tropical cane producers or processing the beet into some of the most costly animal feed that the world has ever known.

So did the experience of the sugar workers justify my sour judgement about the Common Market? At the time, I thought so. However with hindsight comes a different and more mature judgment. For that group of sugar workers, entry into the Common Market was profoundly miserable. But what made it worse was a particularly British failure. In 1975 and the years following, the UK gave no adequate protection and no reasonable support to workers who were damaged by rapid industrial change.

In the 1970s the standard response of British trade unions to a threat of factory closure was that we would use our organisation and industrial strength to protect our members. That policy sounded very fine when delivered with passion and eloquence from the rostrum of a trade union conference, but it took no account of the realities of an industry which had lost much of its raw material. Sugar Refinery workers could go on strike, but that would not change the inexorable arithmetic of the European Sugar regime. The supply of cane sugar was being sharply reduced and that would bring inevitable consequences for the workers who refined it. Strike or no strike, some refineries would close.

The GMB managed to negotiate respectable redundancy terms for our members who lost their jobs. But redundancy payments were not enough. The displaced workers needed proper career counselling, tailor-made retraining packages and regular allowances to maintain their income as they made the transition from the sugar refineries to other jobs. My Union put pressure on Tate & Lyle to provide a complete package of help and we even argued that the Company should create new employment by diversifying into other products. The trouble was that the workers had no legal right to what we were claiming. In British law, all the Company had to do was to sign the tiny redundancy cheques required by the Redundancy Payments Act and walk away.

After 1975 I quickly came to appreciate that, had the sugar closures happened across the Channel in the original six member States of the Common Market, more help would have been given by way of retraining, re-settlement allowances and income protection than was ever available in the UK. The Common Market may well have created the problem for my members but it also had, within its culture, law and practices, policies which would have reduced hardship and created new opportunities. So it was the inadequacies of the British industrial system and of our welfare state that converted a major economic difficulty into the disaster of long term unemployment and blighted lives. The Yes campaigners should also carry some responsibility: they were always keen to talk about the people and industries who would gain from Britain's membership of the Common Market, but never for a moment did they strive to protect and support those people who would be the casualties of British entry.

The economic dislocation in the sugar industry following the 1975 Referendum taught me that the traditional methods of British trade unionism were not enough to protect our members. Of course we needed effective trade unions and the right to strike, but we also needed a framework of legal rights which would protect vulnerable working people in every circumstance and not just when we had industrial muscle to put effective pressure on an employer. When I became General Secretary of my union in 1986, the GMB led a campaign to create fair legal rights for people at work in Britain. By that time there was little opposition in the TUC to such a fundamental change of policy. The recession of the early 1980s had taught us all that few workers had the confidence to strike when unemployment was high and rising. So well before the fall of Margaret Thatcher, the British trade union movement had come to recognise that there was much to admire in the continental approach to industrial relations. Henceforth, there was less claptrap about the efficacy of strike action and, in its place, a more realistic determination to secure for British workers the package of employment rights long enjoyed by workers in France and Germany and Italy.

Most of Europe now recognises that rapid economic change can only be accomplished in a civilised manner if working people are protected by humane social policies and enforceable employment rights. Unfortunately the UK Government has a different agenda. I feel a bitter sense of irony when I observe that, thirty years after the Referendum, it is the original six members of the Common Market who seek to maintain a high level of social protection for people at work and it is a British Labour Prime Minister who argues for deregulation and for measures to reduce employment rights. Looking back I wonder how I could have put such faith in our traditional industrial system and why I glibly decided that the European Social Model had so little to offer the working people of Britain.

Alan Sked

Reflections of a Eurosceptic

At the time of the 1975 Referendum I was a European federalist who was still a D.Phil student at Oxford (under my distinguished supervisor, A.J.P.Taylor), although I had already been appointed lecturer in International History at the LSE. I had had to learn German, Hungarian and Italian for my doctoral thesis, had spent over a year in Vienna, already knew French, (and had studied Latin and Greek), so I thought myself pretty cosmopolitan. Indeed, so cosmopolitan was I, that I had joined Jo Grimond's Liberal Party as a teenager in Scotland and had been active for years as President of the Association of Scottish Liberal Students, Treasurer of the Scottish League of Young Liberals, President of Glasgow University Liberal Club and finally Liberal parliamentary candidate for Paisley in 1970 (at the ripe old age of 22) articulating the case for a United States of Europe. I was as passionate as one could be on behalf of that cause long before we ever entered the EEC. A youthful idealist, I swallowed all the propaganda about peace, unity and prosperity. So when the referendum came along in 1975 there was no doubt which way I would vote: I voted Yes.

Being in London, I took the opportunity to listen to the main speakers. I heard Edward Heath (the real leader of the Yes Campaign) in Trafalgar Square and was surprised by his eloquence. I also heard Enoch Powell for the first time (he was later to speak on my behalf at a memorable by-election meeting at Newbury Racecourse in 1993) and was mesmerised by his oratory, if a little disturbed by the look of some of his supporters. (Nor had I ever seen so many Union Jack flags in one room at one time.)

I was very pleased, needless to say, with the referendum result. It never occurred to me, as a federalist, that the campaign had been totally skewed in favour of the winning side. A decade or so later, I would see it as the sinning side.

In the Liberal Party, I had been in favour of 'a federal Britain in a federal Europe'. However, I soon went off the Liberal Party (partly because I could never feel any enthusiasm for David Steel as leader, although I had worked for him in the Roxburgh, Selkirk and Peebles by-election as a student. The 'boy David' as he was then known always struck me as the 'prig David'. He seemed dour, smug and pedantic.) I also thought that it was time to change the economy around and to tackle the trade unions. But although Grimond had written eloquently of the need for free enterprise values, low tax and small government, his desire to obtain 'a realignment of the left', in short, a Lib-Lab government, had blinded the party to Labour's links with the union barons. And given these links, Liberal clichés about 'co-partnership in industry' were embarrassingly pointless. As a good Scot I also began to fear that a federal Britain would abandon Scotland to the worst sort of Red Clydeside socialism. So, naturally, I became interested in the new Tory Party leader, Margaret Thatcher, although I voted Labour in 1979. (I was still registered in Glasgow, Cathcart, and wanted to get rid of Teddy Taylor, who I then dismissed as appallingly right-wing on account of what I regarded as his 'racist' campaign in support of Ian Smith's Rhodesia. I later confessed this to Teddy (who I don't think forgave me). In any case, I was now politically neutral, although my European federalism was slowly to expire.

The principal reason I became a Eurosceptic was that from 1980–1990 I served as Convener of European Studies at the LSE. In short, I co-ordinated the interdisciplinary MSc programme on contemporary Europe. Indeed, I built it up to be the largest of its kind in the UK. Yet in so doing, I had to chair or attend European research seminar after seminar, mark exams, read dissertations, meet Eurocrats, bureaucrats, Euro-apologists, Euro-spokespersons, Euro-academics galore, until, inevitably, I saw the truth: most of these people, like the system they justified, were mad. British membership of the European Community was unnecessary and damaging. The final straw was a visit from the head of the Brussels DG in charge of transport who verily bounced around the room with a little pointer, shouting 'I say No' before indicating on a map where national governments had suggested road-building schemes. These would only be approved, he made clear, if the roads concerned all led to

Brussels. He spoke for one hour and forty minutes. The students were amazed. But my Euro-enthusiasm did not last.

The 1980s, of course, were also the years in which Thatcher's growing opposition to European practices emerged. The annual struggle over the budget culminating in the famous rebate deal at Fontainebleau in 1984 was the first part. Then came her epic struggle with Delors over the future of Europe. While both could agree on the Single European Act as a means of refining and completing the single market by abolishing non-tariff barriers to trade, the two were soon at loggerheads over EMU and the Social Charter. It was Delors, however, who took the outrageous step, as a foreign, unelected bureaucrat, whatever his title, of visiting the TUC annual congress and telling it that, whatever the policies and achievements of Thatcher's historic, reforming government, Brussels would overthrow the legislation of Britain's democratically elected government. An alliance was then formed by the unelected on both sides of the Channel against the British prime minister. Her response at Bruges, defying the Eurocrats by announcing that she would not extend state power on the European level just to please them, led to the formation of the Bruges Group, which was established at the Reform Club as a non-party group of supporters coalesced around a group of academics, who were to elaborate her themes.

I soon became the most influential pamphleteer and speaker for the group. For example, I wrote the only pamphlet for the Group which was ever unanimously approved by its Council and which attempted to construct an anti-federalist constitution for the EC. (Enoch Powell told me it was the best attempt he had ever read 'to square the circle'. Perhaps the Tories should take it up). Yet with the overthrow of Mrs. Thatcher in 1990 by her colleagues, the most ruthless political assassination in democratic party history, given her electoral record, and the basic cause of the Tory party's misfortunes ever since, I became rather too controversial for Mr Major. A Bruges Group pamphlet on the Germans and the Gulf War written by me, pointed out that there were no grounds in their constitution to prevent them sending troops to the Gulf. This led to great acrimony between the Group and the German government (Baron von Richthofen, the then German ambassador later told me at the Koenigswinter Conference: 'I know who you are Dr. Sked, I know everything about you!'). However, it probably saved the lives of some Kurds and it did help shame the Germans into paying a considerable part of the costs of the Gulf War. Again, the German Constitutional Court later upheld my arguments when the issue was considered there, indeed the *Haus der Geschichte* in Bonn later asked me for a copy of my pamphlet, which, provocatively enough had been entitled *Cheap Excuses.*

My next provocation almost proved my undoing. A press statement criticising Major for doing very little to help the Kurds at the end of the Gulf War was released, which included the line, 'Is the overthrow of Mrs. Thatcher to be paid for with the blood of tens of thousands of innocent Kurds?' This was read out dramatically by John Snow on Channel Four news and Major went ballistic. I was interviewed about the subject as the main guest on the *Today* programme the next morning and Brian Redhead suggested that what I was really saying was that Major was a wimp. After agreeing that he was in danger of giving this impression, the *Evening Standard* that lunchtime came out with the banner headline *Major A Wimp* and carried the text of my interview. ('Dr. Alan Sked, leading spokesman for the Bruges Group, president Lady Thatcher, said this morning etc. etc.') Major then gave a dreadful weekend interview on the subject to Brian Walden, after which in the Monday feature page of the *Daily Telegraph,* Charles Moore's article was headlined 'Major A Flop.' So inadvertently, I put an end to Major's honeymoon with the voters.

Several Bruges Group members were horrified. The Group's secretary and myself were forced to submit our resignations (admittedly, on the condition that they would not be accepted) and there was a huge hue and cry from the media. Eventually, however, it all died down. Still, I soon concluded from this episode that the Group was too pro-Major despite the fact that Major's government was hardly likely to listen to it. So I announced the formation of an Anti-Federalist League (based on the example of the Anti-Corn Law League), with the intention of converting the Tory Party to extreme Euroscepticism (in fact the aim was to quit the EU) by standing candidates against Tory ones at the next general election. I myself declared that I would contest Bath, then held by the arch-federalist and self-styled 'Christian democratic', Tory Chairman, Chris Patten. I still, however, intended to remain a member of the 'non-party' Bruges Group.

Yet it was not to be. Sometime in 1991 I think, after having written the longest Bruges Group pamphlet to date (*Time for Principle,* it was called, ironically, given what was about to happen), I was telephoned by the then chairman of the Group, my LSE colleague, Professor Ken Minogue, who told me not to attend the next Council meeting which was due to take place before a Group meeting at the Reform Club at which the distinguished journalist Lord Rees-Mogg, would be our guest speaker. Minogue told me that I was 'becoming an embarrassment to John Major' and that my position had therefore to be reviewed. I presume he never expected me to attend Rees-Mogg's meeting either.

In any case, after I had squeezed into the back of the crowd in the Reform Club Library, Minogue started proceedings by advertising my pamphlet, claiming it to be the best yet produced by the Group. However, he then went on to say that, regrettably, I had informed him of my wish to retire. I was flabbergasted. I had said no such thing. So I stood up at the back of the room, waited till there was complete silence, and suggested to an embarrassed Minogue, who had not seen me, that he should tell his members the truth, namely that he had just sacked me for becoming an embarrassment to the Prime Minister. The whole affair was written up as the major item in the *Times* diary the next day. Well, that was the end of my connection with the Group, whose fortunes, for a variety of reasons, thereafter appreciably declined.

My next controversial act was to kill off Patten's parliamentary career, helping him to lose his seat in Bath in 1992 and thus stopping him from succeeding Major as Prime Minister. This had nothing to do, I hasten to add, with the few votes I secured there, although my campaign was an extremely robust one. (Daniel Hannan, now a leading Tory MEP provided considerable help; he later became speech-writer to William Hague on European affairs, much to Patten's chagrin.) What happened was that at the main public meeting in Bath, attended by all the candidates and given national publicity thanks to Patten's presence as Tory Party chairman, Patten was asked to apologise for the poll tax. After talking about the rates for a very long time, he then sat down without mentioning the poll tax. So I sprang to my feet and said: 'Chris, in one word, Yes or No, will you now answer the question, will you apologise for the poll tax?' And, of course, he said 'No'. I had slit his throat. All over Bath and all over the country the next day, the headlines ran: 'Patten refuses to apologise for Poll Tax.' So he lost his seat.

After the election, I stood in two by-elections in 1993, first at Newbury and then at Christchurch as an anti-federalist. At Newbury, the Tory candidate was a Europhile, but still got Norman Tebbit to speak for him. ('Half a Tory is better than none,' he supposedly said.) I was supported by Enoch Powell, who was driven down in silence to Newbury from London to save his voice, although when I said I feared we might be late, he told me: 'A speaker should always arrive ten minutes late and with a full bladder. That way, there is a sense of anticipation and he doesn't speak for too long.' The thought of sharing a platform with Enoch was a rather terrifying. In the event, he duly electrified his audience, was very kind and complimentary about me, and when he returned home he told me how much he had enjoyed himself. Surprisingly, I did too. I later discovered that there was a very endearing, warm side to the man, which totally escaped the public.

There were 19 candidates at Newbury, but I came fourth, only 500 votes behind Labour. That is the polite way of assessing my achievement. The same sort of result was repeated at Christchurch a few months later, with a few more votes. Yet clearly I could not stand in every by-election so that a party was needed to further the cause. Also a new name was needed, since League reminded people less of the Anti-Corn Law League than of various fascist bodies in pre-war France. So one weekend in October 1993 along with a number of fellow activists, I summoned a meeting at my office at LSE, which adjourned to the international history common room at the end of the corridor where the UK Independence Party (UKIP) was born. Its constitution provided that all members should sign a declaration stating that they had no prejudices against minorities or nationalities of any kind; it also laid down that it would not take up seats in the European Parliament, since we only acknowledged the sovereignty of the Westminster one, which alone could vote to take us out of the European Union. I ended up writing most of the Party's other policies, since I was emphatic that it should not be a one-issue party; however, most of the colleagues I had to work with were uninterested in other issues. Once I left, they also changed the policy with regard to minorities and on taking up seats on the gravy train.

I led the party into the Euro-elections of 1994, although I had to be hospitalised for appendicitis, and into the General Election of 1997. The media seemed very fair, given our lack of resources and I personally had no grievances. The eurosceptic vote in 1997, however, was split by the advent of the Referendum Party.

This had been set up deliberately to crush UKIP and almost did so, since it was fronted by the extremely wealthy Sir James Goldsmith, whose policy during the campaign shifted from one of 'we don't care which side of the argument you are on, so long as you back a referendum' to a policy of backing withdrawal. Goldsmith did the eurosceptic cause a great service, however, in securing a promise from the Tories that they would hold a referendum on the euro, a promise which Blair subsequently backed. He did it less of a service, on the other hand, by deluding it that it should rely on millionaires rather than on hard work, organisation and intellectual graft to further the cause. I, in any case, after the 1997 election, gave up the leadership of UKIP. I was totally exhausted, confident that Goldsmith would now lead the cause (like everyone else I had no idea how bravely and secretly he had been fighting cancer during the campaign). I was also unhappy about the kind of people who seemed ready to make a take-over bid for the UKIP leadership. I did try to expel the worst of them, but was let down by my national executive. So I left a note for the Party in HQ one day saying goodbye, appointed an acting leader, and took my leave. The best of my colleagues left with me.

The Party did well for a year after I left. Then a new leader, Michael Holmes was elected who seemed to promise wealth and success, but who in fact brought in extreme right-wingers, changed the policy regarding taking up seats in the European Parliament, and in 1999 managed to get him and two others elected as MEPs once the voting system was changed. This was a disaster. In his maiden speech Holmes, to great federalist applause, called for increased powers for the European Parliament. His colleague, Nigel Farage, told him, 'Well done!' when he sat down to more federalist applause. The Party then tried to deny what had happened, but once the film of the Parliamentary session had been released and the truth of the matter was available, there was backlash in the Party and Holmes was flung out.

Later MEPs have been no better or wiser. Holmes's successor, Graham Booth MEP, had to apologise to the Parliament for his incomprehensible maiden speech, while the overall voting and attendance records of UKIP MEPs has been appalling. Meanwhile they take their inflated salaries and expenses, while denouncing the system they profit from. And their main platform nowadays is as much immigration (stopping all and any kind of immigration) as Europe.

If the original idea was that UKIP should subvert the European Parliament from within, the European Parliament has subverted UKIP. The Party now focuses its efforts on retaining its MEPs or securing more (a much easier task, given the List PR electoral system), while neglecting the opportunity of entering the UK

Parliament, the only body empowered to take us out of the EU. For example, in the crop of by-elections that occurred after the 2004 Euro-elections when UKIP was at the height of a popularity wave, it simply refused to put up candidates in two by-elections, where according to opinion polls it could have won! Apparently the leadership was unable to face the prospect of Robert Kilroy-Silk re-entering Westminster and thereby becoming the centre of national attention. In the end Kilroy killed off his own political career by founding Veritas and appearing just as bizarre as any UKIP MEP.

The Conservatives, meanwhile, under the influence of the Bruges Group, UKIP and Tory Eurosceptics changed from being a Europhile to a Eurosceptic party. This forced several Tory Eurofanatics out of the Party altogether. The other dinosaurs (Heseltine, Hurd, Howe and Heath) now simply had to keep quiet. New Tory leaders such as Hague and Duncan-Smith were obvious Eurosceptics, while Kenneth Clarke had no chance of gaining the party leadership, given his extreme and obvious Europhilia. Under these leaders, the Tory party rejected both the membership of the eurozone and the European Constitution. Even New Labour was slow to offer support for the new single currency or the Constitution. Indeed, today, Tony Blair and Gordon Brown while denouncing the economies of the eurozone in the name of free-enterprise are themselves doing everything possible to undermine the free market economy at home. Their game plan seems to be to postpone discussion of the new constitution until Britain is in a better mood to accept it. Their reforming zeal for Europe, however, should not be taken at face value.

So what is a Eurosceptic today to do? My advice is to keep up the pressure over the euro and the constitution, to keep forcing the Tory Party to become even more eurosceptical (its policy of partial re-negotiation of our membership is incoherent) but to avoid the radical right (sadly, now including UKIP) with its obsessions over immigrants and foreigners, obsessions which undermine the eurosceptic cause, which after all is only part of the wider one of democracy and freedom. Events are going our way. In the next referendum, we should be on the winning side.

Tam Dalyell

No Regrets

Then, Now or for the Future

My most lasting recollection of the 1975 referendum is a meeting, widely advertised and solely devoted to European issues, in the 11,000 town of Bo'ness on the River Forth in my then West Lothian constituency. Five people turned up in the large school hall: my wife, myself, the Headmaster who was friend of mine, the janitor who was obliged to open the school anyway and a retired miner from the Kinneis colliery.

The miner made a contribution, 'Tam, what do we pay you for as the Member of Parliament for West Lothian, other than to make the hard decisions for us, in the light of your knowledge and your judgment?' My answer was, I fear, a watery smile. He had a point. It is absurd to have a referendum on complex matters, when the vote may be about all other matters, such as the popularity of the Government.

The day before, attempting to canvas my pro-European views in the village of Fouldhouse, I was asked at least a dozen times, after saying I was at their door for the European referendum, 'Tam, seeing you're here, what can you do to get West Lothian County Council to mend my fence, sort my drain, mend my leaking roof, or fill in the potholes in the road?' Entry into the European Community was far from their thoughts: common currency issues! They relied on me!

It was not as if meetings, as such, were sparsely attended in West Lothian. The five people who came to Bo'ness, the fifteen people who had come to a referendum meeting in Bathgate and the eighteen people who came to a referendum meeting in Broxburn have to be compared to the 350 up-tight, involved constituents who had crowded into the Recreation Centre Hall at Blackburn the week before. They were angry not about the future constitutional arrangements of the United Kingdom in relation to European countries; but because against my better judgment, and out of sheer loyalty to the Labour Government, I had supported measures in a Fresh Water Fisheries Bill which had the effect of limiting fishing opportunities in a matter of riparian rights for weekend working-class anglers! "Tam, you can do what you bloody well like about Brussels, but you are bloody well not to mess around with our fishing for trout, and the occasional salmon on a Saturday night!" There spoke the authentic voice of the serried ranks for the National Union of Mineworkers, who, 30 years ago were so politically important!

This book seeks to determine if anything could have been done differently, and what are the lessons. Hindsight is wonderful, but I do not for the life of me see what could have been done differently, other than to have eschewed the referendum avenue. There was simply no appetite for a vote on issues that were not comprehended, often by people who would rightly consider themselves otherwise well informed.

I still hold the same views on the EU and Britain's membership. Yes. I am as pro-Communautaire as I was on October 28, 1971, when I strode into the same lobby as Edward Heath along with Roy Jenkins and 67 other Labour Members of Parliament, against a 3 line whip, in order to allow Britain to enter into the Community. At the time of writing, February 2005, I am the only remaining Labour Member of the House of Commons to have so voted on that historic occasion.

Furthermore, in terms of those aspects of the EU's development in the intervening period that have surprised me, it is not a fashionable answer that I offer. Between 1976 and 1979, I was one of sixteen Labour Members of the Commons and the Lords to have been elected by my colleagues to serve in the indirectly elected European Parliament. During that period I was a Member of the Budget Committee of the Parliament, chaired by the rigorous and courageous, in his personal history, Erwin Lange from Essen. I was also a Member of the Budget sub-Committee, the Audit Committee of the Parliament, under the expert guidance and chairmanship of Heinrich Aigner of the CSU. These committees were by no means models of harmony. When my neighbour, our names both beginning DA, Kirsten Dahlerup, either disagreed with the Chairman, or got bored, she would bring out her knitting in Committee, taking pleasure in the fact that a Danish woman could make a German chairman apoplectic. But membership of these Committees did allow me to reach the informed opinion that Community funds were not squandered, as many newspapers led European citizens to suppose.

One incident encapsulates my impression that European funds were not misused. Along with the late Earl of Bessborough, a charming, assiduous, and well-informed Conservative Peer, and Martin Bangemann, the German Liberal, who was later to become a distinguished European Commissioner for Industry, I went to Friuli to ascertain whether funds allocated to relief of the appalling earthquake disaster were being significantly misappropriated. When I was told by soaking wet residents, in camps, after midnight, that they thought there was no corruption, I drew the conclusion that the funds had been properly used. If they had not been, the people of Germona and Udine would have been the first to complain!

Tangentially, there was one episode that did surprise me at the time, but which, perhaps, ought not to have surprised me. When I learned that Bessborough, Bangemann and Dalyell had been nominated to represent the European Parliament in Friuli, I went to see Ludwig Fellermaier, Chairman of the Socialist Group of MEP5 (indirectly elected) about nominating an Italian to come with us. With a knowing twinkle in his eye, Fellermaier said, 'Herr Tam, you try to persuade De Labriotta (MEP for the Bolzano area) or any other prominent Italian in the Group to go with you to ascertain if there is corruption in Italy! It's beyond me!' Having failed with my own Group, I then went to the head of the Italian Christian Democrats, with whom I was personally friendly, to ask if their Group would choose an Italian to come to Friuli. I've not been treated like it since I was elected to the House of Commons in 1962, 'Grow up. Don't be a little boy, wet behind the ears. If you think, that I'm going to send any of my colleagues to investigate wrong-doing with European funds in Italy, think again, Signor Tam! My friend's name? Giulio Andreotti. Seven times Prime Minister of Italy and much else.

I came to have a high respect for the dedication and honesty of those employed by the Community around the regions of Europe. Almost all were high quality people. And the Budget Committee was exceptionally well served by officials of superb quality.

However, there is a minority opinion, which I held weakly at the time in the late 1970s, but which I hold most strongly today. Direct elections to the European Parliament were a grievous mistake. It would have been far better to let the old system continue, whereby contingents were deputised to the European Parliament. This is not a matter of personal convenience or advantage since I could not have done more than four years of hexangular life, Edinburgh-Brussels-Luxembourg-Strasbourg-Westminster.

There is a lot to be said for Members of National Parliaments being 'educated' on a rota basis in European Affairs. This is not how it looked, to the overwhelming majority, at the time, who endorsed the report of Schelto Patijn, the Dutch Socialist MEP, later Governor of South Holland, and Burgomaster of Amsterdam, who was the Rapporteur on Direct Elections. The directly elected Parliament seems to me to have little power, and is certainly divorced from day-to-day national politics in Britain.

Another matter was a pleasant surprise where the close inter-Member personal friendships that quickly developed among Members of Party Groups, but also across Party Groups; more than Westminster. In the period of which I have personal knowledge, the European Parliament was a Parliament where members actually talked to each other, candidly and in depth about policies and ideas. I was also impressed by the way in which busy Commissioners such as the German Guido Brunnen (Energy) and the Dane Finn Olaf Gundelach (Agriculture) were willing to come to far away Scotland to speak to my constituents about Europe, and stay the night with my wife and myself at home.

My view on the future of the EU? Bright. I was very touched to go to the Baltic States of Lithuania, Latvia and Estonia in September 2005, and see the joy of the people at being Members of the EU. To think that I had doubts in 1978 about the admission of Greece and was eased out of the European Parliament-Greece Committee for expressing these doubts. Never have I been more misguided in my life!

In terms of the future relationship between the UK and the EU, in the words of an Arsenal supporter on the day the Frenchman Arsene Wenger omitted to name a single Englishman among his team or substitutes, 'I don't care, as long as Arsenal win!' You would get the same comment at Ibrox or Celtic Park in Glasgow. The people feel European now, whatever Rupert Murdoch may feel.

As to potential differences between the 1975 referendum and the forthcoming referendums on the EU Constitution and EMU, there are none. Those who vote will do so out of gut instinct, whilst a tiny minority will vote on the merits, as they see them, or demerits of the European idea. As in 1975, many, many voters will vote for reasons other than what the referendum purports to be about.

Arrogant though I risk sounding, most voters have not even the slightest notion of what the EU Constitution involves, and even less grasp of the pros and cons of EMU. Back to that Bo'ness miner in 1975 who said, 'Tam, why do we pay you, other than to make the hard decisions for us!'

Richard Body

The 1975 Referendum

That the Yes side were able to spend £40 for every £1 that the No campaign had available was undoubtedly a major advantage, but on reflection not so crucial as we believed at the time. With so much money in their hands, they seemed to have little regard for the cost-effectiveness. They were also rather generous to Edward Heath, giving him £4,000 (some £50,000 in today's money) for his help. Their other speakers were also rewarded, whereas on the No side, none were paid and several of us who in the course of the campaign travelled thousands of miles on trains and staying night after night in hotels had to pay out nearly as much as Mr Heath and others were given.

There were, however, several factors which in my opinion did have a decisive effect upon the result. As the common market was to benefit us economically, one would have thought a long line of distinguished economists would have queued up to support the Yes campaign. Yet none of them did so. The one exception was a professor at the University of Warwick, but he conceded that it was the political case that persuaded him. There were, though, plenty to take the contrary view. A few years before the Referendum I had been appointed chairman of the Open Seas Forum, a small think tank to promote the ideal of an open world economy as against the world dividing into trade *blocs* like the common market. As chairman my task was to enlist our leading academic economists and invite them to write monographs all of which were to be implicitly or explicitly critical of the EEC. The task could not have been easier; I asked eight, and they all agreed to do so. Ask ten economists for their opinions and you will get eleven different replies, so the old joke goes but on the EEC they were unanimous. The first monographs were reasonably reported in the quality newspapers, but once it was rumoured we were to have a referendum, a blanket descended. Even papers by James Meade, a Nobel Laureate and professor at the University of Cambridge, and Harry Johnson, professor at the LSE, who both wrote lucidly as well as authoritatively were ignored. Nor was Harry Johnson, as an academic critic of the EEC able to get his views accepted elsewhere, except in the academic press.

That the media were totally and enthusiastically on the Yes side made it difficult enough for us. What was worse was how it distorted whatever we said on the few occasions they gave any space to our views or the facts we stated. Copies of the Treaty of Rome were not available to the public, after all the debate should have been about the Treaty and though we had managed to secure three or four copies several months previously before they went out of print, audiences at public meetings simply would not believe us when we quoted any of its clauses because the BBC and the whole press unanimously reassured everyone it was only about a common market. There was, I should add, one newspaper advocating a No vote, the *Morning Star*, but how we wished it was on the other side. Its opposition to the EEC gave credence to the argument that a common market was serving as a bulwark against the Soviet empire and thus stemming the advance of Communism. No matter how hard we tried to explain the obvious fallacy in that argument, we never succeeded in getting it printed in their pages.

Another theme the newspapers echoed was about the power of the trade unions and the damage they were doing to our industries. Membership of the EEC would bring them to heel. Thirty years on, we have forgotten the dislocation to our lives caused by one large-scale strike after another. To blame the trade union leaders, however, was not altogether fair. When the government expands the money supply by 20–30%, as happened under the Heath government, there is a two-year time lag before the full effect is felt, and our political masters in the early 1970s could not understand that if the increase in the amount of money circulating in the economy was not matched by a similar increase in what money could buy, there was going to be inflation. The cost of living in the last half of the 1970s was soaring upwards and as real wages fell so the trade unions were forced to demand more for their members. Unfortunately, the union leaders rather enjoyed this power to threaten strike action, or at least that was the impression they gave to the public as they came on the television screen. Thus, seen week after week, they became hate figures for the suffering millions, who also had falling incomes, but were often not in a position to claim more.

A notable exception was Jack Jones, the General Secretary of the Transport and General Workers Union, then the largest and most powerful of the unions. He always spoke with some decent humility, and we were delighted when he joined me as the other joint-chairman of the Council of Get Britain Out campaign. Nonetheless, the press tarred him with the brush of 'being one of them'. Whatever they said against the EEC was discounted because of their self-interest; one example will show its effect. *The Times* throughout the campaign had scores of articles, news items and editorial leaders in favour of the Yes side, but were persuaded to have one article setting out our case 'for balance'. The article was to be by both Jack Jones and myself; I wrote the piece and handed it over to Jack to approve which he did without altering a word. Off it went to *The Times*, and when it appeared it had his by-line alone, thus the august 'journal of record' lent weight to the claim that the No campaign was the cause of the Left and the union barons.

Far worse was the way the press portrayed Tony Benn as the leader of the No campaign. Prominent in the CND, seen as someone who would leave us defenceless against the Soviet empire, who wanted all our industries nationalised and the middle classes liquidated, his views were so wilfully misreported that he never spoke to a journalist without his tape-recorder between them. His part in the campaign was quite small; he had no formal link with the campaign and never spoke at any of our meetings. We made a rule that all of these were to be cross-party which proved a futile attempt to show we were not all Lefties and Tony Benn was at none of them as he declined to share a platform with a Conservative. He did speak at other meetings and on the BBC, which threw all impartiality to the winds, was only too happy to have him on as our leader. I remember him making two forecasts: that the Treaty of Rome would lead to a major constitutional change and membership of the EEC would cause a million to lose their jobs, setting out very clearly and logically why both consequences would follow. Of course he was ridiculed for it. His prediction about the loss of jobs was not only correct, but it happened exactly as he said it would.

Business opinion was claimed by the government and the media to be unanimously in favour of a Yes vote. This was far from being true. The chairmen of three well-established public companies told us they wanted to support us. It was decided this could best be done by them signing a joint statement which would be sent to all parts of the media. I met them and helped draft the statement. It should have been newsworthy as it set out factually how three different and important industries would be adversely affected by the EEC. One

newspaper quoted an anodyne passage, the rest ignored their statement totally.

Another incident that ought to be recorded was that Sir John
Hunter, Chairman of Swan Hunter, the shipbuilders, and I had both
contributed to a symposium, *Destiny or Delusion*, he writing on the
effect of EEC membership on industry and I on agriculture. Just
before the campaign began, we met when he said he wanted to play
an active part in it. The Common Agricultural Policy would put up
the price of food by about 50%, he said, wages would have to rise and
as all our heavy industries were much more labour-intensive than
their competitors abroad, they would be unable to compete and collapse (all of which proved to be true). He returned to Tyneside to tell
his fellow directors his intentions. The company, they told him, was
dependent on government aid and already it had been hinted to
them that the company would expect little sympathy if it contra-
dicted the government. Sir John was given a choice: speak his mind
or remain on the board. He felt his first duty was to the company his
forebears had founded and to its many employees.

Fear begets hatred, and it certainly did so as the campaign neared
its climax. The Yes slogan 'Out of Europe, out of Work' went in leaflet form to every household. Three million jobs would be lost if we
voted No. Curiously enough, that was the number that was lost over
the next six years, although two-thirds of other jobs were found.

It was undoubtedly a successful slogan, but the fear it engendered
led to no hatred. But another fear did. The Soviet Union had a huge
army supported by thousands of tanks poised behind the Iron Curtain ready to invade, and behind them were nuclear missiles enough
to destroy Western Europe ten times over.

Carefully selected people were invited to luncheon and dinners to
provide audiences of some twenty or thirty to hear speakers give
what they claimed to be confidential briefings 'off the record'. The
real reason which could not be told publicly for our entry to the common market was because our intelligence service had learnt the
Soviet Union had plans to invade Western Europe and these would
be carried out once the trade unions in Western Europe led by a
Communist Fifth Column had fomented widespread strikes to prevent the invasion being resisted. Thus persuaded, their fear not
unnaturally turned to contempt, repugnance and even hatred for
anyone active in the No campaign.

What happened in the campaign stirred our emotions, too, not at
the time, but shortly afterwards when we resolved to go on with our

opposition. Those few of us still alive, remain convinced intellectually of our case.

John Mills

Recollections of the 1975 Referendum

I had always been interested in the pros and cons of British membership of the Common Market, but at the start of 1975 I was no more
than an interested and sceptical bystander. As the referendum
approached, however, it became apparent that not a great deal was
being done in Camden, the area of London where I have been an
elected member on the Council since 1971, to mobilise a No vote. I
therefore contacted Douglas Jay, whom I had known for some time,
to see whether we should get some sort of organisation going in
Camden. This led to a seminal lunch which had a considerable
impact on the way I have spent my time ever since. It certainly made
a lot of difference to what happened to me over the following weeks.

Although at the time of my lunch with Douglas Jay there was only
about three months until the day when the referendum on whether
Britain should stay in the Common Market was to be held, it soon
became apparent that the relative lack of activity in Camden was
mirrored nationally. There was a certain amount of grass root activity, mostly centred round an organisation called 'Get Britain Out',
run by an engaging by eccentric solicitor called Christopher
Frere-Smith, but no national co-ordination. Get Britain Out had its
qualities, but organisational efficiency was not one of them. Nor was
the situation a great deal better within the newly formed National
Referendum Campaign (NRC), which had been set up as the
umbrella organisation for the No campaign. While this had a tal-
ented cross-party committee under the able and emollient chairmanship of Neil Marten, a Conservative MP, and the executive
management of Bob Harrison, a senior officer seconded from the
T&GWU, to lead the campaign at national level, there was almost no
structure underneath it to mobilise activity outside the small office
in The Strand from which the NRC was run. It was into this void that

I was sucked, leading to one of the most interesting and challenging weeks I have ever experienced.

While the NRC committee was largely interested in policy rather than organisation, it was clear that if we were going to provide ourselves with the best opportunity of winning the referendum vote for the No side, connecting up with the voters was going to have to be a high priority. This was my job. Public meetings had to be re-organised and concentrated on one major conurbation after another, using the best speakers we had to provide a focus every day for press and TV reporting. Speakers needed to be marshalled, halls booked, publicity arranged and the media made aware of what was being planned. We only had a limited budget for posters and leaflets and it was essential that these were used as effectively as possible. This could only be done if some kind of national organisation was created to arrange their distribution, so this had to be set up. Organisers were therefore found for every county, while I ran the London area myself. As referendum day approached, it became increasingly apparent that we would need to have official No campaign representatives at all the counts, so those responsible for activity at county level had to take on an additional role.

While all this activity was being organised throughout the country, at national level there was also an increasing amount to do and I was heavily involved here too. The leaflet setting out the No case, which was distributed to every household, had to be drafted. Policy statements had to be produced. National TV appearances had to be organised. Progress in the polls had to be monitored and appropriate action taken as a variety of issues waxed and waned as priorities in the campaign. As referendum day approached it became increasingly apparent that the tide of national opinion was swinging against us. All the same, I do not recollect any of us anticipating the scale of the defeat which overwhelmed us on 6th June 1975. All our hectic activity led to a two to one vote in favour of continued membership. Looking back from now, thirty years on, what features of the campaign we fought now stand out most clearly in my memory and what lessons might they carry for the future?

Perhaps the most obvious was the huge disparity in funding there was between the Yes and the No campaigns. The best estimate seems to be that the Yes campaigners had about eleven times the funding available to the NRC. This counted against us at every turn. We were grossly under-resourced compared with our opponents. Lack of funding may not dent the enthusiasm of those wholly committed to the cause they are fighting, but it inevitably makes it more difficult to attract the support of those who feel less certain about their convictions. It is impossible to replicate the professionalism of a really well funded campaign with less than one tenth of the money on the opposite side.

This state of affairs was not helped by the well established bias in all referendums towards both the maintenance of the status quo and the tendency for voters to favour Yes answers to ones involving saying No. The question asked was 'Do you think the UK should stay in the European Community (Common Market)?'. A positive answer was for staying in. Had the referendum taken place while we were still outside the Common Market rather than two and a half years after the date when we had become members and had the No campaign therefore had a less obviously negative bias, the result might not have been quite the same as it was.

A problem of a different sort faced by the No campaign was where most of our support was based. Broadly speaking, although there were many important exceptions, it came in 1975 from the left of the Labour Party and the right of the Conservatives. This made for an uneasy coalition and considerable difficulties about providing a single message to appeal to all sections of our support. It also provided organisational problems. Some of our best speakers, for example, would not share a platform with others at the opposing end of the political spectrum. We could only envy the almost seamless uniformity of presentation provided by the right of the Labour Party and the left of the Tories, most of whom looked generally more reassuring and less frightening figures to the uncommitted middle ground than some of the harder edged people who figured prominently in the No campaign.

A more subtle problem of which we were well aware at the time, but which was hard to get across to the public was the impact of the huge amount of propaganda put out by the Yes campaign, much of which we believed — correctly on all the evidence which has subsequently come to light — was, to say the least, economical with the truth. Some of the arguments which appealed to No voters shaded into nationalism and even chauvinism, but the hard core of the NRC campaign case revolved round bread and butter economic arguments and the related political case against remaining in the Common Market, at least on the terms on which membership had been negotiated. What was going to happen to food prices and to inflation generally? What would happen to the balance of payments when tariff barriers between the UK and the continental economies were reduced? Would the Common Agricultural Policy (CAP) benefit the UK by providing us with a more secure supply of food even if it was more expensive or would the CAP simply raise food prices in Britain at great cost to the UK economy and with no corresponding benefit in terms of the availability of supplies on the world market? What was the outlook for the British fishing industry in the light of the future for the UK continental shelf as a Community resource which had been conceded at the last minute at the time of accession? How much would Britain's contribution to the Common Market budget be likely to be over the coming years compared to what we could reasonably expect to receive back?

On all these issues, the Yes campaign had little to say other than to make vague promises which it was clear from all the evidence available even at the time were unlikely to be realised. It was on the political case for staying in the Common Market, however, that the obfuscation of the Yes campaign, as seen by the No side, was at its most mendacious. Continuous assurances were provided that all we were joining was a trading bloc. We were told time after time that our vetoes were secure and that talk on the continent of 'ever closer union' and the building of ever more integrationist structures were mere rhetoric, although it has now been shown beyond all doubt that many leading figures in the Yes campaign knew at the time that this was not true. To argue, as the Yes side relentlessly did, that the creation of the Common Market had guaranteed peace in Europe had a grain of truth in it, even though NATO played the major role in keeping the peace. The claim that the creation of the Common Market was all that the Treaty of Rome envisaged was never an accurate representation of the facts.

When the referendum was over, therefore, and the result declared, even though the majority in favour of staying in the Common Market turned out to be as large as it was, the issues round our membership were not resolved as its proponents hoped they would be. The sentiment among too many of the No camp was that, although they had lost the vote, they had not lost the argument and that events would turn out to show that their reasons for opposing continuing membership were all too well founded. Looking back over the past thirty years, it is hard, at least for me, to avoid the conclusion that this assessment was substantially correct.

Where does this then leave us as possible referendums on the Constitution and even perhaps on the Single Currency loom on the horizon? Surely the most obvious one is that, if decisions as important as these are to be taken, those in political power and controlling the purse strings should not be able to come close to monopolising expenditure on putting across their point of view, however strongly they may be in favour of it, as happened in 1975. It is certainly the case that the vast majority of the British political class at the time were in favour of continuing membership. It also seems possible, nevertheless, that, but for the enormous disparity in spending power and the barrage of propaganda this produced, the judgement of the British people, as expressed in their referendum votes, might have been different from that of most of their political leaders. If it had been, Britain might have enjoyed since 1975 the same independence and prosperity that countries such as Norway and Switzerland have been able to achieve. No doubt, there would have been a price to pay if Britain had been outside the main EU institutions and thus not directly involved in the decisions taken then. This may, however, have been a price well worth paying.

In the end, democracy is not about the maintenance of the status quo favoured by the political leadership's political consensus. On the contrary, it is about the ability of the electorate as a whole to take a view about how it wants to see its future determined. Political leaders always think that they know better and that their judgement of affairs is superior to that of ordinary mortals because of their greater knowledge and experience. History is replete, however, with examples of this sort of cosy consensus being overthrown. Too much of a disparity in resources nevertheless tips the balance too much in favour of the currently favoured consensus being maintained. 1975 may, in the long sweep of history, therefore be seen as an object lesson in how not to have the electorate's opinions swayed unfairly.

Robin Williams

The 1975 Referendum and Beyond

The focus has changed since 1975, it is now much more political and has been since the Single European Act (1986). Since then the speed of European integration has accelerated and continues to do so. This is made clear when one looks at the dates of key treaties in the development of EU:

1957 Treaty of Rome establishes the European Economic Community

1986 Single European Act

1992 (Maastricht) Treaty on European Union

1997 Treaty of Amsterdam

2000 Treaty of Nice

2001 Laeken Declaration: The Future of the European Union

2004 Treaty Establishing a Constitution for Europe

After the Treaty of Rome there was a gap of 29 years before the next treaty, the Single European Act which deepened integration. After it subsequent treaties came every three to six years. Each of these enlarged the law-making powers of what was originally called the Common Market and increased the areas in which decisions are taken by qualified majority voting.

Treaty of Rome

The preamble certainly commenced with the expression of determination to establish the foundation of an ever closer union. Opponents of joining the EEC concluded that further erosions of national sovereignty were in store and campaigned accordingly. However, the actual restrictions at the time were limited. They comprised the establishment of a customs union and a common commercial policy towards third countries, thus we ceased to figure in international trade negotiations, responsibility being transferred to the European Commission. There was also provision for the abolition of obstacles to the free movement of persons, services and capital. The treaty stated that a common agricultural policy was to be inaugurated and also a common transport policy and a system was to be established to ensure that competition should not be distorted in the Common Market.

Supranational institutions were created. But the Assembly, pre-cursor of the European Parliament, was to consist of delegates from the national Parliaments and it was only later when the Assembly became directly elected that the demand grew for it to have more powers. Decisions were taken by the Council and mostly by unanimous vote and, moreover, there was the de Gaulle compromise that qualified majority voting should not be pressed where a country stated its essential national interests were involved.

Hence, the political, academic and business elites in the UK concluded that the losses of sovereignty were not insupportable in view of the supposed economic gains. The important fact that the Commission has the sole power to make proposals to the Council of Ministers was not generally appreciated.

The 1975 Referendum

This was about staying in after Mr Wilson's supposed renegotiation to achieve better terms. The changes were in reality cosmetic. The No leaflet distributed to every household did lead with *The Right to Rule Ourselves – The fundamental question is whether or not we remain free to rule ourselves in our own way.* Nevertheless, a good deal of its argument dealt with the economics of the case. Sub-headings included 'It must mean still higher food prices', 'Your jobs at risk' and 'Huge trade deficit with the Common Market'. The No leaflet went on to recommend returning to EFTA, which by that time had an industrial free trade agreement with the Common Market.

Our defeat in the referendum meant that the subject was off the political agenda until Jacques Delors became President of the Commission and launched his drive for further integration.

Europe's Smiling Mouse

This headline appeared in The Economist on December 7th 1985 above an article describing the agreement reached in Luxembourg by the EEC heads of government. Its major points were:

- Europe has laboured long to produce a mouse. But the animal has a winning smile on its face, and all, including this newspaper, who want a more united Europe to succeed, will be grateful for this new rodent, however small.

- As for the British, Mrs. Thatcher combines a keen desire to create a continental free market with a frank British-first nationalism. She was ready to accept improved decision-procedures for the community as long as she could convincingly tell her Tory backbenchers that this meant no loss of British sovereignty.

- On Tuesday afternoon the important breakthrough was made — the discovery of a form of words on monetary co-operation which all could accept.

- The most striking element of the agreement is the attempt to encourage more decisiveness in the Council of Ministers during its forthcoming campaign to remove barriers to trade within the EEC. Although ministers will still be able to use a veto when their governments believe national interests are at risk, the hope is to increase the number of decisions that the Council can take by majority vote. The new procedures require changes to six of the Treaty of Rome's 240 articles and the addition of one further article. They extend majority voting to decisions on such things as industrial standards and other non-tariff barriers to trade.

- Whether or not to enshrine an article on monetary union in the Rome Treaty almost wrecked the summit. The culprit was the West German Chancellor. On Monday Mr Kohl suddenly announced that he did not after all object to altering the treaty to allow for the steps toward monetary union that some of the ten have taken. Since he had told Mrs. Thatcher that he shared her reservations about such treaty updating when they met in London the previous week, she was naturally startled and rebuked Mr Kohl in front of his peers. A chastened Mr Kohl and his advisers spent most of the next 24 hours drafting language on monetary co-operation that Mrs. Thatcher would accept. 'It does not change anything, she said afterwards; 'If it did, I wouldn't have agreed to it'.

How reassuring The Economist account sounds. It was just about getting rid of non-tariff barriers and enlarging the opportunities for services and the UK is good at providing services, isn't it! The media generally took the same line as The Economist. Thus, Mrs. Thatcher was not the only one who was fooled.

Single European Act

This advanced the integrationist agenda. Its Articles defined the internal market as comprising an area without internal frontiers in which the free movement of goods, persons, services and capital is ensured. The Commission obtained powers specifically relating to health, safety, environmental protection and consumer protection. Decisions by qualified majority appear in articles dealing with social policy. The phrase 'economic and social cohesion' makes its appearance, as does an EEC role in research and technological development and provisions concerning the environment.

Moreover, European Political Co-operation made its appearance with the member countries undertaking to endeavour jointly to formulate and implement a European foreign policy. A clause that was little noticed said that the Commission should be fully associated with the proceedings of Political Co-operation. So that development was not intended to be just intergovernmental co-operation.

It is now generally acknowledged that the Single Act's provisions have been the basis of a very large extension of the legislative authority of the European Community. But this was little appreciated at the time. Amending provisions in the treaty that seemed relatively innocuous have been interpreted in a much wider fashion. What lessons are to be drawn? Surely that if you give the Commission an inch, it will take a mile.

Maastricht Treaty

Emboldened by their success in getting away with so much with so little resistance at the time, the europhiles became ambitious and were repaid by more opposition, particularly on political grounds. The European Union was established, based on the European Communities supplemented by the policies and forms of co-operation established by this treaty. This meant Title V provisions on a common foreign and security policy and Title VI provisions on co-operation in the fields of justice and home affairs. These were proclaimed as inter-governmental, but close students of the text noticed Article

C that the Union shall be served by a single institutional framework. Citizenship of the Union was established. So was economic and monetary union, with the European Central Bank in charge. Lip-service was paid to subsidiarity in areas which did not fall within the European Community's exclusive competence. However, critics noted the provision that the Union was to maintain in full the 'acquis communautaire' and build on it.

For once the Eurosceptics in Britain enjoyed a piece of luck, from Denmark when the voters rejected the treaty in their first referendum. Parliamentary consideration of the necessary legislation by the UK was deferred and for some six months. The effect of this Danish vote was to prolong the period when the treaty was front page news in the UK to well over a year. Conservative eurosceptic MPs took advantage of this and, within the Conservative Party, a process of education occurred about the destination of the European project. Regrettably there was little comparable development within the Labour Party. However, eurosceptic views now spread more widely than hitherto in the country at large. The first Danish vote stimulated membership recruitment of the Campaign for an Independent Britain and, without doubt, the membership of other organisations that came into being alarmed at the speed and apparent destination of the European train.

Opponents of the Maastricht Treaty more and more emphasised the political consequences of European integration. How much of our self-government will we have left? The treaties are complex and difficult to explain. But the point about law-making authority passing increasingly to unelected and unaccountable Commissioners was made with increasing emphasis. The economic case was not overlooked, it could not be in view of the misrepresentations of the Europhiles. But since the Maastricht Treaty, the focus has been more on the political implications.

Who Really Governs Britain?

It is reasonable to try and quantify how much legislative authority has been transferred away from the Parliament we elect. Nirj Deva MEP examined this in a Bow Group pamphlet in 2001 in which he listed the percentage of the legislative programme initiated/authorised in both the EU and in our own Parliament. His analysis showed that overall 55% of our legislation was initiated or authorised in Brussels and Strasbourg. This is not what we were told at the time of the 1975 referendum: for example, the government's leaflet distributed to every household included the statement that, 'no important new policy can be decided in Brussels or anywhere else without the consent of a British Minister answerable to a British Government and British Parliament'.

Two factors are at work. First, there is the desire of Commission staff to be seen to be doing their job. This naturally leads to the drafting of new and supposedly better rules. The flood of regulations and directives is seen as evidence of zeal. If officials are appointed to make rules, rules are what they will make. Otherwise their posts might eventually be deemed to be superfluous. On top of that, there is the gold-plating tendency that appears to be deeply ingrained within the British civil service.

The second and more important factor has been the presence in key positions at important moments of true believers in the project, such as Monnet, Spaak, Spinelli and Delors. Four more such believers were appointed at Laeken to posts that enabled them to become the authors of The Treaty Establishing a Constitution For Europe. They were Valery Giscard d'Estaing, Jean-Luc Dehaene, Giuliano Amato and John Kerr.

The European Constitution

Consequently, in terms of the European Constitution, the misleading term *shared competence* (Article 1–12) states that, *Member States can only exercise their competence when and to the extent that the Union has not exercised or has decided to cease exercising its competence.* This makes provision for the Union to encroach still further into the law-making authority of the member states over a very wide field, including social policy, economic, social and territorial cohesion, the area of freedom, security and justice, not to mention agriculture, fisheries, environment, consumer protection, transport, energy and public health. This not only provides for more government from Brussels, but does so under the friendly term 'shared', which sounds reassuring but the reality will not be.

Conclusion

The greatest difficulty has been explaining the complexity of past treaties and this remains true of the proposed Constitution, whose purpose was described on the BBC News as the need to streamline the EU now it has 25 members. Streamline to what end? to pass more laws more quickly? to throw the EU's weight around in the world when it has a President and a Foreign Minister? Doubtless the reduction in the number of British Commissioners from 2 to 1 could be described as streamlining, but that has occurred in advance of the Constitution.

The increased focus on the political consequences of European integration is due to the fact of that integration. Europhile ambitions are now out in the open. The German Minister for Europe, Hans Martin Burz, was reported by Die Welt on 25th February 2005 saying, 'The EU Constitution is the birth certificate of the United States of Europe'. That should be clear enough even for the BBC. How much more of our self-government are we prepared to lose?

Looking back, I am surprised at the speed of integration from the time of the Single European Act and onwards. Indeed, the train has been accelerating. Explaining what has occurred and what is occurring is not easy, but it has to be done.

Tony Benn

The New Roman Empire[1]

From the time when Julius Caesar landed in 55 BC and brought us into a single currency with the penny, up to the signing of the Treaty of Rome, Britain's relations with Europe have been central to the political debate in this country and divide both parties in a way that has threatened their unity.

The immediate issue is the euro and whether Britain should join the European single currency; a secondary, but more important, question is whether we should accept a new European constitution drawn up under the chairmanship of the veteran French politician Giscard d'Estaing. The constitutional implications of European enlargement, which has brought in many Eastern European countries and produces a union of twenty-five, four times the size of the original six, are huge. A third question relates to whether or not Europe should have a common defence and foreign policy, in order, it is argued, that Europe is more united and can act as a counterweight to the United States.

At the outset of the Common Market I opposed it as a rich men's club; subsequently, as a minister, I concluded that it was probably the only way of providing political supervision and control of multinational companies that were bigger than nation states; and I have now moved to the position where I see the EU's present form as representing a threat to democracy in Britain and throughout all the member states of the Union.

Harold Wilson changed his view on the matter, having first been against and then coming out in favour; and so did Mrs Thatcher, who was passionately in favour of Britain's membership in 1975 and

[1]   From *Dare to be a Daniel* by Tony Benn, published by Hutchinson. Reprinted by permission of The Random House Group Ltd.

signed the treaty that introduced the single market, but later, when out of office, opposed the Maastricht Treaty, the euro and all forms of European integration.

By contrast, Roy Jenkins, Michael Heseltine and Jo Grimond were united in support, as was Ted Heath, who signed the Treaty of Accession in 1972 without the authority of a referendum.

Talking to Ted Heath about this over the years, I have always found his arguments' both simple and plainly political, for I have heard him say, 'Europe has had two major wars costing millions of lives and now we have got to get together.' And his fierce opposition to the Afghan, Iraq and Yugoslav wars confirmed my view that his position on Europe was based partly on his resentment of America dominating our continent.

That is an argument that has to be taken seriously, but since it raises constitutional questions, it would be intolerable if any steps taken to achieve it were slipped through Parliament without referenda to confirm them. Because these are all huge constitutional matters that involve taking away powers from the electors and transferring them into the hands of those who have been appointed.

Over the centuries Europe has seen many empires come and go: Greek, Roman, Ottoman, French and German, not to mention Spanish, Portuguese and British. Many of the conflicts between European states have arisen from colonial rivalry between imperial powers.

The concert of Europe after the fall of Napoleon, in which countries would negotiate alternatives to war, gave way after 1919 to the League of Nations, dominated by the old imperial powers, and broke down in part because Mussolini's Italy launched a colonial war against Abyssinia in breach of the Charter of the League.

After the Second World War, western establishments had to consider how best to cooperate in rebuilding the continent and, as the Cold War began almost immediately, one of their objectives through NATO was to provide armed forces to prevent the Soviet Union from launching a military attack. It could therefore be argued that the EEC was set up to rebuild Europe on safe capitalist lines, and that NATO was set up to arm the EEC against the military threat that we were told was materialising.

Indeed, a few years ago I heard the former American Ambassador in London speaking at a reception in Speaker's House about the Marshall Plan, which, he openly declared, was an investment to prevent the spread of communism.

As Minister of Technology in 1969, facing the massive multinational corporations and wondering how a nation state could cope with them, I did begin to wonder whether the existence of the EEC might offer some opportunity for political control and ought to be considered for that reason. Such a huge step required popular consent, and that was why in 1970 when we were in opposition and I was free to speak, I argued the case for a referendum to seek the consent of the British people. I discovered that the idea of a referendum was absolutely unacceptable to the establishment, which was totally opposed to giving the people direct say in any decisions, least of all one that might frustrate their dream of a Europe controlled by the political elite.

The referendum itself, held in 1975 after Heath had lost the 1974 election, was fought in a way that revealed the imbalance of money and influence on the two sides, the pro-Europe campaign having the support of the establishment and every single newspaper except the *Morning Star*, and able to command enormous resources; while the anti-campaign even had to struggle to find the cash to hold press conferences and meetings.

Wilson moved me from Industry to Energy immediately afterwards and I found myself on the council of energy ministers, where I served until 1979 and had the opportunity of seeing how the Common Market mechanism worked.

During the British presidency in 1977 I was the President of the Council of Energy Ministers. It is the only committee I have ever sat on in my life where as a member, or even as President, I was not allowed to submit a document, a right confined to the unelected Commission, leaving ministers like some collective monarch in a constitutional monarchy, able only to say Yes or No.

The Council of Ministers is of course the real parliament, for the directives and decisions take effect in member states without endorsement by the national parliaments. Because it is in effect a parliament, I proposed during my presidency that it should meet in public, so that everyone could see how decisions are reached and what arguments are used. This sent a chill of horror through the other ministers, who feared that it would bring to light the little deals that were used to settle differences, and I lost.

I also came to realise that the EEC, far from being an instrument for the political control of multinationals, was actually welcomed by the multinationals, which saw it as a way of overcoming the policies of national governments to which they objected. For example, I was advised by the Energy Commissioner that the North Sea oil really belonged to Europe and was told by my own officials that the 1946 Atomic Energy Act in Britain, which gave the then government control of all atomic operations, had been superseded by Euratom (the European Atomic Energy Community) and that we no longer had any power of control. I was warned that national support for industrial companies was a breach of the principle of free trade and was threatened with action if I disregarded their rules.

It became clear over the succeeding thirty years that the European Union, as it became, is a carefully constructed mechanism for eliminating all democratic influences hitherto exercised by the electors in the member states; it presents this as a triumph of internationalism, when it is a reversal of democratic gains made in the previous hundred years.

Now, with the Maastricht Treaty, the Single Market and the Stability Pact, the Frankfurt bankers (who are also unelected) can take any government to court for disregarding the Maastricht Treaty, while the Commission is now engaged in pursuing cases against the elected German and French governments for breaking the strict limits on public expenditure under the Stability Pact.

If the new European constitution comes into effect, other powers will pass from the parliaments we elect to the Council, Commission and Central Bank, and people here and everywhere in Europe will come to realise that whoever they vote for in national elections cannot change the laws that they are required to obey.

This is the most deadly threat to democracy and, if qualified majority voting removes the current veto system, any government could be outvoted and overruled and the people it was elected to represent would have no real say. Moreover, if the development of an independent foreign and defence policy takes place, we could be taken to war by decisions made elsewhere than in our own parliaments.

Not only is this a direct denial of democratic rights, but it removes the power of governments to discourage revolution or riot, on the grounds that a democratic solution is possible. Then the legitimacy and the stability of any political system come into question.

I am strongly in favour of European cooperation, having presented a bill for a Commonwealth of Europe that would include every country in our continent, as the basis for harmonisation by consent of the various parliaments, just as the UN General Assembly reaches agreements that it recommends should be followed.

The case for a European constitution and currency is also presented as a move beyond nationalism, which has brought such anguish to Europe. But I fear that it will stimulate nationalism when angry people discover that they are forced to do things they do not want to and are tempted to blame other nations, when the fault actually lies with the system itself.

Federations come and go, as we have seen in the Soviet Union and Yugoslavia, and I do not rule out the opportunity that the European Federation may break up amidst hostility between nations, which is the exact opposite of what we are told will happen.

The debate about the future of Europe has been reawakened by Gerhard Schröder, the (former) German Chancellor, who is supporting a plan that would absorb all the nations in the EU into a federal superstate with its own central government.

This plan, based on the German model which unites and controls their states (or Lander) would convert the parliaments of Britain and the other member countries into a mixture of regional assemblies and glorified local authorities all subject to the authority of the centre. In this superstate the real power would be in the hands of the president of the Commission, who is appointed and not elected, and he would then have the right to appoint the other, unelected, commissioners to form his Cabinet.

The prime ministers from the separate nations would be bundled together in a second chamber, as a part of the European parliament, with no executive authority over the countries which elected them. The whole concept is political rather than economic. It is the boldest plan yet produced by a European leader and its implications need to be publicly debated, so that we can get clear answers from all our political leaders and candidates.

New Labour hoped that Europe and the euro could be kept out of the election campaign because the Millbank Tower pollsters know very well that the public is strongly opposed to the sacrifices of our independence, and the Tories might well win votes by presenting themselves as the sole defenders of our autonomy and of the pound sterling. This is why the government has cooked up five economic tests that have to be fulfilled before Britain can join the euro, as if some Treasury computer could tell us when to give up the democratic control of our own economy.

The integration of Europe is a political and not an economic question. It must be seen as such, since each step taken in that direction shifts power from the elected to the unelected, and this raises fundamental democratic questions.

It is very important that those on the Left who oppose this do so because it represents a steady erosion of the power of the electors who are not taken in by the crude nationalism of the Right, with their dislike of foreigners and strange commitment to the Queen's image on banknotes. What are the alternatives for those of us who are socialists, democrats and internationalists who do want to cooperate closely with European neighbours?

In theory it would be possible to have a genuinely democratic United States of Europe, along the lines of the American model, with an elected president, Senate and House of Representatives all accountable to the people. But to do so would involve the complete abolition of the Commission, the Council of Ministers and the Central Bank in Frankfurt. For these reasons it would be totally unacceptable to the European establishment because it would reveal their deep dislike of democracy, and would in practice be both unwieldy and unworkable.

What the Left in Europe should be working for is a Commonwealth that brings in all the nations, east and west, committed to cooperate with each other and harmonise their policies, step by step, with the consent of each of their parliaments, rather like a mini UN, with an Assembly and Council of Ministers to oversee it, but with no power to impose on those countries that want to pursue policies that meet their own particular circumstances. This would need to be underpinned by the closest link between the trade unions and other progressive popular organisations across the whole continent.

What we do not want is to go back to the old hostility between the individual countries which led to two world wars and that is the danger of following the Tory Party line.

Internationalism is the proper response to globalisation, and those who believe that a federal Europe would protect us from the power of the multinational corporations are completely wrong, for the European Commission is little more that a regional agent of globalisation, enforcing the diktats of the bankers in our own continent.

We are told that soon after the election we shall have the referendum on the euro, and in some ways it will be a more important choice than the one we made on 7 June 2005, for if Britain s persuaded to join the single currency we shall, forever, have lost the right of self-government through the ballot box and all key decisions will be taken by those we did not elect and cannot remove.

Brian Burkitt

The 1975 Referendum

Its Impact and Consequences

Britain is insular, bound by its trade, its markets ... with the most
varied and often the most distant countries. Her activity is essentially industrial, commercial, not agricultural. She has in all her
work, very special, very original habits and traditions. In short,
the natures, the structure, the circumstances, peculiar to Britain,
are different from those of the other continentals ... How can
Britain, being what she is, come into our system?

Charles De Gaulle, 1963

Introduction

It is strange, in retrospect, seeing what led to what. In 1972 I was a
junior member of the economics department at the University of
Bradford, who inadvertently became a contributor to the current
affairs programme *Calendar* on Yorkshire Television. Some caustic
remarks I made about the benefits of Britain joining the EU[1] led me to
write two reports advocating a No vote in the 1975 Referendum
(Burkitt, 1974 and 1975). Because they attempted an honest analysis,
whose fundamentals I still support, and because of the creative associations to which they led, I re-analyse them here, humbly but without shame.

The UK and the EU: Economics

The economic case I made in 1974 was an early cost-benefit analysis
of the UK's membership of the EU. It demonstrated clearly, as others

[1]   The EU has variously been titled, 'The Common Market', 'European
      Economic Community', 'European Community' and the 'European Union'.
      For ease of exposition, in this Chapter, I refer to its current title, the EU,
      throughout.

have done more recently, such as Hindley and Howe (1996) and Milne (2004), that the costs of membership far outweigh its benefits. Additionally, l believed in 1975 that the UK as an underperforming economy would, through cumulative causation suffer even greater relative economic decline. There my analysis was completely wrong, in that, since the UK joined the EU in 1973, the EU has gone from being a relatively over performing, to an underperforming, industrial economic area. Its situation has worsened since German reunification in 1990 and the adoption of the Maastricht Treaty in 1991.

The key development in the EU's evolution between 1976 and 2005 economically was the acceptance of monetarism incorporated within the Maastricht Treaty. The European Central Bank's sole legal priority is to maintain price stability, without corresponding responsibility for employment or living standards, whilst the Stability and Growth Pact inhibits the use of government budget deficits to pursue expansionary economic policies. The lack of aggregate demand management created low growth and rising unemployment since 1991. Currently the unemployment rate in the eurozone is 8.9% compared to 4.7% in the UK. The weight of evidence indicates that since 1992 the U.K. has outperformed the EU, because it retained the pound and maintained its independent economic policies.

The UK and the EU: Politics

Membership of the EU led to an increasing number of political decisions being taken by an unelected supra-national bureaucracy, which undermines democratically accountable authority. A fundamental principle of democracy is to retain power as close to people as possible. By contrast, the E.U., through its basic methods of operation, takes power away from electors. The crucial decision-taking institutions within the EU lack any semblance of democratic accountability. The EU Commission, the European Central Bank and the European Court of Justice are composed of unaccountable bureaucrats, whilst the Councils of Ministers, whose members are elected, conduct their sessions in secret without any public transparency (save for subsequent public relations briefings). Such a closed system, whilst being undemocratic, is also open to fraud. The Court of Auditors failed to approve the EU's accounts for the last nine years; if it were a private company, the Commissioners would be languishing in jail.

The fact that Britain's leaders were determined to participate in the EU integrationist process revealed a disregard for the views of the majority that would become a running-sore in British politics, capable of endangering the whole project. Unelected bureaucrats never voluntarily relinquish acquired power; yet saying No to the EU Constitution and the single currency are the necessary initial steps to reconnecting citizens with their government, by placing job creation and democracy at its heart.

The 1975 Referendum

Memories of 1975 remain vivid. The obvious conclusion to be drawn is that the vote was determined by the 'power resources' (Horpi, 1983) deployed by the Yes and No campaigns. There was an overwhelming imbalance of funding, whereby the pro-EU forces outspent the No-advocates by at least twenty to one. The Yes vote was supported by almost all of the Conservative and Liberal Parties, and by the leaders of the Labour Party. The main No bloc, apart from Enoch Powell and the Reverend Ian Paisley, were the trade unions and the left of the Labour Party, both of which were unpopular at that time for other reasons.

What was also striking about the 1975 referendum was the Yes support and active role taken by establishment organisations; the only exception was the trade unions (Scholefield, 2001). The centre-stage was taken by the CBI and big business generally, which was totally and vociferously pro-EU. Moreover, the 1975 campaign was conducted with every national newspaper urging a Yes vote except for the *Morning Star*.

Not only were the editorials pro-EU, but many of the main anti-arguments, such as the move to economic and political union plus the continuing loss of democratic accountability, were barely discussed. Indeed the pro-EU campaign, as a matter of tactics, focussed entirely upon economic issues. Such a focus proved a short-term strength in 1975, but became a long-term weakness, because no concept of European Citizenship was developed. Therefore an essential pre-condition for ever closer integration was absent, from Britain's accession to the present day. The press had been publishing pro-EU editorials for some fifteen years before the referendum; their implication was that membership would solve the current economic crisis and alleviate the fear of left-wing socialism. Hence the 'demonisation' of Tony Benn during the campaign (Butler and Kitzinger, 1976).

The UK's Response to EU Membership

After the 1975 referendum, Britain's membership of the EU was seen as desirable, or at least inevitable, until, Margaret Thatcher's 1987 speech in Bruges. However, the relationship between the UK and the EU remained ambivalent; Britain's participation was conceived as an integral part of the managing post-imperial decline. After joining, the Foreign and Commonwealth Office (FCO) focussed upon UK–EU relations. Unfortunately, it accepts the world as it is and seeks what temporary advantage it can accrue by keeping the ship afloat, rather than questioning where it should be heading.

The FCO operates within an intellectual environment, where certain truths are held to be self-evident. The EU was assumed to be following an integrationist path, so that Britain's future lay inevitably in making an accommodation with that process. The strength of the UK's attachment to its traditional freedoms and institutions meant that, from time to time, the electorate had to be assured that some high watermarks or line in the sand had been reached. However, once the specific 'crisis' was averted, Britain's participation could be renewed and arguments about the folly of being marginalised could be resurrected.

The events of summer 2005 overturned all the assumptions, upon which EU–UK relations were based. Britain's continued relative prosperity outside the euro, and the clear rejection of the proposed EU Constitution by two of its founder states, France and the Netherlands, overturns the myth of 'inevitability'. There is nothing inevitable about EU integration, anymore than that it was inevitable that a Habsburg would always be on the throne of Austria or that Communists would indefinitely rule the Soviet Union.

All the diplomatic energy expended upon managing an economically flawed, undemocratic project should have been devoted to create an alternative strategy, which the majority of Europe's people could accept. That is the missed opportunity of the past twenty years, which the next generation of UK and EU leaders need to address.

Future Referendums?

Until the last week of May 2005, it appeared probable that Britain would hold two referendums on its future membership with the EU; one concerning ratification of the draft Constitutional Treaty and a later verdict on membership of the single currency. However, the Dutch and French No votes derailed the ratification process, whilst joining the euro appears to have disappeared over the horizon for the foreseeable future given the Treasury's critical assessments (HM Treasury, 1997 and 2003).

However, the question remains; what would be the likely outcome of such referendums? Opinion polls since Britain left the European Exchange Rate Mechanism in September 1992 consistently indicate that the public is around 66% to 33% opposed to further EU integration. That is why New Labour avoided calling any referendums. Moreover, the balance of power resources has significantly altered since the 1975 referendum; the Conservative Party is now firmly anti-EU integration, the Labour Party possesses significant backbench opposition, whilst business and trade union opinion is spilt. More significantly, media opinion is more divided than in 1975 *The Sun*, *The Daily Mail*, *The Times*, and *The Daily Telegraph* would campaign for a No vote for either referendum. These titles cover more than half the newspaper reading public. Therefore, despite propaganda campaigns by the British government and the EU Commission a pro-EU verdict will be much harder to achieve (Burkitt and Mullen, 2003). Moreover, the former conventional wisdom that Britain faces 'no alternative' to its present relationship with the EU is challenged by recent research, which demonstrates conclusively that a variety of relationships is possible, whether or not the U.K. remains an EU member (Baimbridge *et al.*, 2005). These alternative futures need to be explored, and put to the democratic judgement of the British electorate, before it is unthinkingly accepted that the UK has no choice but to remain 'at the heart of the EU'

Conclusion

Since the signing of the Treaty of Rome in 1957, the central objective of the EU has been to achieve ever closer economic, and subsequently, political integration. This is freely acknowledged by a vast majority of politicians, industrialists, trade unionists and financiers, in all participating countries, except Britain and the Scandinavian members.

When the integrationist process was launched, it seemed to conform to the trends of the age. A united Europe was a crucial bulwark against communist aggression in the Cold War; it removed fears of a continuation of the three wars between France and Germany within seventy years; it also removed tariff barriers between member economies, which were seen as a mechanism to boost prosperity through freer trade. However, in the 21st century, the question arises whether EU integration remains a forward-looking agenda, or whether it becomes increasingly anachronistic, when economic and political circumstances have changed so dramatically during the past 40 years. Is it now merely a shibboleth trapped in the conventional wisdom of past generations?

For the UK, given its problematic history of relations with the EU, those questions are particularly acute. Does it accept that its national interest (or more grandly, its destiny) lies in the full economic and ever greater political, union with much of the continent of Europe? Or will the increased focus by our politicians and diplomats on EU matters detract from the pursuit of Britain's wider global interests? The country faces a crucial strategic decision between an essentially European future, or a global strategy. For EU integration to possess a dynamic, its member nations and peoples need to feel a supra-national bond between them, which currently does not exist. The lack of a European identity is one that EU leaders and bureaucrats have previously ignored, preferring to achieve short-term integrationist measures through unaccountable elite decisions, but in the long-term it cannot be left unaddressed.

Among the UK's greatest assets, underpinning its global economic effectiveness, is the English language. More than 1,400 million people live in officially English-speaking countries, whilst one in five of the world's population speaks English. Currently more than a billion are learning it. It is the main language of books, newspapers, air traffic, international business, academic conferences, science, technology, diplomacy and the Internet. Of all electronically stored information, eighty percent is in English.

The widely held view that Britain possesses 'no alternative' but to participate in European integration is at odds with the facts. Rather a range of possible alternative futures exist, inside and outside the EU, which Baimbridge *et al.* (2005) analyse in detail. Any of these would enable the UK to pursue its historic role of global trader and investor, while at the same time retaining its scope for a largely autonomous economic and social policy. And crucially, outside the unaccountable integrationist process, the choice between and among such strategies would be taken through the mechanisms of democratic politics.

An ironic but historically accurate verdict on the 1975 referendum is that the Yes campaign fought successfully in the short-term to put Britain at the heart of the EU, but the long-term effect of the 1975 vote was the reverse; it put the EU at the heart of Britain and its politics. We wait with bated breath the next phase of this ever-running saga.

Teddy Taylor

1975 Referendum

The calling of the Referendum on whether one should remain within the EU in 1975 was a very skillful initiative by the Prime Minister Harold Wilson. His Party had opposed Britain's membership in 1973 along with a small group of Conservatives including myself and so when they came to power in 1974 it helped the Prime Minister out of a political difficulty to say that the final decision would rest with the British people. Because of this it meant that it would be difficult for MPs in the Commons to accuse the Government of hypocrisy and a change of policy by continuing to work within the EU and at the same time it provided an answer for the numbers of anti-Marketeers who felt they had been unreasonably deprived of giving the people a say on the issue of membership.

It was pretty obvious from the beginning of the campaign, however, that the Referendum would result in a positive decision for Mr Wilson. For a start if there had been a Referendum in 1973, which also argued against membership, we would have been able to point to the unknown and dangerous problems which could arise from membership, while in 1975 it was more difficult to make this point when membership had not produced any serious consequences.

The great difficulty for the No campaigners was that industry and commerce were almost solidly in favour of EU membership, but perhaps more important almost all the sound, solid and respected groups within the political parties appeared to be in favour of continued membership and basically it was the left wing of the Labour Party and the extreme right wing of the Conservatives who were arguing the case for leaving the EU. They had to deal with the argument of what damage would be done to Britain if we decided to leave.

I can well remember the meetings we had in Scotland and perhaps more significant the meetings we had in Trafalgar Square and elsewhere in the South where the speakers were Barbara Castle, Tony Benn and Conservatives like myself. We were clearly regarded as people who were opposed to progress and development and, perhaps more significant, people who were arguing an economic case against the majority of trade and industry and apparently responsible politicians.

It was difficult to argue that our democracy would be undermined when the impact of membership had been of limited impact and it was very difficult to argue the case of economic dangers when there was no apparent evidence of real damage having been caused by membership.

We had the feeling from the beginning of this campaign that the battle was a lost one, but one which had to be fought nonetheless. Even on issues like the Common Agricultural Policy (CAP) which was so fundamentally bad for the consumers and bad for the world, one always had to deal with the argument that now that Britain was a member we could sit round a table with our friends and seek to improve things. And whenever we put forward arguments about long-term dangers it was pointed out that so long as Britain was a member and had a veto we could stop these kinds of things happening.

For all these reasons it was obvious that the result was going to be favourable to Europe and it was only some areas in the islands in the north of Scotland which had the majority against staying within the EU.

Of course there have been dramatic developments since then and there is no doubt that the views of the people have changed. Industry and commerce which used to be totally in favour of membership has changed because the benefits of membership are simply fading away and more significant we are being saddled with the problems of excessive bureaucracy. I think, in addition, some of the arguments put forward for membership are beginning to disintegrate. For example when we had the recent debate on whether Britain should join the Single European Currency, the argument was put forward rigorously and clearly that if we didn't join then British banks would all move over to Frankfurt and other parts of Europe. In fact since we decided not to join banks have come over from Europe to the UK with an increase of around 50%. In the same way countries like Norway and Switzerland which voted in referendums not to join, but which were warned that if they didn't disaster would lie ahead for them, have turned out to be the most prosperous areas of Europe with the lowest rates of unemployment and the highest living standards.

Certainly the views of industry, commerce and the people have changed. In so far as the people are concerned what has obviously worried them is that whereas the veto was a protection against European centralisation this faded away when we moved towards majority voting with the Single European Act and other legislation. In addition it has become abundantly clear that changing basic policies like the CAP is simply something which will not happen.

If we had a referendum now on whether Britain should stay in the EU, I think the result would be different and the debate would be realistic, clear and in my view result in a No vote.

I opposed our membership back in 1971 when Mr Heath, our then Prime Minister, decided to proceed with the application and resigned my post in the Government as Scottish Minister for Health and Education so that I could vote against the Treaty of Rome which I did on the 3rd Reading Debate.

Certainly my views have not changed and I think that the events since then have proved that those who were willing to oppose our membership were correct and wise. For a start Europe's management of its finances has been utterly deplorable and I think it is the only organisation in the world whose auditors haven't approved its accounts for a period of ten years because of the amount of corruption and waste which exists within the organisation.

The economic consequences have been negative without a doubt and our balance of trade with the EU has deteriorated sharply. Apart from anything else the cost of membership has been very substantial indeed and when you think of the hourly amount which we pay into Europe which is now over £1.5 million for every hour in every day of the year it gives some indication as to what the cost really is.

There are huge issues like the CAP, VAT and other issues which are significant, but on the lower level of decision-making the decisions made by Europe are just ridiculous and foolish. For example, we were recently told that we had to apply the Pensioners Heating Allowance to British residents in the Overseas Territories of Europe, which means we have to pay it to people living in Guadeloupe, Martinique and the Azores where there is sunshine all the time, but not if they live in the north of Canada or Iceland where it tends to be freezing. We also have the most ridiculous rules and regulations brought in almost every week which we have to adhere to. I had a Question to the Agriculture Minister who confirmed that if retailers of fruit and vegetables sold bananas that were less than 13.97 cm long or carrots which were less that 1.9 cm at the thick end they could be fined £5000 or sent to prison for three months. In fairness the Government stated that prosecution would be considered only when traders failed to respond to repeated warnings, but existence of this legislation is just ridiculous and no democratic Government would support it.

In terms of more specific and economic issues, the structure of Europe is such that Britain has to give a very substantial financial contribution to its organisation. Germany is the largest contributor, but Treasury documents show net payments of around £4–5bn and in recent years the UK has paid about £11bn per annum direct to the EU receiving about £7bn back in what is called aid, a great deal of this money being spent on foolish and wasteful activities. An interesting issue was the report of the Institute of Directors Survey which found that trading in the EU was on balance unattractive and more costly with more paperwork than before the Single Internal Market.

Probably the area which has caused most concern to the community interested in international affairs is the CAP. The basic principle of EU agricultural arrangements are that we pay the farmers prices well above the world prices and we supply substantial subsidies to enable them to export food to other parts of the world. In addition there are arrangements whereby we offer subsidies to farmers to destroy produce like fruit and vegetables where export is not so easy. Estimates of the cost to Britain vary from £5–15bn and this is a very substantial burden for the people.

However, probably what should worry us as much as anything is what we are doing to the Developing Countries and to places where food should be produced more effectively. The most obvious example is sugar where we pay the farmers about three times the world price and give them subsidies of about twice the world price which means that the production of sugar has increased very substantially in Europe and we are basically wrecking the economies of the countries which are more able to produce these items of our diet. Of course there are constant discussions about the possibility of major reforms, but in practice they never happen and invariably end up by spending more public money.

However, probably the issue which influenced me from the beginning more than anything was the undermining of democracy. I had a group of people who called to see me at one of my weekly surgeries asking what steps we can take to prevent the cruelty involved in the export of live cattle. I had to explain of course that our Parliament could take no action at all. They then asked if they could approach their European MPs and I pointed out, I think fairly, that there would be no point in doing this because if the European Parliament closed its doors tomorrow nobody would notice apart from the taxi drivers of Strasbourg.

The principle of our democracy has always been that the people have the power and can change Government and MPs every five years. However, in so far as the policies of the EU are concerned the people simply have no power whatsoever.

The real difficulty of EU membership, of course, is that far from being a factor which increases or reduces according to circumstances, it inevitably brings an ever increasing transfer of power to the centre. There are two major issues coming up shortly which because of public concern are going to result in a referendum. The problem of referendum votes on European issues is that it is always difficult to identify exactly what will happen because of the changes. We know with Treaties for example that they do appear to be quite soft and reasonable in their approach except that when they are eventually implemented by the Commission and interpreted by the European Court it usually results in a substantial transfer of power to Europe. In the same way with EMU, if we joined the basic control of economic policy would be transferred out of the control of our democratic Parliament. We have seen since the Single Currency was established that both Germany and France have suffered from the most appalling rise in unemployment for which they can really do nothing at all apart from seek to evade the European rules. In the Republic of Ireland by comparison the euro has produced artificial prosperity and this of course also creates many problems. The basic argument against the euro is that it is just really quite impossible to bring in a form of economic management and control which can apply equally to all the democratic countries within the EU. Of course there is an obsession for further centralisation in some countries in Europe.

Hence, the question has become why do they wish to move in this way? I think there is no doubt that in some European countries the memories of the appalling events of the Second World War provide an attraction for an organisation which brings countries together, although in fairness there is a rising tide of Euroscepticism within some countries in Europe.

The basic issue of course is where we go from here and what the future should be for Britain's relationships with the EU. The one advantage of the proposed Constitution, of course, is that for the first time there is a specific provision for countries to withdraw from the EU if they wished to. The procedure is quite a complicated one in that member states can negotiate for two years and if the negotiation is not successful they can then seek to withdraw themselves. However, at least it is something which is clear and precise. There has been a bit of a dispute over the years within the UK Parliament between those who argue that our Parliament could withdraw itself and those who argue that it simply is not possible and legal. My own view is that it would certainly strengthen the EU if there was a specific opportunity for countries to withdraw if they wished to.

However, what is going to happen in the future? The most obvious fact is that countries in Europe have certainly not prospered as a result of membership and the serious economic situation in both France and in Germany at the present makes us think what we would do and what Europe could do if there was to be a general collapse. There is no doubt whatsoever that the ever increasing volume of bureaucracy stemming from the EU is undermining the powers of industry and commerce and of Europe's protectionist policies agriculture is the most obvious example by providing temporary protection it creates enormous long term problems.

Of course there has been a new development in Europe with the expansion of membership to countries in Eastern Europe. I think that for some of these with the history of communism and the abolition of democracy the advantage of Europe is that it appears to be a respectable organisation. There is also the possible attraction of grants and financial incentives which of course would have to be paid for by existing member states.

I think the only certain long term outlook for Europe is that the original member states will have to pay a lot more, that Europe's place in the economic world will not advance, but will decline and that basically democracy will become an irrelevant and useless aspect of our way of life.

I would obviously much prefer to look to a situation when Europe will reform itself and improve by introducing elements of democracy, but the possibility of this actually happening seems to be more than unlikely.

I think change may stem from the potential referendums on the European Constitution and the Single European Currency. My feeling is that if there is a substantial majority for No in both cases, which I think there will be, it might well create a situation in Britain where the Eurosceptic view will become an ingredient in the policies of one of the major parties. However, time will tell but certainly after 25 years I am in no doubt whatsoever that when the decision to join was made I took the right decision in opposing it and I only hope that the countries of Europe will be able to find an effective and positive way out of the democratic and costly organisation which is now being created.

Perhaps the biggest problem for all Europeans is the evidence that the Continent is heading for a crisis regarding population. Whereby a shrinking tax base, more demand for healthcare and pensions and the possible social tensions, which will come from the higher number of immigrants required to compensate for the dramatically falling birth rates could have a cumulative effect.

The UN report on world population forecasts that in 50 years time there will be almost 100 million fewer people living in Europe. Even with an average of 600,000 immigrants a year the population would still fall by 96 million by 2050.

The crisis is a real one, not created by the EU, but the question we should all ask is whether the EU has the democratic basis to cope with it.

Eric Deakins

The Struggle to Preserve British Self-Government

The extent to which, if any, the UK should integrate economically and politically with other European countries has been and continues to be the most divisive issue in UK politics since the Second World War. It is an issue that crosses traditional party lines and divides the mainstream political parties; this has not generally been the case in other EU countries. The main reason is that the British peoples have pioneered the development of parliamentary democracy, thereby ensuring a popular and accountable government, a libertarian legal system and wide-ranging civil rights, by routes very different from those of other EU countries. In England, the long struggle between Parliament and Crown over control of the right to tax culminated in a Civil War, followed by the trial and execution of the monarch. This victory for the people, the first serious challenge anywhere to the doctrine of the Divine Right of Kings, was finally consolidated by the peaceful Glorious Revolution and the Bill of Rights. Then came a struggle between King and Parliament over control of expenditure, with Parliament victorious again.

The growth of the English legal system, based in part on a gradually established system of common law, predated and was confirmed by the thirteenth century Magna Carta. Reinforced by the seventeenth century Bill of Rights, English law and civil liberties have evolved over time and are distinct from continental laws based on the Napoleonic code. The right to jury trial and the writ of Habeas Corpus have been won and safeguarded by and on behalf of the people through the ages; they will not easily be given up for a mess of EU harmonised pottage. Like many British Europhiles, those who do not understand this parliamentary and legal history will not be able to appreciate the fundamental reasons for continued strong objections to the sacrifice of hard-won British parliamentary sovereignty and civil liberties in the dubious cause of EU unity.

When the issue of UK entry into the Common Market arose in the 1960s, the Labour Party was generally opposed and the Conservative and Liberal parties were mainly in favour. By the time that Mr Heath had negotiated British entry, the parties were split, their divisions being echoed in the voting lobbies as the Bill implementing the negotiated terms of entry was debated. A block of nearly 70 Europhile Labour MPs was partly offset by a smaller group of anti-Market Conservatives. As a new backbencher with expertise in agriculture, I was asked to help the Labour frontbench team of Michael Foot, Peter Shore and Ronald King Murray. Agriculture was a very contentious issue and votes critical of aspects of the Common Agricultural Policy were lost by only 5 votes.

After UK entry into the Common Market, increasingly called a Community, the issue of UK membership continued to dominate the political agenda. Back in power in March 1974, Harold Wilson and Jim Callaghan as Foreign Secretary renegotiated the terms of British entry in fulfilment of an election pledge. Their intention was to defuse dissent in the Labour Party and settle the issue once and for all by getting popular approval of the renegotiated terms in a referendum. During this period, Peter Shore and I as Ministers at the Department of Trade made speeches that upset Jim, criticising some Common Market trade policies. Harold was wise enough to know that his Party and Government were split, so agreed that Ministers could openly support the referendum Yes or No campaigns. As a very early Labour Eurosceptic (I had spoken at the inaugural public meeting of the Anti-Common Market League in March 1961), I worked closely with Peter Shore for a No vote during the Referendum. About a week into the campaign, Neil Marten, Conservative MP, leading the Tory No campaign, told me his support was collapsing. He alleged that a Labour Minister was going round the country saying the only alternative to staying in the Common Market was to have a Socialist Britain. This rhetoric was taken seriously by anti-Market Conservatives who disliked the Common Market but hated the prospect of a Socialist Britain. The choice for them was simple; thus, the No campaign suffered.

In these circumstances, it is not surprising that the 1975 Referendum was lost by two to one. The newspapers and broadcasting media were almost unanimous in their backing for the Yes campaign. In addition to leaflets sent out by the YES and No campaigns, the Government helped ensure the right result by sending out its own leaflet recommending continued membership. Each household got three leaflets, but two of them put the Yes case. The Government one gave assurances on the protection of national sovereignty, including a claim, subsequently shown to be unjustified, that proposals for economic and monetary union had been stopped. Many voters' doubts were dispelled and they voted accordingly.

A major error by the No campaign was inadequate consideration of an appropriate answer to the question: 'What is the alternative to staying in the Common Market?' Many people were unhappy about aspects of membership, but they were frightened of the UK being left isolated, outside the Market magic circle. They could not be persuaded that this would not be the case, so they 'clung to nurse for fear of getting something worse'. It is always easier to gain support for the status quo than for radical change. A lesson for all campaigners is to prepare adequately for the obvious questions, agree an appropriate response and stick to it. Co-ordination among different groups campaigning for a No vote in any referendum on either EMU or the EU Constitution is thus a crucial matter, since there is even more at stake than in 1975.

Since 1975, the issue of the UK relationship with other West European countries has continued to simmer away, coming to the boil whenever treaties approving further loss of parliamentary powers and greater EU integration came before Parliament. Despite Europhile rhetoric about shared sovereignty, it became clear that successive British governments were failing to appreciate EU development towards greater centralisation of power in Brussels, at the expense of national sovereignty of member states. Events since 1975 have confirmed the worst fears of the early Eurosceptics. The Single European Act of 1986, greatly extending the use of Qualified Majority Voting on EU legislation, was forced through Parliament by Mrs Thatcher's complacent government and a supine Labour frontbench. Her guillotine of debate on the Bill (a move she lived to regret) ensured its passage. I led the Labour backbench opposition in the House of Commons against what proved to be a disastrous first step on the path to economic union. This Act marked the beginning of an unmistakable trend towards a federal or unitary state. Successive EU Treaties (Maastricht, Amsterdam and Nice) all implemented the principle of 'ever closer union'.

The EU now has many of the constitutional components of a single state and increasingly acts like a state. Economic and Monetary

Union (EMU), accepted in principle by the UK, gave the lie to an important Government promise in the 1975 Referendum that had undoubtedly influenced the result. The establishment of the euro as a common currency marked a significant stage in the process of 'ever closer union'. UK opt out from Stage 3 of EMU has merely delayed, not halted, progress towards harmonised fiscal and economic policies within the eurozone. Since the British Government has chosen not to join the eurozone for the foreseeable future, this progress is likely to be resumed in order to try to rescue faltering national economies that no longer possess major monetary weapons (interest rates and devaluation) that could alleviate their problems. Even their fiscal policy weapons, especially taxation, are under threat from tax judgments by the European Court of Justice and from EU Commission ideas for the harmonisation of corporate tax bases. Significantly, these threats apply to all member states, not just those in the eurozone. More impetus towards fiscal integration can be expected as the economic performance of some member states fails to keep pace with that of other competitors. Further moves towards complete economic integration seem inevitable as the much-vaunted EU social model comes under increased pressure to adapt to the alleged needs of a competitive economy.

These developments could all have been foreseen at the time of UK entry into the Common Market in 1973, but most British politicians failed to do so, partly because they thought that Britain would be able to halt the integration process before it went too far, an assumption both naïve and arrogant. They were also unaware of Mr Monnet's views, at the time of the setting up of the European Coal and Steel Community and the Treaty of Rome, concerning the failure of previous attempts at achieving European unity. He saw that compulsory economic unity had to come first, without mentioning the political unity that would surely follow, because there would be popular resistance to the notion of political unity so soon after the experience of German occupation in the Second World War. Because of this gross deception and the economic trade-off between French agriculture and German industry, subsequent elections in the original six founder members of the Common Market showed no widespread opposition to the Treaty of Rome. Further Treaties increasing political and economic integration have been generally accepted by the peoples of the founder members, except in France for the Treaty of Maastricht, where special factors forced a referendum with a close result. However, the recent breakdown of the Stability and Growth

Pact in the Eurozone suggests that, despite their rhetoric, some members are not yet ready to sacrifice part of their national interest for the alleged greater good of the whole.

The proposed EU Constitution marks a watershed in the story of the so-called 'European project', a term that has never been adequately defined. Some parts of the Constitution, such as further extension of qualified majority voting, could be seen as a continuation of the trend in previous Treaties, but its most important centralising features have no precedent. First, there is the Constitution itself. Under previous Treaties, the EU received additional powers over national governments by virtue of Treaty provisions. The Constitution makes it clear that once the Treaty setting it up is approved, the EU and its institutions will derive their powers not from the Treaty and its predecessors, as in the past, but from the Constitution itself. It is worth emphasising what should be obvious: a Constitution is not a Treaty. Establishing a Constitution rather than, as on previous occasions, member states merely endorsing another Treaty, gives the putative EU state what it has so far lacked: a source of authority that is virtually impregnable because it is stated to be superior to all other authority throughout the EU.

Second, the inclusion of a Charter of Rights in the Constitution, one that in many respects duplicates the existing European Convention on Human Rights, extends the jurisdiction of the European Court of Justice into areas of national life where it previously had no remit or place. We in the UK have seen how the European Convention (not an EU project!) is affecting our legal process by giving further protection to individual rights threatened by the actions of any other person or body. This is good, but the embodiment of the EU Charter in a Constitution with clear legal supremacy means it would take precedence in any clash between its provisions and those of the Convention. There is every prospect of disputes between the two European Courts, with unknown, possibly adverse, consequences for individual rights. Why does the EU need a separate document on human rights, if not to emphasise its supranational nature and to give substance to the concept of EU citizenship?

Third, the creation of institutional structures for common Foreign and Security policies stems from the concern of EU political elites that the EU should wield greater power in the world to compensate for their loss of national power on the world stage. The EU is to get a Foreign Minister and a diplomatic service superior to those of individual member states, enforcing an agreed EU foreign policy. The euphemistic use of 'security' to avoid the use of 'defence' cannot mask EU intentions to build up its own military forces and joint weapons procurement. The risks of undermining NATO, which has kept the peace and protected Western Europe since 1949, will not be removed by honeyed assurances from the EU Council. Although subject to unanimity at present, who can doubt in the light of experience that defence and foreign policy will eventually become matters for qualified majority voting. The EU record shows that, in time, pooling of sovereignty in any area eventually becomes a recipe for abandonment of national sovereignty altogether.

Any future UK referendum on the proposed EU Constitution is something that all Eurosceptics can look forward to, not just because the occasion will provide an opportunity for rejection, but because it will be an ideal chance to expose the deceit in the Yes campaign in 1975. Truth is the daughter of time, as the past thirty years have shown. There is grim determination in the Eurosceptic camp. The forthcoming No campaign should have no difficulty in emphasising the EU's sometimes hesitant steps towards political union, always denied by successive governments. At no stage have the peoples of the EU ever approved this surreptitious goal. Political union, like the proposed Constitution, has been the construct of political elites, well aware of their inability by honest democratic methods to get popular consent for the destruction of self-government in many major areas of national life.

The balance of forces in any UK referendum will be much more even than in 1975. The press is no longer united in support of the government line and the broadcasting media less susceptible to Establishment bias. Where the EU is heading is abundantly clear from the provisions of the proposed Constitution. Government soft soap and obfuscation are now not so easily applied to a less gullible and less trusting electorate than in 1975. Then people were asked by the Government to vote for the status quo i.e. for continued membership of a Common Market; in the future, they will be asked by the Government to vote against the status quo and for radical change, psychologically a much more difficult proposition. Just as the proposed Constitution is a watershed in EU development, so the UK Referendum result will mark a watershed in the relations between the British people and their European neighbours.

David Stoddart

Reflections on the 1975 Referendum

In the early 1960s when pressure was building up for Britain to join
the European Economic Community (EEC), or Common Market as it
was popularly known, the driving considerations were that Britain
had become ungovernable and that the economy needed to feel the
'chill wind of competition' if it was to grow and prosper. It was this
gutless attitude of the ruling elite which sent Mr Heath cap in hand
to the EEC begging them to accept Britain as a member. The attempt
failed, as did further attempts by the Labour Government between
1966 and 1970.

In the run up to the 1970 General Election, Edward Heath, who
had by then become leader of the Conservative Party, stated that
Britain should join the EEC only with the full hearted support of
Parliament and people and that he wanted a mandate to negotiate,
no more and no less. He and his Party won that election and without
much delay and with little consultation signed the Accession Treaty
(in which our fishing waters were handed over to the EEC as a community resource). The European Communities Bill to ratify the
Treaty was forced through Parliament without the full hearted consent of the people, an amendment for a referendum having been
refused, and with only the grudging consent of Parliament. Indeed,
that consent would not have been obtained at all but for the defec-
tion of Europhile Labour MPs defying three line whips on critical
amendments and, in fact, at Second Reading when the majority in
favour of the Bill was only eight.

The Bill finally received Royal assent and Britain joined the Community on 1st January 1973. So the British people, unlike the Danes,
the Irish and the Norwegians who all had referendums, were denied
any say in what was a huge change in the British Constitution. This
change accepted the superiority of EEC law over British law and

enforcement by a European Court of Justice which would have superiority over British courts in the matter of EEC decisions. Thus it was that in the General Elections of February and October 1974 the Labour Party was in favour of withdrawal unless fundamental changes could be achieved through re-negotiation. On that basis and the expectation of a referendum, Enoch Powell recommended voters to support the Labour Party in the elections and many thought his intervention was crucial in the defeat of Heath in February and his replacement by a minority Labour Government which in the October election was converted to an overall majority of three.

The subsequent re-negotiation was a farce and nothing of substance in the Treaty was changed. Parliament endorsed the modest concessions and went on to agree to a referendum as to whether Britain should remain in the EEC. The Europhiles, who had previously been opposed to a referendum, now supported it because they realised that the voters were being swung over to their side by the sham re-negotiation which Parliament had endorsed and that the Government would be bound to support and recommend remaining in the EEC. Indeed, it was a bitter blow to the anti-EEC camp when the Government did just that, in spite of the fact that the official policy of the Labour Party was still for withdrawal.

The Cabinet had voted by two to one to recommend a Yes vote, but it was a different story in the case of junior ministers, of whom I was one. At a meeting of the junior ministers called by Harold Wilson (Prime Minister) and James Callaghan (Foreign Secretary) at which I was present it became quite clear that a substantial number of those ministers were opposed to the policy as one by one they stood up to disagree with the Cabinet's decision.

Certainly, by the time Wilson brought the meeting to an abrupt end, he could not have been in any doubt that, outside the Cabinet, his Government was seriously split with a majority of junior ministers opposing his policy to recommend a Yes vote. Dispensation was, however, given to Ministers, MPs and party members to campaign on which side of the argument they chose.

On the No side, we had the odds stacked against us from the start. Added to the Government policy to recommend a Yes vote, we were out-financed not only during the referendum campaign itself but also in the run up period. It is not possible to accurately assess the disparity between the two camps but, taking into account the large financial resources of Britain in Europe at the beginning of the campaign plus the large donations to the Yes side from industry and commerce, the farming industry and private individuals, it is estimated that the Yes campaign out-financed the No campaign by twenty to one. The No side had little money over and above the grant of £125,000 made available to both sides except for a few donations from Trade Unions and some private donations. So they were considerably constrained in their activities by the lack of funds which meant that they could not employ people at national level to run and coordinate a first class campaign and to ensure that an efficient hard hitting press office was available.

The press itself, apart from the Daily Express and the Morning Star, were supporting a Yes vote and press coverage in favour of remaining in the EEC was two to one. Advertisements were about three to one in favour of Yes. In addition to the one-sided coverage in the national press, radio and TV tended to support the status quo. Indeed, the Today Programme actually had breakfast meetings with Britain in Europe to plan radio coverage for that day. The No campaign was also seriously disadvantaged by the decision of the Government to back up their recommendation to stay in, by sending out their own pamphlet recommending people to vote Yes. That meant that voters had two pamphlets urging a Yes vote, but only one urging a vote for No. So we were put at a serious disadvantage by the misuse of power and taxpayers money by HM Government. In my own view the Government recommendation and the distribution of their pamphlet were decisive in swinging the vote to Yes.

But that was not all; added to the powerful support of the Government the Yes campaign had the overwhelming support of British industry. They warned that if Britain did not remain in the EEC it would be a disaster for industry which would result in a massive loss of jobs. The same was true of farming which saw the Common Agricultural Policy as the champion and saviour of the farming industry and a prosperous living for farmers. It is ironic that manufacturing industry as a proportion of GDP in the UK has fallen from 32% in 1972 to 17.5% in 2004 and that it is now beset by large additional costs and onerous regulations emanating from the EU. As for farming, it is a shadow of its former self. In 1972 there were 500,000 farmers. Now there are only 150,000 and their incomes have never been smaller except, that is, for the big farmers who do best out of EU subsidies.

During the referendum campaign itself my activities were mostly confined to my own constituency of Swindon. As I have already said the national No campaign was strapped for cash and could give little financial aid to individual campaigns in the country. On the other hand the Yes campaign, being so much better financed, were able to run a more professional campaign at local level as well as at national level. We, in the No campaign, had to rely on local donations and voluntary help to run the campaign.

The Labour Party organisation and facilities were not available to us because, although the Labour Party was in favour of withdrawal, it had been decided that its machine nationally and locally should be neutral during the referendum campaign.

For myself, I tried to organise my campaign as if it were a General Election; door to door canvassing, street corner loudspeaker meetings, leaflet distribution and indoor public meetings. To the best of my recollection we also organised at least one major motorcade and there would have been others at a more local level.

Our reception by the general public was friendly and seemed quite supportive and that gave rise to the feeling that we could win. Public meetings were well attended and, again, there seemed to be great enthusiasm for the No cause. Indeed, our final meeting at the Swindon Technical College was full with standing room only. Again there was overwhelming support in the audience which gave rise to a feeling of euphoria which, unfortunately, was to prove mistaken.

Many local trade union branches and individual members of the Labour Party were supportive of the No position and did what they could to help but, of course there were others working for the Yes camp. The Yes campaign was supported by the local Tory Party which was overwhelmingly in favour of the Yes side, as were the Liberals. Local business and commerce were heavily in favour of staying in and we did what we could to counter this bias by holding factory gate meetings and meetings of workers inside the factories themselves when this was possible. Some firms wrote to their employees advocating a Yes vote and others used their in house publications to push the Yes cause, although there were others who gave space to both sides.

Metal Box, which had two factories in Swindon at the time of the Referendum, gave me the opportunity to write a near full page article to say 'why we should come out' and this was replied to by Alex Page, the then Chairman of Metal Box, in the following issue, who believed we should stay in. I have to say that the arguments I used in that article are just as relevant today as they were in April 1975 when I wrote it. Metal Box no longer exists.

One of the most depressing incidents during the campaign in Swindon concerned a letter by Sir Donald Stokes (now Lord Stokes),

Chairman of the British Leyland Motor Corporation (BLMC), to all 5000 employees at the car plant in Swindon warning them that if they voted No in the Referendum, the car industry and their jobs would be at risk. That warning from such a distinguished and powerful source certainly had an effect on BLMC employees and their families in Swindon and adjoining areas and its effect spread wider than that firm itself. In the event, of course, there is no longer an indigenously owned car maker left in Britain which, like so much of our manufacturing industry, have felt Harold MacMillan's 'chill wind of competition' and have perished by it. But at least Lord Stokes has had the good grace to say that he now believes his letter was a mistake.

And so polling day arrived and I toured Swindon urging people to come out and Vote No and the turn-out was quite reasonable. At 64% the turnout nationally was higher than at the 2005 General Election and the one preceding it in 2001. The result was a great disappointment the No campaign having been beaten by two to one. But, in retrospect, it is remarkable that in spite of the huge weight of resources on the Yes side, which completely eclipsed those of the No camp and included the huge resources deployed by the Government, 33% of the electorate still voted to come out of the EEC.

One of the consequences of that vote is that it has been used by the Europhiles to claim that the British people voted to join the EEC/EU. But that is a false claim since the people were never given the opportunity to say whether Britain should join, only whether they should remain in, and that is quite a different question.

For myself, and many others, the referendum solved nothing. I had been against Britain joining and my opposition went back as far as 1962 when I was the Labour candidate for the Newbury Constituency. It was clear to me that joining a bloc of countries whose ultimate aim was ever closer union leading to a European superstate, was bound to progressively undermine the UK's status as a fully independent nation free to run our country to suit its own needs, not those of a clutch of other countries with interests inimical to those of the UK.

Successive governments have consistently denied that the EEC was graduating towards statehood, a country called Europe. Yet goaded on by the European empire builders they have agreed to a greater number and more significant powers being transferred to the institutions of Europe. In a House of Lords written answer I elicited the information that the EEC/EC/EU had produced over 100,000 regulations between 1973 and 2003 and the Government now accepts that 55% of all measures now emanate from the EU.

In 1977 I resigned my position as a Lord Commissioner of the Treasury (senior whip) in the Labour Government over the issue of direct election to the European Assembly, converted to the European Parliament in the Single European Act, because I would not respond to a three line whip on the Third Reading of the Bill to bring this policy into law. I realised that a directly elected assembly (parliament) would become more powerful and ambitious than an appointed one and that it would constitute a further threat to the sovereignty of the British Parliament and so it has proved. The Parliament has had greater powers conceded to them and yet they demand more, including an input into foreign affairs and security policy and for the longer term taxation powers. They clearly believe that they have attained ascendancy over national parliaments and the supine attitude of the national parliaments, in the face of the creeping power of the European Parliament, never ceases to amaze me. They either don't know or don't care that the European Parliament is one of the engines of the drive towards a single European state and the relegation of national parliaments to the status of provincial assemblies at best.

But, oddly enough, the most significant boost to European integration was the Single European Act (SEA) agreed by Margaret Thatcher, the then Prime Minister, in 1986. That was the Act that created the single market, boosted the use of qualified majority voting and enabled a significant widening of the Community's powers over a new range of policies including, health, employment, the environment and even education. It also introduced the spectre of economic and monetary union including a single currency and laid the foundations of co-operation in foreign and security policy and justice and home affairs, albeit on an intergovernmental basis rather than a Community one. Thus the skeleton was provided for the next stages of integration which soon arrived in 1992, through the Maastricht Treaty, which would put flesh and muscle onto those bones.

The SEA was forced through the House of Commons in spite of the fight put up by the Labour Opposition and some Tories and, when it arrived in the House of Lords, Lord Bruce of Donington and I were given the task of opposing it from the Labour Front Bench . We and others of their Lordships, including former Lord Chief Justice, Lord Denning warned that this was a highly significant and dangerous measure which was bound to affect Britain's sovereignty and was not simply about the creation of a single European market. But our arguments were not taken seriously and our amendments were simply swept aside, sometimes with Labour Peers either voting against us or abstaining in divisions. We tried to convince the Government that the preamble to the SEA really meant what it said viz:

> The contracting parties are moved by the will to continue the work undertaken on the basis of the European Communities Treaties and moved by the will to transform relations as a whole among their states into a European Union, in accordance with the Solemn Declaration of Stuttgart of 19th June 1983.

But our warning was simply dismissed by the assertion that the preamble was mere verbiage and the words didn't really mean what we said they meant.

And so the SEA reached the Statute Book and was implemented and it wasn't too long before Mrs. Thatcher realised what an appalling mistake she had made in supporting the measure and pushing it through Parliament. In 1988 in her famous speech in Bruges she said 'We have not successfully rolled back the frontiers of the state in Britain in order for them to be re-imposed at a European level'. But it was too late and she was soon to be swept, ignominiously, from office by a coup, undoubtedly organised by the Europhiles in her Government.

A further consequence of the SEA was the decision of Neil Kinnock, the Leader of the Labour Party, to shift the Party's policy on the EC from one of opposition and withdrawal to one of enthusiastic support. I was one of a deputation sent by the Labour Euro Safeguards Committee to persuade him not to go ahead with such a change, but he was unwilling to alter his decision. His view was that it was necessary for the Labour Party to abandon its opposition to the EC if they were to win power at the next election. In the event Kinnock not only lost the election in 1987 but also the subsequent one in 1992.

So the SEA provided the impetus for a great leap forward for European integration and it was not long before the integrationists were once again on the march anxious to consolidate and build on their achievements so far. Hence the Edinburgh Summit which led to the Maastricht Treaty. John Major, the new Prime Minister, had always been considered rather Eurosceptical but he embraced the new Treaty with alacrity and forced it through the House of Commons against fierce opposition from some Conservative MPs, eight of whom (the 'Bastards' as Major described them) subsequently had the Whip withdrawn from them. Whilst it was true that Major had obtained opt outs on joining the single currency, he agreed to extend the influence of the EU over foreign affairs and security policy and justice and home affairs, although these remained on an inter-governmental basis. He also flourished the new 'concession' subsidiarity which, he claimed, would limit the transfer of power to Brussels and enable powers to be returned to Member States. In the event, there has been a constant transfer of power to the EU and not one scrap of power has been returned to Member States.

When the Bill came to the House of Lords the 'Usual Channels' agreed to drive it through the House in three days but a number of Lords formed themselves into an opposition group under the name the 'Maastricht Study Group', of which I was joint chairman with Lord Pearson of Rannoch whose persistence and negotiating skills obtained a further seven days for the Bill's consideration in the House of Lords. The Group virtually took over the role of the official Opposition and whilst no amendments were won the House of Lords was made to have a proper and serious discussion of the Bill and the profound issues at stake. Lady Thatcher was a member of the Group and attended many of its meetings where she made spirited and useful contributions. An amendment calling for a referendum was put down and led by the late Lord Blake but it was defeated by a large majority, the Government having brought in its backwoodsmen as well as their regular supporters. The voting figures were 176 in favour of the amendment and 445 against. Not a bad result for that period and since then there has been an increasing number of peers joining the Eurorealist ranks.

But those who thought that Maastricht would settle European issues for a long time were in for a nasty surprise. No sooner were the provisions of Maastricht being enacted than a new treaty was being worked on and that culminated in the Treaty of Amsterdam which strengthened the EU provisions on foreign affairs and security and set up a new post of High Representative of the Common Foreign and Security Policy (nascent EU Foreign Minister) and the setting up of a policy Planning and Early Warning Unit. By this means progress towards a Common Foreign and Defence Policy would be created. But even this advance could not satisfy the EU's insatiable lust for more power and the Nice Treaty, intended simply to put the finishing touches to accommodate the accession of ten new Member

States, went much further than that by envisaging further constitutional changes which included a Charter of Fundamental Rights.

The Laeken European Council decided that deeper constitutional change was essential, falsely claiming that the absorption of the ten new Member States required it, and a decision was taken to set up the Convention on the Future of Europe to consider a future constitution for Europe. The Convention numbering some 130 representatives from national parliaments, governments, the European Parliament, the Commission and others was set up under the presidency of Valery Giscard d'Estaing, who had always believed in a federal European State. The Convention laboured for two years but by the time it ended there was little change from the proposals set out by d'Estaing and the Presidium at the outset. The final draft was considered by Member States but there was little material change to the Convention draft and the Treaty Establishing a Constitution for Europe was signed in Rome on 29th October 2004.

The Treaty, including declarations and protocols, is 511 pages long, is extremely complicated and difficult for the ordinary reader to follow and understand. It imposes on all the Member States including the UK a written constitution which will be interpreted not by the British Government or British Courts, but by the European Court of Justice. The Constitution extends the powers of the EU institutions and confirms that EU law is superior to national law. The EU will have the major say in what powers they wield and those which will be allowed to be exercised by Member States and will also have a legal personality, enabling it to negotiate international agreements which will be binding on Member States. In addition, the Constitution abolishes the intergovernmental arrangements in respect of foreign and security policy and justice and home affairs which are all subsumed into the competence of the EU. Foreign policy will be led by an EU Foreign Minister and Member States will be expected to loyally support EU foreign policy decisions and promote them in any international bodies of which they are members, eg the UN.

The system of six monthly presidencies is scrapped and, instead, a President of the EU will be elected for a period of up to five years by the European Council. He will speak and act for the EU on the world stage and drive the work of the Union forward. The Charter of Fundamental Rights famously described by Mr Keith Vaz, when he was the British Minister for Europe, as 'having no more relevance than the Beano' has been incorporated into the Constitution and will thus be justiciable by the ECJ. It is astounding and shameful that a British

Government should agree to such a Constitution which is bound to have a fundamental and far reaching effect on our own flexible Constitution, if not undermine it completely, and considerably constrain the powers of the British Parliament and Government. People such as Blair who trumpet their British patriotism are the ones who are most anxious to sell their country down the river.

It is even more astonishing that the British Government, which originally opposed most, if not all, these radical measures contained in the Constitution now describe them as mere tidying up operations. Other Member States certainly take a completely different and opposite view from the British Government. For example, Hans Marten Bury, the German Europe Minister said 'The Constitution is the birth certificate of the United States of Europe' (Die Welt 25 February 2005). Also, Mr Miguel Angel Maratinos, Spanish Foreign Minister, declared 'Accepting the EU Constitution means the surrender of Member States' sovereignty', adding that 'we are witnessing the last remnants of national sovereignty'. Meanwhile Jacques Chirac has been telling the French people that the Constitution is a French Construction and will a build a Europe capable of confronting the USA. From this the obvious question that arises is why are British New Labour Government Ministers so ready to cede such vital powers to the EU Empire?

Tony Blair did, of course, agree to a referendum being held before final ratification, but he only agreed to it for his own ends, not in the interests of democracy. He didn't want the issue to figure in the 2005 General Election and he succeeded in this because the timorous Tories failed to challenge his silence and to make the Constitution a major issue in the election campaign. Blair also believes that, by the blatant and immoral use of taxpayers money and the government machine between now and twenty eight days before the referendum actually takes place and the purveying of misrepresentation and lies, he will be able to win a Yes vote. He can also be sure of support from the TUC and some of the trade unions, a good proportion of the national and local press and, of course, the BBC, if their behaviour at the 1975 Referendum is anything to go by.

Workers will be told that their jobs are at risk and the Tories will be accused of wishing to withdraw from the EU altogether. If only that were so! Blair's counterparts in Europe will ride to his assistance. So will the European Commission and if anyone believes that they will not intervene in Britain's domestic politics, they should recall that at the 2005 General Election they publicly challenged the Conservative leader on his asylum and immigration policy which, they said, could not be implemented under European law.

So, make no mistake, the referendum cards remain stacked in the Government's favour and although the opinion polls at present show a healthy majority for those against the Constitution, that could easily change during a lengthy well financed campaign using Government resources to persuade people to change their minds.

The No Campaign must recognise that the next referendums on EMU and the (revised) Constitution will be no pushover for them and it is essential that all those forces who are opposed to these developments are welded into a hard hitting, co-ordinated force able to take the fight to every part of the UK. The No campaign will be once again wildly out financed by the Government and their allies between now and when the referendums take place and this imbalance should be tackled straight away. The Electoral Commission should be pressurised to intervene, as should MPs who are supposed to represent their electors and not simply serve their political party. After all, MPs are supposed to be the guardians of taxpayers' money and to see that it is spent properly and fairly.

Although the No campaign is likely to be better financed during these referendums than it was in 1975, even so, the resources must be used efficiently, and as far as possible, evenly throughout the country. There will also be more balanced national newspaper coverage, but the local press must not be forgotten in getting the message across. A watchful eye will have to be kept on the TV and radio media to ensure balanced reporting and debate over the air waves. Government Ministers should not be given preferential treatment on air time nor should they be allowed to be treated with kid gloves by TV and radio interviewers. Neither should TV and radio time be hogged by the political parties. These issues transcend party politics and will affect the lives of everybody in the UK.

Uwe Kitzinger

Plus ça Change

Yet the verdict of the referendum must be kept in perspective. It was unequivocal but it was also unenthusiastic. Support for membership was wide but it did not run deep. The referendum was not a vote cast for new departures or bold initiatives. It was a vote for the *status quo*. Those who had denounced referenda as instruments of conservatism may have been right. The public is usually slow to authorise change; the anti-Marketeers would have had a far better chance of winning a referendum on whether to go in than one on whether to stay in. Before entry, to vote for going in would have been to vote radically. But after entry, it was at least as radical and unsettling to vote for leaving. To come out a few years after joining would be yet another disruption in the country's life. So the verdict was not even necessarily a vote of confidence that things would be better in than out; it may have been no more than an expression of fear that things would be worse out than in.

Nor should the psychological impact of the referendum result in Britain be over-estimated. For the rest of 1975 there was little evidence that the British government had become more Community-minded than it was before. Over a whole range of issues, from energy policy and the direct election of the European Parliament to pollution control and lorry drivers' hours, they showed themselves as nationalist as ever and perfectly ready to take over France's old role as the recalcitrant of the Community. The logic of the argument that Britain needed a strong Community was not carried over into any obvious efforts to speed up its strengthening.

As far as the ongoing processes of British party politics were concerned, the effects of the referendum seemed by the end of 1975 to be much smaller than most observers had expected. Certainly in the months that followed there was no movement towards the coalition that some thought they had discerned taking shape under the BIE umbrella. There is no doubt that the inter-party co-operation both at the national and the local level left a legacy of understanding and trust between individuals. For occasional crusades on local or non-partisan issues the associations built up in 1975 would certainly be invoked, and in some future crises the cross-party links forged at the top might prove important. But otherwise the unexpected and enjoyable camaraderie of the campaign seemed unlikely to leave a major mark on the British political scene.

The Conservative party emerged virtually unaffected by the referendum. None of the anti-Market MPs encountered serious trouble with their constituency associations. The frontbench pecking order seemed uninfluenced by campaign performance. There was no echo of the criticisms of Margaret Thatcher's inactivity in May when she faced her first Party Conference as Leader at Blackpool four months later. Only the Conservative party machine was left with a somewhat ambiguous lesson. On the one hand it could feel mildly reassured as to its efficiency; BIE had had to turn to it for an enormous amount of help, for it was the only available organisation with an effective nationwide field force, able to arrange meetings and conduct other basic administration. Yet the evenness of the results in spite of the unevenness of the efforts could not but cast doubt on the ultimate effectiveness of much of their traditional electioneering activities.

For the Labour Party the referendum was of course of far greater importance. The party comprises so wide a range of views that the possibility of a split must always be there, but somehow for forty-five years there had been no major breakaway whether to the right or to the left. But by 1975 the European issue had divided Labour politicians for thirteen years, and though it never entirely coincided with the basic division between right and left in the party, it had for much of the time helped to crystallise and exacerbate the normal conflicts of ideology and struggles for power. In the 1970s, as the NEC and the Party Conference became more clearly dominated by forces opposed to the parliamentary leadership, schism was seen as a growing hazard and Europe as the issue that could most easily precipitate a split. Too many Labour politicians had taken up irreconcilable positions from which they could not simply withdraw in the interests of party unity. The referendum thus removed a serious threat to the party's future. Once the decision on the issue was, by common agreement in the party, transferred to the electorate at large, agreements to differ within the party could ease the tension.

Moreover, the fact that the verdict was Yes, and by a majority that must have included more than half of the Labour party's own voters, meant that in intra-party terms the moderates, a minority among the activists, were seen to represent the majority of the party's supporters in the country. The result was thus a major boost to the morale of the centre and the right of the Labour Movement in the face of the left's perennial claim to be the true and ideologically pure voice of the working people of the country. For the past three years the European issue had been used as a test of faith at selection conferences and a number of potential MPs (and ex-MPs) had been denied selection because of their pro-Market stand. There was thus lost ground to be made up in the composition of the parliamentary party as well as other party bodies, notably of course the National Executive.

For the Liberals the referendum provided a brief period of cross-party prominence. But the alliances of the campaign did nothing to help the party out of a bad period. Their dilemmas of leadership, finance and active membership were, if anything, worse at the end of 1975 than at the beginning. As far as the other parties were concerned, the referendum results were of course a defeat for the SNP, Plaid Cymru and the Ulster Unionists. But the referendum did not significantly change the position of these parties in their own segments of the UK. Despite their public stand none of them was really deeply committed on the issue and each was well known to have pro-Marketeers among its leading figures. In Scotland there were speedy warnings against interpreting the result as a repudiation of the SNP and opinion polls and local elections soon confirmed that the SNP had not declined.

In Ulster divisions over Europe may have contributed to the split with the main body of the Ulster Unionists in September 1975. But perhaps the chief casualty of the referendum was Enoch Powell, who had so linked his career both to Ulster and to the referendum. Already in an isolated position among his new Unionist colleagues his interventions in the 1974 general elections may well have been decisive in bringing Labour to power in February and even in giving it its narrow majority in October.

The referendum gave attractive demonstrations of spontaneous voluntary endeavour, yet the lesson drawn by many was the need for professionalism and the dominance of central, national persuasion through the media. In BIE hard-headed top politicians moved in and largely took over from the European Movement; for good or ill, publicity was placed in the hands of highly experienced technicians; in the field increasing reliance had to be put on the nationwide Conservative machine. The anti-Marketeers suffered not only from lack of money, but also from lack of the professionalism that money can buy: the real impact of their campaign came essentially from their leading politicians as they deployed the skills acquired over the years in making their case on the platform and on radio and television.

To say this is not to endorse all the professional activities. Indeed if the polls were right in detecting an anti-Market movement in the last days of the campaign, it would suggest that the expensive and expert planning of BIE reaped less reward than the more ramshackle and restricted efforts of NRC. But the point can never be proved. Without the BIE efforts the last minute slippage in Yes support might have been much greater. The effectiveness of the £400,000 spent by BIE on advertising, and still more of the £105,000 spent on the four Guggenheim television programmes, will long be argued over by those who have to plan campaigns. But they will no doubt use the relatively high referendum turnout as an argument for spending money on central publicity activities rather than on traditional local campaigning.

Looking back, there were a number of fears and expectations which, in the event, were not fulfilled. Firstly, many had feared public apathy. Yet the evidence of the opinion polls, the audiences for meetings and broadcasts, the voluntary work and the final turnout, almost everywhere tell a different story. Nor did the behaviour of the electorate reflect any general alienation.

Secondly, many had expected the campaign to get dirtier as it went along. Yet, though Tony Benn might justly complain of the vilification which he suffered, there was no general blackening of characters. The argument over 500,000 jobs was conducted mildly by the standards familiar in some other genuinely democratic countries. The guilt by association propaganda which some pro-Marketeers were at least contemplating was never used

Thirdly, no significant sub-groups emerged with an economic interest which made them dissent almost unanimously, beyond the fishermen of Shetland who provided the one clear-cut but minute exception. The solidarity of the business community and the farmers' organisations was notable and the uniform results across the nation showed how little sectional appeals would probably have achieved had either side really sought to use them.

The fourth perspective on the referendum, concerns its importance as a constitutional innovation. In terms of political logistics it demonstrated the feasibility of a referendum. Nothing went wrong with the administrative machinery. The *ad hoc* campaign arrangements succeeded in offering people over most of the country a chance to hear the arguments from a public platform, while on radio and television there was a balanced presentation of the rival cases.[1]

The referendum also showed itself to be a less revolutionary constitutional innovation than many had feared. For one moment on one issue Parliament in a partial way abjured its sovereignty. The referendum was only advisory, in that Parliament would have had to give effect to a No vote, but the government had promised to abide by the popular decision. There was, however, no evidence during or after the referendum that MPs felt their status diminished by referring this one issue to the people.

The referendum had for the first time seen the official acceptance of a public cabinet split within a one-party government. But ministers showed restraint in taking advantage of the permission to differ on this one issue.

Finally, just how the public saw the European issue is not fully clear. It is certain that few electors regarded themselves as recording a judgement on the success or otherwise of renegotiation. If quite different figures had emerged on the budget contribution or on New Zealand butter, with everything else held constant, hardly a vote would have been cast differently. The issue was not how much the terms had been altered, but whether Britain should stay in or get out.

The way in which the issue of membership was resolved may have had a fair amount to do with the advocates on both sides, but that was inevitable in this referendum, and would no doubt be inevitable in any future referendum on as complex an issue such as EMU or an EU Constitution in which a good deal of the facts and the figures, the logic and the probabilities had to be taken on trust. Yet there was also a further element underlying the vote. There were echoes in the referendum of the same theme that had been at the root of the February 1974 election: 'Who governs?'. And to that extent the referendum

---

[1] Various basic problems of referenda were left undecided. The broadcasting authorities worked broadly on a principle of equal time for the two sides. But the principle of equality is not self-evident if there were a referendum on an issue where all parties were agreed but on which the endorsement of the people was thought necessary would political justice require that the 10% who were on one side should have equality on the air or in the press or on the platform with the 90% who were on the other? And should the political parties abjure their role as the prime organisers of mass opinion when a referendum is called on an issue that cuts across normal party lines?

could not be divorced from the right-left dimension of the normal political battle.

And to that extent, though in many ways the referendum might be said to have set a successful precedent, it was a precedent that exhibited distinct limitations on the extent to which a single issue can be isolated for popular decision independently of the party political context.

In the country at large, the referendum did seem popular. In the final week an ORC poll found that 58% of people thought it right to hold a referendum and only 35% thought it wrong. Almost every other poll on the subject found a similar or greater majority for putting the EEC issue to a popular vote.

On the other hand at the centre there was no enthusiasm for repeating the experience. Immediately after the referendum, the myths of parliamentary sovereignty resumed their sway. What would have happened if the people had taken a decision contrary to the government's and Parliament's recommendation remained an untested dilemma? All had been well this time, but that was no reason to take the same risks again. Few politicians wanted the balance upset permanently to the detriment of their own role. They may publicly pay their respects to the common sense and good judgement of their electors, but they have dismal memories of the demagogic exploitation of plebiscites in other countries, and they know full well the complexities of modern government, the interrelationships between issues, and the need for clearly defined responsibility in the political management of economic and social change. The 1975 referendum may have removed one barrier to future referenda, the argument that 'we've never had one here'; but it engendered no enthusiasm for the innovation, certainly not among Britain's political leaders.

Britain's New Deal in Europe

Her Majesty's Government have decided to recommend to the British people to vote for staying in the Community (Harold Wilson, Prime Minister)

Dear Voter

This pamphlet is being sent by the Government to every household in Britain. We hope that it will help you to decide how to cast your vote in the coming Referendum on the European Community (Common Market).

Please read it. Please discuss it with your family and your friends.

We have tried here to answer some of the important questions you may be asking, with natural anxiety, about the historic choice that now faces all of us.

We explain why the Government, after long, hard negotiations, are recommending to the British people that we should remain a member of the European Community.

We do not pretend, and never have pretended, that we got everything we wanted in these negotiations. But we did get big and significant improvements on the previous terms.

We confidently believe that these better terms can give Britain a New Deal in Europe. A Deal that will help us, help the Commonwealth, and help our partners in Europe.

That is why we are asking you to vote in favour of remaining in the Community.

I ask you again to read and discuss this pamphlet.

Above all, I ask you to use your vote.

For it is *your* vote that will now decide. The Government will accept *your* verdict.

Harold Wilson

Your Right To Choose

The coming Referendum fulfils a pledge made to the British electorate in the general election of February 1974.

The Labour Party manifesto in the election made it clear that Labour rejected the terms under which Britain's entry into the Common Market had been negotiated, and promised that, if returned to power, they would set out to get better terms.

The British people were promised the right to decide through the ballot box whether or not we should stay in the Common Market on new terms.

And that the Government would abide by the result.

That is why the Referendum is to be held. Everyone who has a vote for a Parliamentary — that is, everyone on the Parliamentary election register which came into force in February 1975 — will be entitled to vote.

Polling will be in the normal way, at your local polling station, from 7 a.m. to 10 p.m. (Your poll card will remind you of the date and give other details.) You will get a ballot paper, and be asked to mark the ballot paper in one of two clearly marked places, in order to record a Yes or No vote about Britain's continued membership of the European Community (Common Market).

The Government have recommended that Britain should stay in on the new terms which have been agreed with the other members of the Common Market.

But you have the right to choose.

Our Partners In Europe

With Britain, there are nine other members of the Common Market. The others are Belgium, Denmark, France, Germany, Ireland, Italy, Luxembourg, the Netherlands.

Their combined population is over 250 million.

The Market is one of the biggest concentrations of industrial and trading power in the world.

It has vast resources of skill, experience and inventiveness.

The aims of the Common Market are:

- To bring together the peoples of Europe.

- To raise living standards and improve working conditions.

- To promote growth and boost world trade.

- To help the poorest regions of Europe and the rest of the world.

• To help maintain peace and freedom.

The European Community and its world-wide links
[Illustration: map marking 'Countries which have special trading links', with an alphabetical list]

The New Deal

The better terms which Britain will enjoy if we stay in the Common Market were secured only after long and tough negotiations.

These started in April 1974 and did not end until March of this year.

On March 10 and 11 the Heads of Government met in Dublin and clinched the bargain. On March 18 the Prime Minister was able to make this announcement: 'I believe that our renegotiation objectives have been substantially though not completely achieved.'

What were the main objectives to which Mr Wilson referred? The most important were FOOD and MONEY and JOBS.

Food

Britain had to ensure that shoppers could get secure supplies of food at fair prices.

As a result of these negotiations the Common Agricultural policy (known as CAP) now works more flexibly to the benefit of both housewives and farmers in Britain. The special arrangements made for sugar and beef are a good example.

At the same time many food prices in the rest of the world have shot up, and our food prices are now no higher because Britain is in the Market than if we were outside.

The Government also won a better deal on food imports from countries outside the Common Market, particularly for Commonwealth sugar and for New Zealand dairy products. These will continue to be on sale in our shops.

This is not the end of improvements in the Market's food policy. There will be further reviews. Britain, as a member, will be able to seek further changes to our advantage. And we shall be more sure of our supplies when food is scarce in the world.

Money and Jobs

Under the previous terms, Britain's contribution to the Common Market budget imposed too heavy a burden on us. The new terms ensure that Britain will pay a fairer share. We now stand, under the Dublin agreement, to get back from Market funds up to £125 million a year.

There was a threat to employment in Britain from the movement in the Common Market towards an Economic & Monetary Union. This could have forced us to accept fixed exchange rates for the pound, restricting industrial growth and putting jobs at risk. This threat has been removed.

Britain will not have to put VAT on necessities like food.

We have also maintained our freedom to pursue our own policies on taxation and on industry, and to develop Scotland and Wales and the Regions where unemployment is high.

Helping the Commonwealth

It has been said that the Commonwealth countries would like to see us come out. This is not so. The reverse is true.

Commonwealth Governments want Britain to stay in the Community.

The new Market terms include a better deal for our Commonwealth partners as well as for Britain. Twenty-two members of the Commonwealth are among the 46 countries who signed a new trade and aid agreement with the Market earlier this year.

Britain is insisting that Market aid for the poorer areas of the world must go to those in most need.

Here is what Commonwealth leaders have said about Britain's role in the Market:

Mr Gough Whitlam

Prime Minister of Australia, speaking in Brussels on December 18, 1974:I do not want to give any impression that the present Australian Government sees any advantages for Australia, for Europe or for the world in Britain leaving the Community.

Mr Wallace Rowling

Prime Minister of New Zealand, said in Paris on February 22, 1975, that it would not be in the long-term interest of the New Zealand economy if Britain were to withdraw from the Common Market.

Mr Donald Owen Mills

Jamaican Ambassador to the UN, New York, February 28, 1975, talking about the Lomé Convention for trade and aid between the Common Market, including Britain, and 46 developing countries: The Convention is a major move towards the establishment of a new international economic order and demonstrates the considerable scope which exists for the creation of a more just and equitable world.

Will Parliament Lose its Power?

Another anxiety expressed about Britain's membership of the Common Market is that Parliament could lose its supremacy, and we would have to obey laws passed by unelected 'faceless bureaucrats' sitting in their headquarters in Brussels.

What are the facts?

Fact No. 1 is that in the modern world even the Super Powers like America and Russia do not have complete freedom of action. Medium-sized nations like Britain are more and more subject to economic and political forces we cannot control on our own.

A striking recent example of the impact of such forces is the way the Arab oil-producing nations brought about an energy and financial crisis not only in Britain but throughout a great part of the world.

Since we cannot go it alone in the modern world, Britain has for years been a member of international groupings like the United Nations, NATO and the International Monetary Fund.

Membership of such groupings imposes both rights and duties, but has not deprived us of our national identity, or changed our way of life.

Membership of the Common Market also imposes new rights and duties on Britain, but does not deprive us of our national identity. To say that membership could force Britain to eat Euro-bread or drink Euro-beer is nonsense.

Fact No. 2. No important new policy can be decided in Brussels or anywhere else without the consent of a British Minister answerable to a British Government and British Parliament.

The top decision-making body in the Market is the Council of Ministers, which is composed of senior Ministers representing each of the nine member governments.

It is the Council of Ministers, and not the market's officials, who take the important decisions.

These decisions can be taken only if all the members of the Council agree. The Minister representing Britain can veto any proposal for a new law or a new tax if he considers it to be against British interests. Ministers from the other Governments have the same right to veto.

All the nine member countries also agree that any changes or additions to the Market Treaties must be acceptable to their own Governments and Parliaments.

Remember: All the other countries in the Market today enjoy, like us, democratically elected Governments answerable to their own Parliaments and their own voters. They do not want to weaken their Parliaments any more than we would.

Fact No. 3. The British Parliament in Westminster retains the final right to repeal the Act which took us into the Market on January 1, 1973. Thus our continued membership will depend on the continuing assent of Parliament.

The White Paper on the new Market terms recently presented to Parliament by the Prime Minister declares that through membership of the Market we are better able to advance and protect our national interests. This is the essence of sovereignty.

Fact No. 4. On April 9, 1975, the House of Commons voted by 396 to 170 in favour of staying in on the new terms.

If We Say 'No'

What would be the effect on Britain if we gave up membership of the Common Market? In the Government's view, the effect could only be damaging.

Inevitably, there would be a period of uncertainty.

Businessmen who had made plans for investment and development on the basis of membership would have to start afresh.

Foreign firms might hesitate to continue investment in Britain. Foreign loans to help finance our trade deficit might be harder to get.

We would have to try to negotiate some special free trade arrangement, a new Treaty. We would be bound by that Treaty. Its conditions might be harsh. But unless and until it was in force, Britain's exports to the Common Market would be seriously handicapped.

We would no longer be inside the Common Market tariff wall—but outside.

For a time at least, there would be a risk of making unemployment and inflation worse.

Other countries have made these special arrangements with the Community. They might find Community decisions irksome, even an interference with their affairs.

But they have no part in making those decisions.

The Common Market will not go away if we say 'No'.

The countries of the Common Market would still be our nearest neighbours and our largest customers. Their policies would still be important to us. But Britain would no longer have a close and direct influence on those policies.

More than that, decisions taken in Brussels — in which Britain would have no voice — would affect British trade and therefore British jobs.

Britain would no longer have any say in the future economic and political development of the Common Market. Nor on its relations with the rest of the world — particularly on the help to be given to the poorer nations of the world.

We would just be outsiders looking in.

If We Say 'Yes'

Let us be clear about one thing: In or out of the Common Market, it will be tough going for Britain over the next few years.

In or out, we would still have been hit by the oil crisis, by rocketing world prices for food and raw materials.

But we will be in a much stronger position to face the future if we stay inside the Market than if we try to go it alone.

Inside, on the improved terms, we remain part of the world's most powerful trading bloc. We can help to fix the terms of world trade.

Inside, we can count on more secure supplies of food if world harvests turn out to be bad. And we can help to hold down Market food prices — as we have done since we joined in 1973.

Inside the Market we can work to get more European Community money spent inside Britain:

- More from the Social Fund for retraining workers in new jobs. Since we joined we have benefited from this Fund to the tune of over £20 million a year.

- More from the Community's new Regional Fund, which already stands to bring us £60 million in the next three years.

- More from the Farm Fund when world prices are high. For instance, up to now we have obtained £40 million from this Fund to bring down the price of sugar in the shops.

- More from the Coal & Steel funds and the European Investment Bank. Since we joined, arrangements have already been made for loans and grants of over £250 million.

The long period of negotiation between Britain and the other Market countries has proved that the Market is not a rigid organisation.

It is flexible. It is ready and able to adapt to changing world conditions.

It can, and does, respond to the differing needs of member states.

The Market is aware of the need to help the poorer nations of the world outside Europe.

Whether we are in the Market or not, Common Market policies are going to affect the lives of every family in the country.

Inside the Market, we can play a major part in deciding these policies.

Outside, we are on our own.

And Now — The Time For <u>You</u> To Decide

When the Government came to power in February 1974 they promised that you, the British voter, should have the right to decide — FOR continued membership of the European Community (Common Market) or AGAINST.

It is possibly the most important choice that the British people have ever been asked to make.

Your vote will not only affect your life and your neighbours' lives. It will affect your children's lives. It will chart — for better or for worse — Britain's future.

We are only at the start of our relationship with the Community. If we stay inside we can play a full part in helping it to develop the way we want it to develop. Already Britain's influence has produced changes for the better. That process can go on. The Common Market can be made better still.

The Government have made THEIR choice. They believe that the new terms of membership are good enough for us to carry on INSIDE the Community. Their advice is to vote for staying in.

Now the time has come for *you* to decide. The Government will accept your decision — whichever way it goes.

The choice is up to YOU. It is YOUR decision.

Your Vote Counts — Use It

This booklet is being distributed to all households by the Post Office. Extra copies will be available in main Post Offices during the days immediately before the Referendum.

Issued by HM Government

Why You Should Vote Yes

Why We Should Stay in the European Community

On Wednesday, 9th April 1975, the House of Commons approved, by 396 votes to 170, the Government's recommendation that we should stay in the European Community. For years we argued: should Britain join or not? At last we did. The question now is whether, after years of striving to get in, under both Conservative and Labour Governments, we should go through the agony of pulling out. This tearing apart would be a major upheaval. The main brunt of it would fall on Britain, but it would also damage the whole of the West, at a dangerous time in a dangerous world. So the arguments against coming out are even stronger than were those for going in; that's why many people say 'Yes' now who were doubtful in 1971. And hardly anyone has moved the other way. Our case is not just a negative one — stay where we are for fear of something worse. It is based on the real advantages for Britain and Britain's friends of our staying in.

It makes good sense for our jobs and prosperity. It makes good sense for world peace. It makes good sense for the Commonwealth. It makes good sense for our children's future.

Being in does not *in itself* solve our problems. No one pretends it could. It doesn't guarantee us a prosperous future. Only our own efforts will do that. *But it offers the best framework for success, the best protection for our standard of living, the best foundation for greater prosperity.* All the original six members have found that. They have done well — much better than we have — over the past 15 years.

'I believe that both the security and the prosperity of the country depend upon a Yes vote. Not to have gone into Europe would have been a misfortune. But to come out would be on an altogether greater scale of self-inflicted injury. It would be a catastrophe. It would leave us weak and unregarded, both economically and politically.' Roy Jenkins, 26th March 1975

Our friends want us to stay in

If we left we would not go back to the world as it was when we joined, still less to the old world of Britain's imperial heyday. The world has been changing fast. And the changes have made things more difficult and more dangerous for this country. It is a time when we need friends. What do our friends think? *The old Commonwealth wants us to stay in.* Australia does, Canada does. New Zealand does. *The new Commonwealth wants us to stay in.* Not a single one of their 34 governments wants us to leave. *The United States wants us to stay in.* They want a close Atlantic relationship (upon which our whole security depends) with a Europe of which we are part; but not with us alone. *The other members of the European Community want us to stay in.* That is why they have been flexible in the recent re-negotiations and so made possible the improved terms which have converted many former doubters. Outside, we should be alone in a harsh, cold world, with none of our friends offering to revive old partnerships.

'I do not want to give any impression that the present Australian Government sees any advantage for Australia, for Europe or for the world in Britain leaving the Community — we regard European economic and political integration as one of the great historic forward movements of this century.' Gough Whitlam, Prime Minister of Australia, 18th December 1974

> Our government recognizes the emerging fact (of Europe) and we applaud. We applauded last week in Brussels just as we applauded two years ago on the occasion of the entry into the Community of Britain, Ireland and Denmark (Pierre Trudeau, Prime Minister of Canada, 13th November 1974).

Question 'Would you agree that if Britain does decide to withdraw from the Common Market it would be very much in the long-term interests of New Zealand?' *Answer* 'No.' *Question* 'Why do you say that?' *Answer* '1 think that New Zealand's interest must in the long-term be in the strongest possible Europe and the strongest possible U.K.' Wallace Rowling, Prime Minister of New Zealand, answering questions on 22nd February 1975

Why can't we go it alone?

To some this sounds attractive. Mind our own business. Make our own decisions. Pull up the drawbridge. In the modem world it just is not practicable. It wasn't so even 40 or 60 years ago. The world's troubles, the world's wars inevitably dragged us in. Much better to work together to prevent them happening. Today we are even more dependent on what happens outside. Our trade, our jobs, our food, our defence cannot be wholly within our own control. That is why so much of the argument about *sovereignty* is a false one. It's not a matter of dry legal theory. The real test is how we can protect our own interests and exercise British influence in the world. The best way is to work with our friends and neighbours. If we came out, the Community would go on taking decisions which affect us vitally — but we should have no say in them. *We would be clinging to the shadow of British sovereignty while its substance flies out of the window.* The European Community does not pretend that each member nation is not different. It strikes a balance between the wish to express our own national personalities and the need for common action. *All decisions of any importance must be agreed by every member.*

Our traditions are safe

We can work together and still stay British. The Community does not mean dull uniformity. It hasn't made the French eat German food or the Dutch drink Italian beer. Nor will it damage our British traditions and way of life. The position of the Queen is not affected. She will remain Sovereign of the United Kingdom and Head of the Commonwealth. Four of the other Community countries have monarchies of their own.

English Common Law is not affected.

For a few commercial and industrial purposes there is need for Community Law. But our criminal law, trial by jury, presumption of innocence remain unaltered. So do our civil rights. Scotland, after 250 years of much closer union with England, still keeps its own legal system.

> I am proud to have been a member of the Cabinet that took Britain into Europe. At that time there were those who did not want us to join. I believe that many of them today have changed and now consider that once we are in, it would be catastrophic to withdraw (William Whitelaw, 26th March 1975).

Staying in protects our jobs

Jobs depend upon our industries investing more and being able to sell in the world. If we came out, our industry would be based on the smallest home market of any major exporting country in the world, instead of on the Community market of 250 million people. It is very doubtful if we could then negotiate a free trade agreement with the Community. Even if we could it would have damaging limitations and we would have to accept many Community rules without having the say we now have in their making. So we could lose free access not only to the Community market itself but to the 60 or more other countries with which the Community has trade agreements. *The immediate effect on trade, on industrial confidence, on investment prospects, and hence on jobs, could well be disastrous.*

> If we were to come out of Europe this summer I can see no other result except even fiercer inflation and even higher unemployment (Jo Grimond, 26th March 1975).

Scotland, Wales, Northern Ireland and the less prosperous English regions will benefit if we stay in. We shall pursue our own national development area policies and continue to receive aid from the Community's Regional Fund.

Secure food at fair prices

Before we joined the Community everyone feared that membership would mean paying more for our food than if we were outside. This fear has proved wrong. *If anything, the Community has saved us money on food in the past two years.* Why? Not just by accident, but because stronger world demand has meant that the days when there were big surpluses of cheap food to be bought around the world have gone, and almost certainly gone for good. Sometimes Community prices may be a little above world prices, sometimes a little below. *But Britain, as a country which cannot feed itself, will be safer in the Community which is almost self-sufficient in food.* Otherwise we may find ourselves standing at the end of a world food queue. It also makes sense to grow more of our food. That we can do in the Community, and it's one reason why most British farmers want to stay in.

> If we left the European Community tomorrow, we could not expect any reduction in the overall cost of our food as a result (Shirley Williams, 27th March 1975).

Britain's choice: the alternatives

The Community is not perfect. Far from it. It makes mistakes and needs improvement. But that's no reason for contracting out. *What are the alternatives? Those who want us to come out are deeply divided.* Some want an isolationist Britain with a 'siege economy' — controls and rationing. Some want a Communist Britain — part of the Soviet bloc. Some want us even closer to the United States than to Europe — but America itself doesn't want that. Some want us to fall back on the Commonwealth — but the Commonwealth itself doesn't want that. Some want us to be half linked to Europe, as part of a free trade area — but the European Community itself doesn't want that. So when people say we should leave, ask them what *positive* way ahead they propose for Britain. You will get some very confusing answers. There are also differences amongst those of us who say 'stay in'. Some of us are Labour, some are Conservative, some are Liberal, some are non-party. But we all agree on the fundamental question before us. The safety and prosperity of this country demand that we stay in the European Community. So do our duty to the world and our hope for the new greatness of Britain. We believe in Britain — in Britain in Europe. For your own and your children's future it makes good sense to stay in.

> Are we going to stay on the centre of the stage where we belong, or are we going to shuffle off into the dusty wings of history? (Edward Heath, 5th April 1975).

Why You Should Vote No

Re-negotiation

The present Government, though it tried, has on its own admission failed to achieve the 'fundamental re-negotiation' it promised at the last two General Elections. All it has gained are a few concessions for Britain, some of them only temporary. The real choice before the British peoples has been scarcely altered by re-negotiation.

What did the pro-Marketeers say?

Before we joined the Common Market the Government forecast that we should enjoy: a rapid rise in our living standards; A trade surplus with the Common Market; Better productivity; Higher investment; More employment; Faster industrial growth.

In every case the opposite is now happening, according to the Government's figures. Can we rely upon the pro-Marketeers' prophecies this time? The anti-Marketeers' forecasts have turned out to be all too correct. When you are considering the pro-Marketeers' arguments, you should remember this. Remember also that before the referendum in Norway, the pro-Marketeers predicted, if Norway came out, just the same imaginary evils as our own pro-Marketeers are predicting now. The Norwegian people voted NO. And none of these evil results occurred.

Our legal right to come out

It was agreed during the debates which took us into the Common Market that the British Parliament had the absolute right to repeal the European Communities Act and take us out. There is nothing in the Treaty of Rome which says a country cannot come out.

The Right to Rule Ourselves

The fundamental question is whether or not we remain free to rule ourselves in our own way. For the British people, membership of the Common Market has already been a bad bargain. What is worse, it sets out by stages to merge Britain with France, Germany, Italy and other countries into a single nation. This will take away from us the right to rule ourselves which we have enjoyed for centuries. The Common Market increasingly does this by making our laws and by deciding our policies on food, prices, trade and employment—all matters which affect the lives of us all. Already, under the Treaty of Rome, policies are being decided, rules made, laws enacted and taxes raised, not by our own Parliament elected by the British people, but by the Common Market—often by the unelected Commissioners in Brussels. As this system tightens—and it will—our right, by our votes, to change policies and laws in Britain will steadily dwindle. Unlike British laws, those of the Common Market—which will take precedence over our own laws—can only be changed if all the other members of the Common Market agree. This is wholly contrary to the wishes of ordinary people who everywhere want more, not less, control over their own lives. Those who want Britain in the Common Market are defeatists; they see no independent future for our country. Your vote will affect the future of your country for generations to come. We say: Let's rule ourselves, while trading and remaining friendly with other nations. We say; No rule from Brussels. We say: Vote No.

Your food, your jobs, our trade: We cannot afford to remain in the Common Market because:

It must mean still higher food prices. Before we joined, we could buy our food at the lowest cost from the most efficient producers in the world. Since we joined, we are no longer allowed to buy all our food where it suits us best. Inside the Common Market, taxes are imposed on food imported from outside countries. For instance, we now have to pay a tax of over £300 a ton on butter imported from outside the Market and over £350 a ton on cheese. Our food is still cheaper than in the rest of the Common Market. But if we stay in, we will be forced by Common Market rules to bring our food prices up to Common Market levels. All of us, young and old alike, will have to pay. For example, the price of butter has to be almost doubled by 1978 if we stay in.

If the vote is Yes, your food must cost you more. Not merely do the Common Market authorities tax food imports or shut them out, but they also buy up home-produced food (through Intervention Boards) purely to keep the prices up. Then they store it in warehouses, thus creating mountains of beef, butter, grain, etc. Some of this food is deliberately made unfit for human consumption or even destroyed, and some is sold to countries like Russia, at prices well below what the housewife in the Common Market has to pay. The Common Market has already stored up a beef mountain of over 300,000 tons, and all beef imports from outside have been banned. If we come out of the Market, we could buy beef, veal, mutton, lamb, butter, cheese and other foods more cheaply than if we stay in. World food prices outside the Market are now falling. There is no doubt that the rise in food prices in Britain in the last three years has been partly due to joining the Common Market. For example, between 1971 and 1974, food prices rose in Britain and Ireland (which joined) by over 40%. In Norway and Sweden (which stayed out) they rose only by about 20%.

Your jobs at risk

If we stay in the Common Market, a British Government can no longer prevent the drift of industry southwards and increasingly to the Continent. This is already happening.

If it went on, it would be particularly damaging to Scotland, Wales, Northern Ireland and much of the North and West of England, which have suffered so much from unemployment already.

If we stay in the Common Market, our Government must increasingly abandon to them control over this drift of industry and employment. Far-reaching powers of interference in the control of British industry, particularly iron and steel, are possessed by the Market authorities.

Interference with the oil around our shores has already been threatened by the Brussels Commission.

Huge trade deficit with Common Market

The Common Market pattern of trade was never designed to suit Britain. According to our Department of Trade, our trade deficit with the Common Market was running, in the early months of 1975, at nearly £2,600 million a year — a staggering figure, compared with a very small deficit in 1970 when we were free to trade in accordance with our own policies. Yet before entry, the pro-Marketeers said that the 'effect upon our balance of trade would be positive and substantial'. If you don't want this dangerous trade deficit to continue, vote No.

Taxes to keep prices up

The Common Market's dear food policy is designed to prop up inefficient farmers on the Continent by keeping food prices high. If we stay in the Market, the British housewife will not only be paying more for her food but the British taxpayer will soon be paying many hundreds of millions of pounds a year to the Brussels budget, largely to subsidise Continental farmers. We are already paying into the Budget much more than we get out. This is entirely unreasonable and we cannot afford it.

Agriculture

It would be far better for us if we had our own national agricultural policy suited to our own country, as we had before we joined. We could then guarantee prices for our farmers, and, at the same time, allow consumers to buy much more cheaply. In the Common Market, the British taxpayer is paying as much to keep food prices up as we used to pay under our own policy to keep them down. The Market also have their eyes on British fishing grounds because they have over-fished their own waters.

Commonwealth links

Our Commonwealth links are bound to be weakened much further if we stay in the Common Market. We are being forced to tax imported Commonwealth goods. And as we lose our national independence, we shall cease, in practice, to be a member of the Commonwealth.

Britain a mere province of the Common Market?

The real aim of the Market is, of course, to become one single country in which Britain would be reduced to a mere province. The plan is to have a Common Market Parliament by 1978 or shortly thereafter. Laws would be passed by that Parliament which would be binding on our country. No Parliament elected by the British people could change those laws. This may be acceptable to some Continental countries. In recent times, they have been ruled by dictators, or defeated or occupied. They are more used to abandoning their political institutions than we are. Unless you want to be ruled more and more by a Continental Parliament in which Britain would be in a small minority, you should vote NO.

What is the alternative?

A far better course is open to us. If we withdraw from the Market, we could and should remain members of the wider Free Trade Area which now exists between the Common Market and the countries of the European Free Trade Association (EFTA) — Norway, Sweden, Finland, Austria, Switzerland, Portugal and Iceland. These countries are now to enjoy free entry for their industrial exports into the Common Market without having to carry the burden of the Market's dear food policy or suffer rule from Brussels. Britain already enjoys industrial free trade with these countries. If we withdrew from the Common Market, we should remain members of the wider group and enjoy, as the EFTA countries do, free or low-tariff entry into the Common Market countries without the burden of dear food or the loss of the British people's democratic rights.

The Common Market countries would be most unlikely to oppose this arrangement, since this would neither be sensible nor in their own interests. They may well demand a free trade area with us. But even if they did not do so, their tariffs on British exports would be very low. It is scare-mongering to pretend that withdrawal from the Common Market would mean heavy unemployment or loss of trade. In a very few years we shall enjoy in North Sea oil a precious asset possessed by none of the Common Market countries. Our freedom to use this oil, and our vast coal reserves, unhampered by any threatened Brussels restrictions, will strengthen our national economy powerfully.

For peace, stability and independence

Some say that the Common Market is a strong united group of countries, working closely together, and that membership would give us protection against an unfriendly world. There is no truth in this assertion. The defence of Britain and Western Europe depends not on the Common Market at all, but on the North Atlantic Treaty Organisation (NATO), which includes other countries like the United States, Canada and Norway, which are not members of the

Common Market. Any attempt to substitute the Common Market for NATO as a defence shield would be highly dangerous for Britain. Most anti-Marketeers rightly believe that we should remain members of NATO, the Organisation for Economic Co-operation and Development, EFTA, and the Council of Europe, as well as of the UN and its agencies. In all these, we can work actively together as good internationalists, while preserving our own democratic rights.

The choice is yours

It will be your decision that counts. Remember: you may never have the chance to decide this great issue again. If you want a rich and secure future for the British peoples, a free and democratic society, living in friendship with all nations—but governing ourselves: VOTE NO.

Results of the Referendum on the Continued EEC Membership (%)

	Turn-out	Yes	No	Yes lead (in % points)
United Kingdom	64.5	67.2	32.8	34.4
England	64.6	68.7	31.3	37.4
Wales	66.7	66.5	33.5	33.0
Scotland	61.7	58.4	41.6	16.8
Northern Ireland	47.4	52.1	47.9	4.2
English Counties				
Avon	68.7	67.8	32.2	35.6
Bedfordshire	67.9	69.4	30.6	38.8
Berkshire	66.4	72.6	27.4	45.2
Buckinghamshire	69.5	74.3	25.7	48.6
Cambridgeshire	62.2	74.1	25.9	48.2
Cheshire	65.5	70.1	29.9	40.2
Cleveland	60.2	67.3	32.7	34.6

	Turn-out	Yes	No	Yes lead (in % points)
Cornwall	66.8	68.5	31.5	37.0
Cumbria	64.8	71.9	28.1	43.8
Derbyshire	64.1	68.6	31.4	37,2
Devon	68.0	72.1	27.9	44.2
Dorset	68.3	73.5	26.5	47.0
Durham	61.5	64.2	35.8	28.4
Essex	67.7	67.6	32.4	35.2
Gloucestershire	65.4	71.7	25.3	43.4
Greater London	60.8	66.7	33.3	33,4
Greater Manchester	64.1	64.5	35.5	29.0
Hampshire	68.0	71.0	29.0	42.0
Hereford and Worcester	66.4	72.8	27.2	45.6
Hertfordshire	70.2	70.4	29.6	40.8
Humberside	62.4	67.8	32.2	35.6
Isles of Scilly	75.0	74.5	25.5	49.0
Isle of Wight	67.5	70.2	29.8	40.4
Kent	67.4	70.4	29.6	40.8
Lancashire	66.4	68.6	31.4	37.2
Leicestershire	67.2	73.3	26.7	46.6
Lincolnshire	63.7	74.7	25.3	49.4
Merseyside	62.7	64.8	35.2	29.6
Norfolk	63.8	70.1	29.9	40.2
Northamptonshire	66.7	69.5	30.5	39.0
Northumberland	65.0	69.2	30.8	38.4
Nottinghamshire	63.1	66.8	33.2	33.6
Oxfordshire	67.7	73.6	26.4	47.2
Salop	62.0	72.3	27.7	44.6

	Turn-out	Yes	No	Yes lead (in % points)
Somerset	67.7	69.6	30.4	39.2
Staffordshire	64.3	67.4	32.6	34.8
Suffolk	64.9	72.2	27.8	44.4
Surrey	70.1	76.2	23.8	52.4
Sussex, East	65.8	74.3	25.7	48.6
Sussex, West	68.6	76.2	23.8	52.4
Tyne and Wear	62.7	62.9	37.1	25.8
Warwickshire	68.0	69.9	30.1	39.8
West Midlands	62.5	65.1	34.9	30.2
Wiltshire	67.8	71.7	28.3	43.4
Yorkshire, North	64.3	76.3	23.7	52.6
Yorkshire, South	62.4	63.4	36.6	26.8
Yorkshire, West	63.6	65.4	34.6	30.8
Welsh Counties				
Clwyd	65.8	69.1	30.9	38.2
Dyfed	67.5	67.6	32.4	35.2
Glamorgan, Mid	66.6	56.9	43.1	13.8
Glamorgan, South	66.7	69.5	30.5	39.0
Glamorgan, West	67.4	61.6	38.4	23.2
Gwent	68.2	62.1	37.9	24.2
Gwynedd	64.3	70.6	29.4	41.2
Powys	67.9	74.3	25.7	48.6
Scottish Regions				
Borders	63.2	72.3	27.7	44.6
Central Scotland	64.1	59.7	40.3	19.4

	Turn-out	Yes	No	Yes lead (in % points)
Dumfries and Galloway	61.5	68.2	31.8	36.4
Fife	63.3	56.3	43.7	12.6
Grampian	57.4	58.2	41.8	16.4
Highland	58.7	54.6	45.4	9.2
Lothian	63.6	59.5	40.5	19.0
Orkney	48.2	61.8	38.2	23.6
Shetland	47.1	43.7	56.3	–12.6
Strathclyde	61.7	57.7	42.3	15.4
Tayside	63.8	58.6	41.4	17.2
Western Isles	50.1	29.5	70.5	– 41.0
Source: King (1977)				

Bibliography

Albert, M. (1993) Capitalism against capitalism, Whurr, London.

Anderson, P.J. and Weymouth, A. (1999) *Insulting the public? The British press and the European Union*, London: Longman.

Baimbridge, M., Burkitt, B. and Whyman, P. (2005) *Britain and the European Union: alternative futures*, London: Campaign for an Independent Britain.

Ball, G. (1968) *The Discipline of Power*, London: The Bodley Head

Barclay, R. (1960) Memorandum, 26th June, London: Public Records Office, FO 371/150360

Bell, L. (1995) *The Throw that Failed: Britain's 1961 Application to Join the Common Market*, London: New European Publications

Benn, T. (1989) *Office without Power: Diaries 1968–72*, London: Arrow

British Management Data Foundation (2000) 'Document: A Letter to *The Times*', Transcript of BBC Radio 4 Programme broadcast on Thursday 3rd February 2000, Stroud (Gloucestershire): British Management Data Foundation

Broad, R. and Geiger, T. (1996) 'The 1975 British Referendum on Europe', Contemporary Record, 10 (3) pp 82–105.

Burkitt, B. (1974) *Britain and the European Economic Community: an economic re-appraisal*, Skipton: British Business for World Markets.

Burkitt, B. (1975) *Britain and the European Economic Community: a political re-appraisal*, Skipton: British Business for World Markets.

Burkitt, B. and Baimbridge, M. (1990) The performance of British agriculture and the impact of the Common Agricultural Policy: a historical review, *Rural History*, 1(2), 265–280.

Burkitt, B. and Mullen, A. (2003) European Integration and the Battle for British Hearts and Minds: New Labour and the Euro, *The Political Quarterly*, 74 (3), 322–336.

Butler, D. and Kitzinger, U. (1976) 'Polls'; in *The 1975 Referendum*, London: Macmillan, pp. 246–262.

Butler, D. and Kitzinger, U. (1976) *The 1975 Referendum*, London: Macmillan.

Butler, D. and Ranney, A. (1978) Referendums: A Comparative Study of Practice and Theory. Washington DC: American Enterprise Institute.

Butler, M. 'The EU Budget Problem', http://www.euromove.org.uk/features/rebate

Cabinet Office (1952) Memorandum by Sir Anthony Eden, 15th February, London: PRO, CAB 129/49C (52) 40

Cabinet Office (1955) Minutes of the Cabinet Mutual Aid Committee, 24th October, London: PRO, CAB 134/1030, MAC (55) 200

Cabinet Office (1960a) 'Future Policy Study, 1960–1970', January, London: PRO, CAB 21/3847

Cabinet Office (1960b) 'The Six and the Seven: Long-term Arrangements', 25th May, London: PRO, CAB 134/1852, EQ (60) 27

Cabinet Office (1960c) Minutes of the Cabinet European Economic Association Committee, 27th May, London: PRO, CAB 134/1819

Cabinet Office (1960d) 'The Six and the Seven: The Long-term Objectives', 6th July, London: PRO, CAB 129/102 pt.1, C (60) 107

Cabinet Office (1961) Minutes of Cabinet Meeting, 20th April, London: PRO, CAB 134/1821

Cabinet Office (1962a) Minutes of Cabinet Meeting, 5th July, London: PRO, CAB 128/36, CC (62) 44

Cabinet Office (1962b) Minutes of Cabinet Meeting, 27th September, London: PRO, CAB 128/36, CC (62) 48

Camps, M. (1964) *British and the European Community, 1955–63*, Oxford: Oxford University Press

Clarke, R. with Cairncross, A. (Ed.) (1982) *Anglo–American Economic Collaboration in War and Peace, 1942–1949*, Oxford: Clarendon Press

Council of the European Union (2005) *Financial Perspectives 2007–2013, Presidency Discussion Paper on the structure of the EU budget*, 14118/05, CADREFIN 2333, 8 Nov 2005.

Denman, R. (1996) *Missed Chances: Britain and Europe in the Twentieth Century*, London: Indigo

Dorril, S. (2000) *MI6: Fifty Years of Special Operations*, London: Fourth Estate

Esping-Andersen, G. (1990) *The three worlds of welfare capitalism*, Polity Press, Cambridge.

European Commission (1995) *Eurobarometer: Public Opinion in the European Union, Trends 1974–1994*, Table B4 (Attitudes towards the Unification of Western Europe), Brussels: European Commission

Evans, D. (1975) *While Britain Slept: The Selling of the Common Market*, London: Gollancz

Foreign Office (1945) Memorandum from Alfred Balfour to Ernest Bevin, 9th August, *Documents on British Policy Overseas*, Series 1, Vol.III, London: HMSO

Foreign Office (1947) 'Stocktaking' Memorandum, January 1947, London: PRO, FO 371/66546,

Foreign Office (1949a) 'Third World Power or Western Consolidation', March, London: PRO, FO371/76384

Foreign Office (1949b) Report by Sir William Strang, 17th March 1949, *British Documents on the End of Empire*, Series A, 2 (2), 338

Foreign Office (1955) Memorandum from Sir Ivone Kirkpatrick to Sir Gladwyn Jebb, 25th November, London: PRO, FO 371/16054

Foreign Office (1956) Report of working group of officials from the Board of Trade, Commonwealth Relations Office, Foreign Office and the Treasury, 20th April, London: PRO, FO 371/122075

Foreign Office (1960) Memorandum from Lord David Kilmuir to Edward Heath, 14th December, London: PRO, FO 371/150369

Foreign Office (1961) Report of meeting between George Ball, Edward Heath and Sir Frank Lee, 30th March, London: PRO, FO 371/158162

Foreign Office (1964) 'Regional Studies', September, London: PRO, FO 49/302

Foreign Office (1965) Memorandum from Michael Palliser, April, London: PRO, FO 371/182377

Foreign Office (1966) 'How to get into the Common Market', August, London: PRO, FO 371/188346

Gallup (1968) 'Public Opinion and the EEC', *Journal of Common Market Studies*, 6 (3), 231–249

Heath, E. (1998) *The Course of My Life*, London: Hodder and Stoughton

Her Majesty's Government (1971) *The United Kingdom and the European Communities*, Cmnd.4715, London: HMSO

Her Majesty's Government (1945) *Statistical Material presented during the Washington Negotiations*, Cmnd.6707, London: Her Majesty's Stationary Office [HMSO]

Hindley, B. and Howe, M. (1996) *Better off out?: the benefits or costs of EU membership*, Occasional Paper 99, London: Institute of Economic Affairs.

HM Treasury (1997) UK membership of the Single Currency: an assessment of the five economic tests, London: HMSO.

Hofstede, G. (1980) *Culture's consequences*, Sage, London.

Kent, J. (1989) 'Bevin's Imperialism and the Idea of Euro-Africa, 1945–49', in Dockrill, M. and Young, J. (Eds.) *British Foreign Policy, 1945–56*, Basingstoke: Macmillan

King, A. (1976) *Britain says Yes: the 1975 Referendum on the Common Market*, Washington DC, American Enterprise Institute.

Kisch, R. (1964) *The Private Life of Public Relations*, London: MacGibbon

Korpi, W. (1983) *The democratic class struggle*, London: Routledge and Kegan Paul.

Lippmann, W. (1922) *Public Opinion*. New York: Macmillan.

Lodge, J. (1975) Britain and the EEC: exit, voice or loyalty?, *Cooperation and Conflict*.

Macmillan, H. (1959) Memorandum to Sir Anthony Eden, 22nd October, London: Public Records Office, PREM, 11/2985, 22

Milne, I. (2004) *A cost too far?*, London: Institute for the Study of Civil Society.

Morgan, D. (1999) *The European Parliament, mass media and the search for power and influence*, Aldershot: Ashgate.

O'Neill, C. (2000) *Britain's Entry into the European Community: Report on the Negotiations of 1970–1972*, London: Frank Cass

Price, V. (1992) *Public Opinion*. Newbury Park, Ca: Sage.

Schoen, D. (1977) *Powell and the Powellites*, London: Macmillan.

Scholefield, A. (2001) *Why Mr. Blair will not win a euro-referendum*, Futures.

Shore, P. (1993) *Leading the Left*, London: Weidenfeld and Nicolson

Shore, P. (2000) *Separate Ways: The Heart of Europe*, London: Duckworth

Teer, F. and Spence, J. (1973) *Political Opinion Polls*, London: Hutchinson.

Wistrich, E. (2001) 'Lessons of the 1975 Referendum', in Beetham, R. (Ed.) *The Euro Debate: Persuading the People*, London: Federal Trust

Worcester, R., Dionne, E. and Schoen, D. (1975) *Referendum Polling Presentations*, May-June 1975, London: MORI.

Young, H. (1998) *This Blessed Plot: Britain and Europe from Churchill to Blair*, London: Macmillan

Zakheim, D. (1973) 'Britain and the EEC – Opinion Poll Data, 1970–72', *Journal of Common Market Studies*, 11 (2), 191–233

Index